Corporate Strategies of the
Top UK Companies of the Future

Corporate Strategies of the Top UK Companies of the Future

The Corporate Research Foundation

HarperCollinsBusiness

HarperCollins*Publishers*
77–85 Fulham Palace Road,
Hammersmith, London W6 8JB

Published by HarperCollins*Publishers* 1999
1 3 5 7 9 10 8 6 4 2

Copyright © Corporate Research Foundation

Corporate Research Foundation
Lauderdale House,
25, Duke Street,
London W1M 5DB
+44 (0) 171 486 2603

The Corporate Research Foundation asserts the moral right to
be identified as the editor of this work

A catalogue record for this book
is available from the British Library

ISBN 0 00 257039 4

Set in Linotype Meridien by
Rowland Phototypesetting Ltd, Bury St Edmunds, Suffolk

Printed and bound in Great Britain by
Clays Ltd, St Ives plc

Contents

Introduction

Businesses can learn much from what works well in the present, but it remains imperative to consider what will work best in the future. This book looks at companies in the UK that do this exceptionally well.

Corporate Research's principal aim is to consider those companies whose strategic management, growth orientation or sheer appetite for innovation and success will have a major impact – perhaps as far away as ten years' time. Our approach rests on the assumption that certain key factors – customer demand, structural flexibility, human resources, and the successful application of technology – will precipitate changes to the list of leading companies. The big names of today will not necessarily be the big names of tomorrow. Our aim therefore is to find businesses – of all shapes and sizes, from all sectors and regions of the UK – that are truly companies of the future. British ownership is not essential; what matters is that the company contributes to the UK economy.

Of course, many companies by virtue of their success will become attractive to other companies. And smaller ones may choose to merge with larger enterprises in order to gain access to capital, expertise, technology or markets in a time frame shorter than would be achievable through organic growth. We are not trying to predict the FTSE-100 index in 15 years' time, nor are we making recommendations for investment portfolios. But in one way or another, we expect the companies in this book to make an impact on the UK, and probably the international, economy.

We have drawn from many sources, employing a panel of specialist consultants, academics, company analysts and financial journalists to establish a list of businesses that are leading the way in best-practice strategic management and future orientation. Our choices may be controversial. Some well-known companies do not appear while some of our selections are not yet household names and, by virtue of their products, may never be.

The panel was asked to list businesses that are advancing in key areas. Our criteria were structural flexibility, innovation, human resources, growth markets, quality of management and international orientation. Some 1,500 companies were pre-selected at the initial stage of the research process, from which the final selection was made. A number of companies declined to participate, for reasons varying from restructuring, the imminent publication of cautionary announcements in respect of mergers and acquisitions, or sensitivity over strategic and prevailing market issues. Some companies even requested to withdraw at the later stages of the process for one or other of these reasons.

The final profiles of the companies were prepared by a team of 11 leading financial writers. Company executives were interviewed and all facts were checked with the companies – but the in-depth assessments and evaluations are the writers' own.

In turn, our writers appreciated that they do not set or own a company's business strategy – each company does. In that sense, we have allowed senior executives to enlarge on their strategy for future success, what it is based upon and how it will be delivered. Time will provide the real litmus test.

CORPORATE RESEARCH FOUNDATION

Foreword

In considering UK plc, it is not surprising that some sectors come to the fore while others are less evident. The British advertising, marketing services and brand management industries are much revered worldwide and certainly some leading lights are featured in this book. The financial services industry is not only enormous, but has an enormous future. Consolidation, deregulation and the governmental trend to outsource the provision of 'stakeholder pensions' is creating opportunity for some very significant players. Britain leads the world in deregulation and privatisation, and many companies – in electricity generation, water, other utilities and in transport – have overcome the initial transformation into free spirits and have now embarked on serious expansion, acquiring companies, moving into new activities and expanding into new countries. The information technology industry has very strong roots here, and even if a company is US-owned, its UK subsidiary is often its second-largest worldwide. In management consulting, telecommunications, aerospace engineering to name but a few, British companies are up there with the best in the world.

And if that points to a single common denominator of future success, it is the need to *be competitive*. In a country whose history has not necessarily taught it to be servile and customer-facing, it is those companies which really do address the needs of their customers – and assess and then beat the competition – which are succeeding. If there is one vocational factor that we would recommend is incorporated into any national educational curriculum, it is to stress that no-one owes anyone a living – success in business comes to those who are better than the next guy. And to the companies and their employees, we would suggest that entrepreneurs are not one-man operations or start-ups with a totally new idea – everyone, in even the largest organisation, can be entrepreneurial in behaviour.

Because the competitive marketplace is not an individual market or country – it is the entire world. 'Globalisation' and 'worldwide' are hardly new words, but they are here to stay. And the world is shrinking, as transportation, telecommunications, IT and e-commerce make it easier and quicker to do business anywhere in the world. This also means that you may not even be aware of your competitor, let alone see him.

If the world is getting smaller, the players are getting bigger. The large corporations are showing an insatiable appetite to enter new markets, forge new alliances, find more customers and acquire other companies. Big is not necessarily best, and less likely beautiful, but it is still big.

The UK has some specific international issues to address over the next few years. Often finding itself halfway – culturally and economically – between Europe and the US, the UK is watching the trend towards European Monetary Union gather pace. The single European currency has been launched, at this moment for cashless transactions only, and the UK has to live with that whether it wishes to join or not. And it doesn't need us to tell people that opinion is divided among politicians, among businesses, and among the general public. Some business leaders regard it as an imperative that Britain joins the single currency as soon as possible. Others view it with horror, treating the euro as 'just another currency', but with attendant bureaucracy and social employment laws that impinge on business efficiency.

With a currently strong pound, some have argued that it has been a good time to 'stay at home'. The economic crisis racking South-east Asia has highlighted the necessity of structural and operational flexibility within businesses when just a few years ago exposure to this region was a prerequisite for rapid growth.

Businesses are realising that their workforces are huge pools of creative resource. Yet so many businesses stifle creativity and therefore deny themselves the opportunity to innovate in the truest sense. Many make the mistake of regarding innovation as meaning the use of the latest technology – particularly of the information variety. But this would be to miss the point. IT is just a means, a tool. Innovation is a way of thinking, of doing things differently, smarter, more flexibly. It can apply just as equally to people working in accounts or supply-chain management as in technology and computing.

But technology is very important of course – harnessing it even more so. A business does not, or should not, replace a man with a machine or computer unless that act increases the productivity of the business. The Internet, digital technologies, electronic data interchange, telecommunications, surface physics and materials science are transforming the way in which the world does business.

No surprises then that innovative companies which create and provide the technologies of today and tomorrow are as likely to be as successful as the companies which apply their technologies effectively in production, information exchange, marketing, business integration and supply.

When the next recession is always just around the corner, depending on what you read or who you listen to, how best to enter it is an interesting question. Do you see Michael Schumacher brake early or late as he approaches a tight corner? In past recessions, smart and nimble companies have not only set survival as their goal, but have plotted how to emerge in a position of strength.

For many, it is often too late by then to make a difference – the important decisions have been taken years earlier when businesses had the courage to invest. In previous economic downturns, so many companies have cut costs that one wonders how much fat there is on top of the muscle. Investment, as it probably always has done, seems to hold the key.

Investment is not restricted to technologies, plant, and systems. People remain the constant factor in any successful business. In a fast-changing world, the flexibility and commitment of the workforce is a prime asset for any company. Unfortunately, there may not be enough good people to go round at present. In a zero sum game, every company cannot hire the best people, even if they all wish to – or claim to!

Without raising contentious issues about the educational system, it is readily apparent that there are skill shortages in many specialist areas, particularly in computing and technology; people are not always as prepared for commercial life as they might be; and the psychological contract between employer and employee is changing out of necessity. When all the discussion is over, it may be that the top UK companies of the future are those which really do find, develop, motivate and keep the best people.

CORPORATE RESEARCH FOUNDATION

Research Team

Writers:

Lisa Buckingham
Alex Brummer
Roger Cowe
Paul Donkersley
Jim Dow
Sue Hayward
David Kirk
Kevin Pratt
Roger Trapp
Barry Turnbull
David Vickery

Sources and Advisers:

Charterhouse Tilney
Grant Thornton
Greig Middleton
The London School of Economics – Professor Terry Gouvish
Oxford University – Professor Mary Benwell
Panmure Gordan

Companies of the Future

3M United Kingdom plc

3M is one of the world's leading technology companies. 3M manufactures more than 50,000 innovative products, including adhesive tapes, pharmaceuticals, abrasives, reflective materials, fibre optic connectors, respirators and fabric protectors. 3M uses over 100 different technologies in over 40 business units in the manufacture of products for a variety of industrial, commercial, healthcare and consumer markets. US-owned 3M had worldwide sales of $15 billion in 1998 and over 70,000 employees. In the UK and Ireland, 3M employs over 4,200 people in 15 locations with an annual turnover in excess of £600 million.

Scorecard:

Flexibility	★★★★★
Innovation	★★★★★
Human resources	★★★★
Growth markets	★★★★
Quality of management	★★★★
International orientation	★★★★

Biggest Plus:
One of the truly great innovating companies

Biggest Minus:
Ethical, caring approach needs to be balanced with commercial need

Key Figures:
(worldwide, to 31 December 1998)

Sales	$15.021 billion
Net Income	$1.526 billion*
R+D expenditure	over $1 billion
Employees worldwide	over 70,000
Employees UK	4,200

*Excludes the impact of charges relating to restructuring costs in 1998 and a gain on the sale of national advertising in 1997.

3M United Kingdom plc
3M House, PO Box 1, Market Place
Bracknell, Berkshire RG12 1JU
Tel. 01344 858000   Fax. 01344 862367
e-mail: innovation@uk.mmm.com
website: www.3M.com

3M United Kingdom plc

Company Background

At 3M the story is often told about how this struggling sandpaper company grew to become one of the world's largest innovative companies. Since the Minnesota Mining & Manufacturing Company was founded in 1902, the company has built an unwavering legacy of innovation at every level, and a dedication to developing new products that make the lives of its customers easier and better.

There's no better illustration of 3M being ahead of its time than a quote from William McKnight, chairman and CEO of the company back in 1944:

'Those men and women to whom we delegate authority and responsibility, if they are good people, are going to want to do their jobs their own way. Mistakes will be made. But if a person is essentially right, the mistakes he or she makes are not as serious in the long run as the mistakes management will make if it undertakes to tell those in authority exactly how they must do their jobs. Management that is destructively critical when mistakes are made kills initiative. And it is essential that we have many people with initiative if we are to continue to grow.'

Operations and Markets

3M has real worldwide presence. It has operations in 60 countries and sells its products in over 200 countries. Some two-thirds of the products that it sells abroad are produced locally. 3M in the UK and Ireland is one of the largest subsidiaries outside of the USA, and is involved with the vast majority of 3M's incredible 50,000 product range.

3M is a market leader in most of its businesses, frequently creating new markets by developing products that fill unarticulated customer needs. A test of innovation? Thirty per cent of each year's sales are expected to come from products less than four years old. The company looks to produce around 1,000 new products every two years. Previous generations include easily recognisable names – like Post-it® Notes, Scotchgard™ products and the signature Scotch™ tape brand.

3M takes innovation seriously. And it is guided by 'technology with purpose' – it doesn't matter what the technologies are, it's what they do that matters. 3M has documented more than 100 technologies, and claims about 30 technology platforms (technologies that produce multiple products for multiple markets). New developments happen at a frantic pace. Around $1 billion is invested in R&D annually and the company makes substantial capital investments.

Successful technologies include micro-replication; adhesives; non-woven fibres; pharmaceuticals, fluorochemicals; mechanical fasteners, and optical fibres and connectors. 3M's Customer Technical Centre in Bracknell welcomes some 3,000 visitors each year looking for technology-based solutions to their business or manufacturing problems. Not surprisingly, 3M keeps patent offices busy. In 1997, the company was awarded no fewer than 578 US patents.

Strategy and Management

3M's objective is to continue growth – which is internally driven – and earn high returns on capital, and produce strong, sustainable cash flow. At the heart of 3M's strategy is listening to customers, developing stronger relationships with them, and accelerating the development of high-impact new products.

The 'Pacing Plus' programme seeks to identify new products which have real global potential to take 3M clearly above the competition. Such products enjoy an accelerated form of process management, where the company puts the appropriate levels of resources and priorities behind those products which are going to win.

There is never a shortage of candidates for new products at different stages of advancement and involving different degrees of complexity. 'At some point, when the shape and scope of a product emerges from the earlier stages of its development, someone has to stand back and say that this is going to be a home run for the company,' says Wayne Brown, managing director of 3M in the UK.

In business to business, the 3M brand is all-powerful, but less so with the end-consumer. Having built up thousands of trademarks and secondary brands, 3M is now taking more of a rational and market-led approach to branding, rationalising secondary brands and increasingly using 3M as the product's primary brand. Powerful brands in their own right, such as Post-it® products, will remain exceptions.

3M organises its three main business groups around common industries, markets and distribution channels: industrial and consumer markets; healthcare markets; and transportation, safety and chemical markets. 3M's structure and global reach also mirrors its increasingly multinational customers, leading to a form of business unit/regional matrix.

'It's vital that 3M leverages its many technologies,' says Dr John Howells, technical director, 3M UK and Ireland, 'and we do. There is no room for jealously guarded discoveries. The technologies belong to the company and must be shared.' Luckily, 3M has a sharing culture.

But there are still rules and devices. 'Technical audits' of 3M's 70 major laboratories worldwide are made regularly by groups of people drawn from across 3M. Technical forums and fairs allow the 3M technical community to gather, display and discuss their work and ideas with one another, while an array of awards, recognition schemes and publications foster the sharing culture of 3M technology.

Take micro-replication – a great technology for 3M which is showing up in some of the company's most promising and advanced products. The technology creates microscopic, precise, three-dimensional patterns on a variety of surfaces which has led to an explosion of many revolutionary products, with many more possibilities just waiting to be discovered. Sales of products that rely on micro-replication – from 3M™ Scotchlite™ Diamond Grade Sheeting, 3M™ Dual Brightness Enhancement Film for computer screens, to 3M™ Trizact™ Abrasives – have doubled in each of the past four years.

Values are extremely important to 3M. It wants to be a company which its employees are proud to be a part of. The customer is king, and the company must always satisfy customer expectations. Those of its shareholders too, in meeting their expectations of growth. And at all times, 3M maintains a respect for its social and physical environment.

This is a very ethical company, and the company provides a clear set of values so that employees are in no doubt what is expected of them in terms of ethical business behaviour. 3M's culture also values teamwork, continuing education, and people who show a willingness to change and an aptitude for innovation. Importantly, innovation is not the sole preserve of 3M corporate scientists but applies to all forms of working.

The Future

3M is running with some important business trends. And some big mysteries lie ahead. Global customers are looking for fewer suppliers to deal with in search of business simplification. Product life cycles are shortening and the pace of getting products to market is quickening. The advent of the euro will inevitably mean that multinational companies will seek price harmonisation across countries. 'And with most of 3M's products sold through the channel of distribution, the transforming world of electronic commerce asks a lot of questions of the manufacturing/distribution role,' says Peter Knight, logistics manager, UK and Ireland.

3M's response as distribution consolidates and as manufacturers recognise that the value of a product is not what you pack into a box but the speed with which you get it to the customer, will be to work smarter through three drivers. First, its Pacing Plus programme gives it a commercial 'get-go' perspective at an early stage of a promising product cycle. Secondly, the need for supply chain excellence is already firmly ensconced, with 3M paying close attention to smarter, faster distribution, recognising that a lot of a product price is cost not value. Thirdly, to earn greater customer loyalty, 3M will be putting more effort into the branding identity of its products – one thing that can ensure the quality of the product irrespective of its distributor is the 3M name on the label.

It is the compulsive spirit of innovation though – working intuitively or in practical and commercial partnership with its customers – that is 3M's real trump card. There is a genuine joy in innovation and invention at 3M. It has always been willing to invest in research for its own sake, 'for the happy outcomes which emerge from the most unpromising of starts'. That 3M has increased revenues and profits in almost every single year since 1985 suggests that this innovative company knows precisely what it is doing.

AMV Group

Abbott Mead Vickers is one of the largest advertising and marketing services groups in the UK. Abbott Mead Vickers·BBDO is the
leading advertising agency in the UK, and BBDO Worldwide is
the world's fourth largest agency network. The group's other
areas of activity include media planning and buying, direct
marketing, customer magazines, promotional marketing, public
relations and investor communications. Now owned by Omnicom, Abbott Mead Vickers plc has a good record of consistent
growth in turnover, profits and earnings year on year.

Scorecard:

Flexibility	★★★★★
Innovation	★★★★★
Human resources	★★★★★
Growth markets	★★★★
Quality of management	★★★★
International orientation	★★★★★

Biggest Plus:
Highly creative, highly successful – a leading light in
UK marketing services

Biggest Minus:
Advertising is still the largest business, although decreasing
as a proportion all the time

Key Figures:
(to 31 December 1997)

Revenue	£431 million
Operating profit	£16.5 million
Pre-tax profit	£17.2 million
Employees UK	1,450

Abbott Mead Vickers plc
151 Marylebone Road
London NW1 5QE
Tel: 0171 616 3500
Fax: 0171 616 3600
website: amvbbdo@amvbbdo.co.uk

AMV Group

Company Background

Abbott Mead Vickers (AMV) was created in 1977 by the three people in the company's name, and was listed on the London Stock Exchange in 1985. In 1991 Abbott Mead Vickers bought BBDO London and AMV·BBDO is now the number one advertising agency in the UK with billings of £366 million. In 1999 Omnicom, BBDO's parent which already owned 25% of Abbott Mead Vickers PLC, acquired the rest of the equity in the company.

Today AMV is one of the largest marketing services groups in the UK, a web of related companies linked by the craft of persuasive communications. It is the result of the popular cocktail of organic growth and a series of selective acquisitions (some 18 in 13 years). While advertising agency AMV·BBDO is still the largest company in the group, and often seen as the flagship operation, more than 60% of total profits now come from other companies.

Prominent company names in the AMV stable include New PHD (media), Barraclough Hall Woolston Gray (direct marketing), Redwood Publishing (customer magazines), Fishburn Hedges (corporate PR) and Freud Communications (consumer PR).

Over the past five years, group revenue has grown by 30% compound each year – significantly better than the market and significantly better than its competitors.

Operations and Markets

AMV has an enviable esprit and a unifying commitment to outstanding creativity. Quality is valued above size, people over systems. There is a sharing of operating principles and beliefs and no little affection between the constituent members of the group. In developing its business in the wider market for persuasive communications, AMV has sought companies that enhance the quality and width of the service it offers its clients, and whose businesses will in turn benefit from being part of a larger group.

Nearly all AMV companies are located in the UK, the vast majority in London. And why not? London is one of the foremost advertising and marketing capitals of the world, if not *the* capital. AMV's client base is far more international, of course, and the relationship with BBDO has proved to be a fruitful one. One third of the advertising agency's income is now international, with opportunities increasing all the time.

Abbott Mead Vickers·BBDO is the brand leader in UK advertising, yet still has less than 4% of this fragmented market. Creative awards are certainly not in short supply, however – some 21 were scooped during 1998. And *Marketing Week's* annual reputations survey of the people who matter – the clients – had AMV as second best agency overall and first for creativity, the highest valued criterion.

In marketing services, a company's reputation and track record of creative and effective work is everything. AMV's is second to none.

Strategy and Management

At the time of the advertising agency's twentieth birthday in 1997, *Campaign* magazine wrote: 'Throughout its history, Abbott Mead Vickers·BBDO has never pursued size for its own sake, but focused only on achieving excellence. Yet, by concentrating on the latter, it has achieved the former. By hiring the best people and treating them with respect and decency, AMV has created a cycle in which virtue brings success. It is hard to see how that virtuous circle could be broken.'

And there's the key. People. There is probably no business on earth that relies on people and their intuition and creativity more than marketing services. According to Michael Baulk, chief executive, 'Our people are our principal asset, and it is their talent, their intelligence and their energy that solve our clients' problems. The better we do that, the better our competitive edge.'

What remains as a beacon throughout the AMV group is the primacy of ideas. AMV believes that to lose sight of this, to be distracted by technology or the intellectualising of communications and techniques as a substitute for ideas, would be wrong. AMV will remain a strongly creative business.

AMV estimates the UK market for the full range of communications services to be worth some £25 billion. The communication spend of many companies is at least double their advertising spend with sectors like direct marketing, data consultancy and consumer loyalty marketing growing well ahead of inflation.

Advertising tends to be more vulnerable to downturns than direct marketing, and AMV has recognised the importance of keeping pace with new opportunities to insulate itself against over-exposure to economically sensitive areas.

The obvious route has been selective acquisition of companies with proven management teams, and in the last two years AMV has bought Aurelia Public Relations (brand PR consultancy), Horseman Cooke (design), The O'Connell Partnership (marketing planning), Irish International (advertising), Telecom Express (telemarketing) and acquired the remaining shareholding in Drum (media consultancy).

Direct marketing is an extremely buoyant sector of the marketing communications business, estimated to be worth some £7 billion in the UK. AMV has strengthened its position by acquiring Craik Jones, a prolific prizewinner, to complement Barraclough Hall Woolston Gray.

'However this expansion is not just based on a "filling in the boxes" approach to company growth,' says Peter Mead, chairman. 'Although there are gaps in our communication portfolio, we will only fill them when we meet people who are running companies in those areas which we believe will contribute towards the long-term success of our group, in that they share our principles and beliefs as well as our long-term fiscal ambitions.'

Chief executive Michael Baulk points to three key drivers of the consistent and underlying growth across the AMV group:

Firstly, AMV's client list is outstanding, and a prime source of organic growth. AMV counts many of the UK's most successful companies as clients and, for most of these companies, advertising remains the primary stimulus for growth in sales and market share. Their commitment to advertising is consistent and long-term – and increasing.

Secondly, all group companies have an excellent new business record, winning major pieces of 'flagship' business including BT, Prudential, ICI Dulux, WHSmith, *The Economist*, Guinness, Duracell and Royal Mail. One year's new business underwrites the next year's growth.

Thirdly, AMV has successfully expanded the range of services it can provide to clients, creating valuable opportunities for client referral.

The drive towards integrated communications is coming as much from clients, as from marketing services companies. There might be the temptation for one individual company to say 'yes, we can do everything'. But at the centre, AMV convinces its companies that it is in their best interests to work jointly with other group companies and that in the long run, there will be more opportunities for business development through recognising their own strengths and weaknesses. 'Once you acquire the habit of working together it's easier to appreciate each other's strengths,' says Adrian Vickers.

Proof of encouraging companies to work together? The number of clients using three or more AMV companies and generating in excess of £100,000 income each year has risen from five in 1994 to 31 in 1999.

Growth has not come at the expense of investment. AMV group

has increased staff levels by 20% in 1997 and by 9% in 1998, excluding acquisitions. Group companies undertook a series of property moves aimed at creating a better working environment for its people (the ad agency has been referred to as 'the fun factory' by clients only too happy to visit the offices). All are located in separate buildings – AMV management encourages independence – but balanced with a strong sense of togetherness.

Despite the entrepreneurial history of spirited people in companies acquired by AMV, belonging to the group has not only given them status and financial management, but the growth in co-operation has changed the nature of the group.

AMV has tried carefully to avoid an overlap of companies and clients, having spent time carefully choosing the companies in the first place for their management skills. Group management still maintains a keen involvement though, without ever applying a heavy directional hand. Fortunately, it is dealing with mature people.

The objective is to ensure that client business finds the right home in the group without placing any restrictions on companies going for accounts in their own sector. It is important that all AMV people know the other disciplines, companies and the people in the rest of the business. AMV does a lot to ensure that people familiarise and work with each other, and the process runs smoothly.

The Future

Creativity and ideas will remain absolutely fundamental to AMV's business, with everyone motivated, driven and fascinated by the creative product.

The combination of a quality client base, new business success and a developing cross-referral programme has fuelled AMV's excellent record of revenue growth. All AMV companies continue to excel in their individual markets, receiving craft awards, winning new assignments in their own right, and collaborating successfully with other group companies on joint pitches and joint projects.

Yet AMV estimates that its share of the total UK marketing services market is less than 3%. Building its share of a market that is itself growing healthily offers a very active and exciting agenda.

Andersen Consulting

Andersen Consulting is one of the world's largest, and fastest-growing, consultancies. Though best known for implementing large-scale information technology projects, it is also increasingly active in strategy and other more traditional areas of consulting.

Scorecard:

Flexibility	★★★★
Innovation	★★★★★
Human resources	★★★★
Growth markets	★★★★
Quality of management	★★★★
International orientation	★★★★

Biggest Plus:
Ability to embrace change and anticipate business needs

Biggest Minus:
Hard-driving culture inevitably leads to staff retention challenges

Key Figures:
(to 31 August 1998)

Revenue	$7.8 billion
Profit	Not disclosed
Employees worldwide	63,000
Employees UK	5,000

Andersen Consulting
2 Arundel Street,
London WC2R 3LT
Tel: 0171 438 5070
Fax: 0171 831 1133
website: www.ac.com

Andersen
Consulting

Andersen Consulting

Company Background

Andersen Consulting grew out of the 'Big Five' accounting firm Arthur Andersen. The business was established in the 1950s, and in the late 1980s the consulting operation was made a separate unit within the Andersen Worldwide Organisation, which in 1998 had total revenues of $13.9 billion. Though that is still the case, the firm believes it is likely to be a completely separate entity by the end of the year 2000 as a result of the ongoing arbitration of its long-running dispute with the accounting firm over conflicts of interest and profit-sharing arrangements.

The firm is particularly well known for its implementation of large and complex information technology projects for large international companies and governments around the world. However, it has also become a significant player in the increasingly important outsourcing market and involves itself in strategy advice and other key traditional areas of consulting.

With a mission to 'help clients change to be more successful', the firm now says it can help with all the major components of organisations, 'aligning technology, processes and people in support of an organisation's overall strategy'. It claims to serve nearly 75% of *Fortune* magazine's global 200 largest public companies and all but one of the magazine's most profitable companies.

Since becoming a separate business unit in 1989, growth has been phenomenal. Revenues have risen from $1 billion to nearly $8 billion – giving the firm an average annual growth rate over the period of more than 20 per cent. In that decade, the size of the workforce has trebled, from 21,000 professionals to 63,000, serving clients around the world. As a partnership, Andersen is not obliged to publish profit figures, but the firm is widely acknowledged to be highly profitable.

Operations and Markets

Like the accounting firm that spawned it, Andersen Consulting began as a quintessentially middle American organisation. But over the years it has transformed itself into a mirror of the multinational organisations that it serves, with offices in about 50 countries. The Americas remain the most important region in revenue terms, but the Europe/Middle East/Africa/India grouping is closing fast, while Asia Pacific has also seen significant growth.

To many people, Andersen Consulting is largely an implementer of large-scale information technology projects for leading international businesses and government bodies. However, in recent years it has sought to stress that, though this high-earning and labour-intensive business has been immensely successful for it, it is not the only thing it does.

Consequently, while it is usually competing with specialist organisations such as EDS and the consulting arms of computer companies such as IBM as well as other leading accountancy firms for IT work, it also rivals strategy firms and other specialist consultancies for a broad range of consultancy assignments to the world's largest companies. But, as one manager says, 'Technological capability and expertise underpin a lot of what we do.'

Always determined to see strong growth in fees, the firm has set great store by what it calls its Business Integration Client Service Model and its four core components of strategy, technology, change management and process. Indeed, Andersen says it has gone so far down this route that it is difficult to break down revenues into geographical or industrial segments. Projects typically call on people who have a broad range of expertise and come from all over the world.

Strategy and Management

Change is a watchword at Andersen. When it was established as a business in its own right in 1989, the partners were determined to create what current managing partner and chief executive George Shaheen describes as 'an organisation like no other'. This meant undergoing dramatic change in order to rewrite the rules of its industry and to establish a new measure for success, he says. And true to the aim of serving clients in new and innovative ways, that process has been going on ever since. In the fight to build 'the consulting firm of the future' organisational structures are constantly evolving.

In particular, the firm has used its strength in technology, coupled with an obsession with the future, to be ahead of the game in such areas as developing databases dedicated to knowledge management and helping clients anticipate and plan for future trends in their industries and society in general. Moreover, by taking over the running of IT systems and other non-core but still vital operations for global companies, the firm sees itself as being in the vanguard of the creation of a new kind of business entity.

'Consulting is becoming the fabric of international industry,' says one insider, pointing to the ever closer working relationships between firms like Andersen and key clients. 'We're becoming facilitators, helping large-scale organisations achieve goals that they haven't been able to achieve by themselves.'

For the moment, only a few organisations have the ability to provide this level of service rather than the traditional one-off project approach to consulting. And Andersen believes it is in the vanguard of assisting the world's largest corporations in managing their increasingly complex and wide-ranging operations in this way.

It sees this approach working in six central areas: helping organisations shift their fundamental strategy or strategic approach to products, services and processes; helping them change relationships with customers or business partners by looking at such developments as electronic commerce; assisting with a change in the approach to people by finding fresh opportunities for employees to contribute to the organisation in the most effective ways; looking at structures with the aim of helping organisations position themselves for success amid market changes; examining processes with a view to develop better ways of doing business; and helping companies to explore new territory or attempt to alter the competitive landscape of their industries in order to affect and shape their futures.

At the same time as attempting to deliver on all these promises, the firm is also setting about the practicalities of itself being a large organisation. Conscious that Andersen is widely perceived to be 'a juggernaut that you either get on board or get run over by', the firm has launched an initiative aimed at 'keeping a sense of community'. The idea is that rather than being part of a 'faceless structure', employees are inspired and motivated by being members of communities of 150 people or less. There is also a conscious effort to communicate through such means as meetings, Lotus Notes and the development courses for which Andersen is famed.

The Future

First and foremost, Andersen Consulting is dedicated to maintaining high growth. It believes it can achieve this through its constant readiness to change itself – most recently through establishing 'a new global organisation that can speedily deliver the best expertise and the best approaches to its clients anywhere in the world'.

Though proud of its achievements, Andersen is not an organisation to stand still or to be complacent. George Shaheen – who believes that 'the future will be reserved for those who choose to invent it' – says he often tells Andersen Consulting people that they must continue to have enough pride in the firm to have the courage to change it. 'This sentiment has served us well through the years,' he says, adding: 'We look for ways to improve. We keep striving for new and better ways to operate so that we may best serve our clients.'

Consequently, if it sets out – as it has done – to position itself as 'the premier partner' with the insights and capabilities to assist organisations in meeting their own goals, the competition had better look out.

ARM Holdings

ARM is an international high technology company which licenses high-performance, low-cost, power-efficient microprocessors for use in an extensive range of applications such as mobile telephones, portable computers and engine management systems. The company has offices in the UK, United States, Germany, France, Japan and Korea. In April 1998 it achieved simultaneous listing on the UK Stock Exchange and the technology-oriented NASDAQ in the US. Both turnover and profitability have increased significantly in recent times; for the year ended 31 December 1998, pre-tax profits stood at £9.4 million, a increase of 108% over 1997's £4.5 million.

Scorecard:

Flexibility	★★★★
Innovation	★★★★★
Human resources	★★★
Growth markets	★★★★
Quality of management	★★★★★
International orientation	★★★★★

Biggest Plus:
ARM provides a key building block for tomorrow's technology

Biggest Minus:
Fortunes are linked to general appetite for new devices

Key Figures:
(to 31 December 1998)

Annual turnover:	£42.3 million
Pre-tax profit:	£9.4 million
Employees worldwide:	354
Employees UK:	267

ARM Holdings plc
90 Fulbourn Road
Cambridge CB1 9JN
Tel: 01223 400500
Fax: 01223 400700
website: www.arm.com

ARM

ARM Holdings

Company Background

ARM was established in November 1990 as a joint venture between technology leaders Apple, Acorn and VLSI. Its speciality is the development of intellectual property based on RISC processors (Reduced Instruction Set Computing); the ARM* architecture was revolutionary because it placed the emphasis on providing high performance through a low-cost, power-efficient medium. Competing architectures focused more on maximising performance and therefore did not offer the same range of benefits to manufacturers of today's lightweight, portable equipment.

The company has grown rapidly, achieving stock market listings in the UK and US in 1998. It has established an extensive network of partnerships with many leading technology companies throughout the world to help exploit the capabilities of ARM's ground-breaking technology. The company has 11 offices worldwide.

Operations and Markets

ARM is an intellectual property provider. As such, it does not manufacture items; rather, it licenses its designs to electronics companies for use in their own products. ARM also sells software and development systems and provides consulting, maintenance and training services to support its architecture. In addition to fees from licensing agreements, ARM also earns royalties on the use of its technology in end products. These include portable communications devices, digital television equipment, multi-media and other cutting-edge applications.

ARM is structured into six Business Units:

Product Licensing – licenses ARM's various products, including its architecture, processor cores, microprocessors and, working with the other business units, system chips, peripherals, software tools and methods.
Development Systems – provides product designers with a fully-

integrated development environment, combining software tools, hardware/software co-design support and system development boards.

Electronic Design Automation – working with partners, this unit provides ARM licencees with models, model generators and automated design tools.

Software Systems – two areas are covered by this unit: the porting of operating systems to the ARM* architecture; and working with specialist application software vendors to deliver software solutions for industry applications on the ARM* architecture.

Design Consulting – again working with partners, this unit delivers ARM expertise to companies that want to design integrated solutions based on the ARM* processor core and peripherals. The design goal is to reduce system cost, design time and power consumption while improving quality and reliability.

Support Services – provides support, maintenance and training to ARM partners and systems companies, assisting with design issues, software applications and porting.

Given the international nature of ARM's clientele, the services provided through these units are distributed through the company's global network of offices.

Strategy and Management

As the product of a collaboration between three leading players in the electronics and computer industry – Apple, VLSI and Acorn – it is hardly surprising that ARM's strategy since its creation in 1990 has been to forge a global network of partnerships with other organisations. These links enable work to proceed on the development of products which exploit the ARM* architecture – the fast, powerful, energy-efficient microprocessors which are at the heart of contemporary communications technology.

ARM's chairman, president and chief executive officer is Robin Saxby, who has been with the company since the beginning. As head of a company that deals in intellectual property, he realises that his greatest asset is his people; his strategy, therefore, is to create an environment where the brightest minds are able to flourish: 'Our culture is one of hard work and fun,' he says. 'If people do not enjoy what they are doing, they won't be able to perform to their best ability. We need to design the next generation of systems before the competition does. That takes flair and imagination. You have to be prepared to cultivate those characteristics.'

The fast-moving nature of the electronics and computing industry also necessitates a flat management structure where decisions can be made at high speed. ARM has also embraced the international nature of its operations, establishing a physical presence in all its key markets. Robin Saxby says that ARM is a global business run in real time, with senior managers constantly travelling to meet partners and customers. He appreciates the irony of the fact that, even though his company is at the forefront of electronic communications, he might still visit three continents within a week: 'Face to face contact remains of key importance,' he says.

The extensive network of ARM offices means the company is potentially exposed to regional economic problems. For example, it has offices in Korea, a country which felt the full effect of the economic downturn which swept Asia in 1998. However, the global reach of the company means that, if one area is depressed, another can be buoyant. Thus in 1998 ARM experienced significant growth in Japan, securing three new licensing agreements.

ARM has recorded impressive growth during its nine years of operation and the company is ambitious for more. Given the brainpower contained within the organisation, Robin Saxby deems it appropriate to consult staff on possible routes forward. To this end, he held a series of strategy workshops early in 1999 during which everyone from the company was invited to contribute ideas and suggestions. Periodically, ARM will effectively cease operations for a day to allow individuals to refresh lines of communication and discuss macro issues, rather than their more immediate concerns.

With ideas of such value at ARM, the company jealously guards its corporate secrets, using patents and other legal machinery to keep competitors at bay. It attracts and retains its staff with competitive remuneration and an employee share-ownership scheme which enables everyone in the business to share in its success. Robin Saxby says that, in terms of corporate strategy, it is vital that the company harnesses the skills of the top people in the field: 'This is an area where people respond to the challenges you give them. If you provide the right tools, the right environment and the right projects, they will give you their best.'

The strategic direction of the company also aims to reflect the needs of end-users – the people using the portable computers, mobile phones, digital televisions and legion other appliances and applications which rely upon ARM technologies. According to Robin Saxby, this involves 'knowing what the customer wants before he knows he wants it'. Again, close links with product manufacturers ensure that ARM is able to anticipate demand and respond with the necessary techniques, tools and services.

The Future

ARM secured its leading position in its sector of the semiconductor industry by recognising before anyone else that the most important features of microprocessors would be their energy-efficiency and cost-effectiveness. While rivals ignored the issue of power usage and simply concentrated on increasing their offerings' performance capabilities, ARM delivered precisely the right product for the 'small is beautiful' 1990s marketplace. The company can take a large degree of credit for the fact that today's portable appliances are lighter, more powerful and last for longer on a modest battery supply.

Inevitably, ARM's triumph has obliged its competitors to mimic its market-beating approach. Thus the future will see the company working hard to defend its current lead. With partnerships already in place with the world's leading semiconductor, software and systems companies, it is well placed to continue to show the competition a clean pair of heels.

An example of the might of the partnerships with which ARM is involved is the work it is doing with Symbian, the alliance between Psion, Nokia, Ericsson and Motorola. ARM's microprocessors are at the heart of the smart-phones currently being developed, giving the business a greater than 50% share of the digital mobile phone business in 1999. With billions of units expected to be in use by 2005, the prospects for ARM look more than encouraging.

Ove Arup & Partners

Ove Arup & Partners (Arup) is an international firm of consultants, providing engineering design, planning and project management services for civil, industrial, building and transport developments.

Scorecard:

Flexibility	★★★★★
Innovation	★★★★★
Human resources	★★★★
Growth markets	★★★★
Quality of management	★★★★
International orientation	★★★★★

Biggest Plus:
Creative pursuers of excellence

Biggest Minus:
Still repositioning its corporate identity in the marketplace

Key Figures:
(to 31 March 1998)

Turnover:	£217 million
Profit on turnover:	£9.3 million
Reserves:	£37 million
Employees:	4,200

Ove Arup & Partners
13 Fitzroy Street
London W1P 6BQ
Tel: 0171 636 1531
Fax: 0171 580 3924
website: www.arup.com

Ove Arup & Partners

Company Background

Ove Arup & Partners was founded in 1946 by Ove Arup, a British engineer of Danish descent. The firm started life by handling structural engineering for buildings: from there, it expanded into mechanical and electrical engineering, and thereafter into more specialised work such as civil engineering, industrial engineering, car design, acoustics, fire safety design, risk analysis and much more. Throughout its operations, the firm is known as a highly innovative business which invests considerably in research.

Among its many projects, Arup is a London & Continental Railways consortium member for the Channel Tunnel Rail Link: responsible for engineering design and commissioning, the firm sponsored the route which was adopted by the government. It also handled project planning, structural, mechanical and electrical engineering and fire safety design for Heathrow's Terminal 5; did structural, mechanical and electrical engineering, communications and IT for the John F Kennedy International Airport, New York; and structural engineering for the 800-bedroom Shanghai Hilton.

In 1977, the founding partners vested their interest in a trust for the benefit of all employees. Part of the earnings are now shared among members of staff. In 1998, for instance, £6.9 million was set aside for profit-sharing.

Today, 50% of the firm's work is UK-based, with the remaining 50% from its worldwide operations: Arup has offices in 73 countries. The London office is the largest, followed by Hong Kong.

Operations and Markets

Arup's services to clients cover every stage of a project, from inception to completion and afterwards. The firm works with its clients in multi-disciplinary teams to enhance co-ordination. Overall, the policy is to pursue continual improvement in all its products and services.

The firm today handles a wide array of services. These include urban redevelopment, regenerating derelict sites for modern use. Services here may include geotechnics, civil and infrastructure engineering, transportation planning, highways and drainage, maritime engineering and much more. For example, the firm's redevelopment of the Euralille site in Lille, France, included masterplanning, geotechnics and infrastructure, transportation planning, engineering feasibility studies, concept design of civil engineering structures and fire safety design.

Arup is also heavily involved as engineers, planners and project managers of offices, laboratories and industrial facilities: for instance, on the British Airways Heavy Maintenance Hangar in Cardiff. Its environmental services include pollution control through computer-aided dispersion modelling of atmospheric emissions, and redevelopment of contaminated land.

Transportation planning is another service. This includes traffic engineering and development planning, and the firm handles projects from movement studies for single buildings to planning strategies for regions or even countries.

The firm also handles activities such as economics and planning. For instance, work undertaken to support Cape Town's bid to host the 2004 Olympic Games included management of the entire bid process, preparation of the sports plan, capital expenditure estimates, economic benefit analysis, community consultation, urban planning and communications engineering studies.

Arup is perhaps best known to many as an engineer of large-scale projects: highways, bridges, railways (such as Hong Kong's Mass Transit Railway, where work included geotechnical, civil and structural engineering commissions), airports and public buildings, retail, sports and leisure, exhibition centres, resorts, hotels and conference centres among others. An important and more recent development is in the energy field, where the firm provides a wide range of services to the oil and gas industry.

Strategy and Management

The firm has a highly unusual ownership structure, coupled with a belief in excellence. Although important, the concept of profit has traditionally been secondary to the firm's striving for outstanding work and its desire to nurture its people. Its belief in continuous improvement has led to a rolling out of knowledge management.

In 1995, the chairman, Duncan Michael, set out a list of 12 targets for the firm to achieve by the year 2000. These include having highly motivated people working together; to have good leaders in all parts of the firm; to recruit and retain excellent people from diverse sources; to deliver financial performance; to develop ongoing relationships with clients; and to achieve significant and continuing improvements in the quality of work. Together, these 12 targets represent a significant step to a truly modern management basis, working towards a more structured, quantifiable approach.

Another strategic change is to move towards creating global businesses. In 1997, the firm set up two global businesses, Arup Transport and Arup Energy. These have done well, and more may follow on the same model. Transport now accounts for around 20% of Arup's turnover. Global teams mean that the firm can draw on the skills of its people around the world, giving it 24-hour working if necessary, with the work following the sun. This approach means that time and distance become invisible.

For many of the firm's activities, however, local working will always be more appropriate; and here, a strong part of its strategy is to employ local people and truly understand conditions in its various areas. Arup has been in Japan for ten years and is the only foreign registered design engineering business there. It has followed the same route in Moscow and is one of the very few Western companies to have a Russian Federation design licence.

Other strategic initiatives are to define more precisely the way the firm wants to be seen in 10 and 20 years' time. An independent study of four years ago looked at the construction industry and found that Arup was the only firm with a recognisable brand. But this brand will need to develop, especially now that advertising and marketing is permitted within the professional sector.

Many of the firm's clients today are global, heavily branded businesses. The objective is to be more like those clients, without compromising the firm's distinctive cultural identity.

Finally, part of the firm's strategy is to shape its industry rather than be shaped by it. The Egan Report, commissioned by John Prescott, looks at the industry as a whole and has identified some improvements needed in cost, speed, delivery and other areas. Various senior people at the firm are involved in this process. Similarly, one director sits on the board of the Urban Task Force, another government initiative. Influencing events at a high level is part of the firm's culture.

The Future

The firm's strategy is undoubtedly forward-looking; an international firm is clearly better placed to survive local recessions. Currently very well represented in Africa, Asia, Australasia and Europe, if the firm has a geographical weakness, that weakness is in the Americas: it has offices in San Francisco, Los Angeles, Detroit, Boston and New York, but none in Canada, Central America or South America. It intends to address this gap in the next few years.

Another change will be the positioning of the firm. As marketing

and PR manager Olivia Gadd puts it, 'This is all about how we want
to be seen, and the key to that is the pursuit of excellence and delivery
of value. We believe strongly that our work is creative. Creativity is
close to the hearts of all our people, and therefore to the future shape
of the firm.

'We're also keen to continue conceiving of new ways to do things.
We believe we're able to react more quickly to change than some
of our competitors because we have lots of people thinking about
possibilities, and sharing their thoughts across a wide skill base. This
must be a strength for the future: because in our business, time scales
only get shorter.'

Overall, the company's vision of the future is threefold. It aims to
provide clients with an excellent service; to be widely known and
respected for the quality of its work, its concern for the environment,
and its ability to deliver; and to operate as a highly successful international firm. Based on its past achievements and its strong strategy,
this vision looks eminently achievable.

The W & G Baird Group

The W & G Baird Group is the dominant force in printing, book manufacturing and document management in Northern Ireland, with major publishing subsidiaries in England, a position achieved through continued and substantial investment in the most modern technology, staff development and 'the pursuit of excellence in our operating companies'. It is on course to achieve its target of a £45 million turnover by the end of the year 2000 and the development of a wider base in the communications industry through acquisitions and alliances and the development of advanced document management techniques.

Scorecard:

Flexibility	★★★
Innovation	★★★★
Human Resources	★★★★★
Growth markets	★★★★
Quality of management	★★★★
International orientation	★★★

Biggest Plus:
Excellence in technology and skills and a motivating vision

Biggest Minus:
Need for development of greater group cohesion and strategy

Key Figures:
(1997)

Annual turnover	£34 million
Operating profit	£3.2 million
Pre-tax profit	£2.7 million
Annual investment	£5.3 million
Number of employees	568

W & G Baird (Holdings) Limited
Caulside Drive
Antrim BT41 2RS
Tel: 01849 463911
Fax: 01849 466266

The W & G Baird Group

Company Background

It was a circuitous route, with a brief foray into the world of multinational corporations, that brought W & G Baird to its position as one of Northern Ireland's leading companies and an increasingly significant player in the United Kingdom printing industry – with a reach that is extending well beyond the British Isles.

In 1862 brothers William and George Baird, 'craftsmen printers, enterprising, resolute and industrious', opened a tiny print shop in Belfast.

Eight years later they launched Northern Ireland's first halfpenny newspaper, the *Belfast Evening Telegraph*, which over the years established a position as the province's 'national' newspaper. Nearly a century later, in 1964, the company was acquired after a bitter takeover battle by empire-building media baron Lord Thomson. In 1967, however, the print firm W & G Baird Limited, along with a collection of others around Britain, was sold to the British Printing Corporation where it languished in a state of under-investment until 1977 when its present chairman Roy Bailie led a management buy-out and returned it to Ulster ownership.

If ever the phrase 'it never looked back' is appropriate, it is here. Continual investment in leading-edge printing and digital technology, investment in people and investment in developing new markets have resulted in solid foundation organic growth. Enhanced later by a series of strategic acquisitions, they have driven sales from £400,000 to group sales of £34 million.

The excellence of its products has won it many accolades in the annual Irish Printers Awards and in 1995 it was voted North West Regional Printer of the Year by the British Printing Industries Federation.

Operations and Markets

Since it made its first acquisition in 1983, W & G Baird has become a group of six companies. Over the past few years these have received capital investment in new technology to the tune of £8 million.

Related, but diverse in their range of activities, they are:

W & G Baird Limited of Antrim has an enviable reputation as one of the UK's most sophisticated and technically advanced printing facilities. It is a leading supplier of high-quality colour printing, academic journals, trade and technical journals, social and fashion 'glossies' and books. Fifty per cent of output goes outside Northern Ireland.

Textflow Services in Belfast started as a joint venture with Queen's University in 1984, but is now wholly owned. Using digital technology it can convert information in any format to digitally printed 600 dpi form for a wide range of 'on demand' printing. A 100-page A4 book can be printed, collated and bound in a matter of minutes.

MSO Limited of Belfast designs and manufactures printed packages, boxes and presentation packs and is a leading manufacturer of packaging for the food industry, with 75% of total production being exported. It offers a complete service from original concept through design to the finished product, which range from folding carton to rigid box or combinations of both. Multi-media packaging is a rapidly growing sector.

Biddles Limited of Guildford and King's Lynn is a major British book manufacturer and an acknowledged leader in the production of illustrated non-fiction books for publishers across Europe in a huge range of formats and sizes. Its new short-run book division uses the latest digital technology.

Blackstaff Press, although the smallest member, is a jewel in the crown of the group. One of Ireland's most highly regarded, most exciting book publishers, focusing on history, politics, fiction, humour and poetry, it has won the *Sunday Times* UK Small Publisher of the Year award.

Thanet Press – formerly Eyre & Spottiswoode of Margate, this venerable company was founded in 1770 and today is a leader in the field of academic, legal, scientific and security printing. Acquired out of receivership in 1995, it has since enjoyed a major capital investment programme including the installation of a £1.5 million Komori Lithrone four-colour press. Its services range from small-format, multifold leaflets to technical journals and security/confidential printing.

Strategy and Management

When Roy Bailie led his successful management buy-out in 1977 he laid down just one operating principle – 'to be the best at what we do'.

Since then, dedication to providing personal service with technical excellence has been at the core of the management target of £45 million sales by the end of the year 2000. The development of existing and new export markets, mainly in the Republic of Ireland and Europe but also the United States, is also a key element of the strategy.

Managing director of the Antrim company is Bryan McCabe, who has spent his lifetime with the company. He says: 'The mainspring of our synergy is flexibility, an ability to anticipate change. Our whole management team has shown a remarkable ability to recognise the right time to seize the investment opportunity, the right time to forge a new alliance, and the time when it is wise to mark time.'

Harnessing technology and managing change are skills at which the company excels, and investment in state-of-the-art equipment helps keep it centre stage in the printing industry.

This flexibility and quick response is ensured by carrying out all its operations 'in house' from pre-press to warehousing and distribution.

There are probably few other industries where as much competition from a range of previously unthought-of sources has grown, and to remain the best has required continual investment in technology that allows a company to offer 'that something extra', including speed of delivery.

This has been the Baird strategy, an example of which was the £1 million investment in 1998 where a combination of Swiss leading-edge technology and training put it ahead of the field in binding and finishing equipment. The new equipment trebled finishing speeds for magazine and book production – and to ensure that it obtained maximum benefit from it, a team was flown to Zurich for exclusive, hands-on training from the Swiss manufacturers.

Baird operations director Henderson Allen says: 'This has been an innovative step forward. We are committed to developing our people and by taking the team away from production pressures and deadlines they were able to fine-tune their own personal skills on the machines. While on the course, they also had the chance to network with printing companies from Russia and the United States, all of which was useful to us.'

It is now looking at state-of-the-art technologies to maintain forward momentum into the new millennium. Speed of production turnaround without loss of quality is increasingly demanded and the technology for this, both in the form of hardware and software, is developing at a bewildering pace. The W & G Baird association with the Computer

Science Department at Queen's University through its subsidiary Textflow Services gave it a head start in this area, and also in the technology for making short-run printing jobs economically feasible.

The Future

The W & G Baird 'recipe' of new technology, new skills and new markets has served it well over the past two decades and is not going to be changed. However, new opportunities have been identified as being 'where the future is' and the same principles will be applied to the exploitation of these.

Centred round the concept of 'document management' they are a logical extension of the information management expertise that the company has built up and include the production and distribution of corporate printed and electronic documents and archival and retrieval systems. It can be expected that further acquisitions or alliances will be designed to strengthen its position in these areas. Mailing and call-centre operations are other areas under consideration as areas of opportunity.

The development of packaging technology, especially for the food production and retailing sectors in the light of changing legislation, is another area regarded as having great potential for future growth, centred on its group member, MSO. An example of the type of innovative work being carried out there is the development of a new user and customer friendly recyclable tray of coated craft board to replace the traditional polystyrene tray used for retailing chicken and meat products.

Bristol & West plc

Bristol & West is the leading financial institution in the West Country and also has a national presence through its branch network, its intermediaries and its other distribution channels.

Scorecard:

Flexibility	★★★★★
Innovation	★★★
Human resources	★★★★★
Growth markets	★★★★
Quality of management	★★★★
International orientation	★★★

Biggest Plus:
Has a distinctive strategy which gives it a strong sense of direction

Biggest Minus:
Operates in an ever more competitive marketplace

Key Figures:
(to year ending 31 March 1998)

Group profit before tax:	£91.2 million
Gross residential and commercial mortgage lending:	£1,802 million
Mortgage assets:	£10.8 billion
Return on capital:	20%
Share of national residential mortgage lending:	3.5%
Employees UK:	2,500

Bristol & West plc
PO Box 27
Broad Quay
Bristol BS99 7AX
Tel: 0117 979 2222
Fax: 0117 929 3787
website: www.bristol-west.co.uk

Bristol & West plc

Company Background

Bristol & West was founded in the mid nineteenth century as a building society. It converted to a bank in 1997 when it became part of the Bank of Ireland group, creating a major new force in the British personal finance market.

The merger brought a range of benefits to Bristol & West. The relationship is such that Bristol & West enjoys considerable autonomy in its operations while gaining from its parent's strengths. John Burke, chief executive: 'We have better treasury back-up as a result of being part of the Bank of Ireland group and also now have a first-class commercial lending department. This allows us to relationship-manage situations we would probably have had to turn away before.'

Bristol & West's strategy remains unchanged by the merger. That strategy, one of the clearest in its industry, is to focus on just three product types: mortgages, savings and investments. In so doing, it positions itself as a specialist rather than a generalist financial services company. Underlying this strategy is the company's belief that consumers would rather buy the best financial planning products than opt for one-stop shopping. The company's successful growth, to the point where it is now holding more than twice its natural market share, certainly appears to bear this strategy out.

Operations and Markets

In line with its strategy, Bristol & West operates in just three marketplaces: mortgages, savings and investments. The natural question is whether this will suffice for such an ambitious company. Ian Kennedy, group operations director: 'If an area of our market is not doing so well for a while, there is a temptation to add in other business lines. But we've resisted that temptation. As our strategy has developed, it's made us look more carefully at our markets. The impact of this scrutiny has led us in two directions: to develop new distribution channels and to find new niche markets.'

The company's southern bias geographically may even have been an advantage, since it has forced it to develop new means of distribution. It now has a very broad range, allowing it to address different parts of the market. Its approach is to set up a separate unit to deal with each channel. For instance, its mortgage business has five different distribution channels: Bristol & West branches, intermediaries, telephone, post and Internet. Each has its own sales and marketing functions, allowing significant concentration of resources.

In the same way, its savings market initiative has three channels: its branches, postal and telephone marketing, and Bristol & West Professional Intermediaries (which targets stockbrokers and other professionals). There is also a Guernsey-based offshore subsidiary, Bristol & West International, which has been developed considerably in the last few years.

The investment side until recently had just one distribution channel, the company's branches: but new developments in this sector include Direct Investments, a means of calling on existing customers who ask for investment advice, piloted over the last 12 months.

In terms of products, the company is currently revamping its entire range. Tied to Eagle Star, it is now engaged in designing a new range of Bristol & West products which are set to launch in 1999. Instead of the traditional capital growth, income growth or geographically based investments, for instance, the company will be focusing on risk profiles and offering low, medium and high return products. In the mortgage field, the company also offers commercial mortgages, a product line which has been highly successful in recent years.

The company does sell related products, for instance, life assurance for mortgages – but only on the back of its core products. Ian Kennedy: 'Our related products are there for one reason: to make our main products more effective. We're happy to offer them; but we're equally happy for our customers to go elsewhere for them.'

Bristol & West has a record of successful niche marketing. One is the buy-to-let mortgage, designed for people who buy retail properties as investments. Another initiative planned is the subprime mortgage, aimed at those who have experienced credit problems. Jeff Warren, deputy chief executive: 'Some people are genuinely bad risks; but some have suffered problems through no fault of their own – for instance, marital breakdown, recession, or whatever – and have subsequently rebuilt their lives. This is a higher risk sector, but it also offers higher margins. We will be one of the first mainstream lenders into this sector when we launch our product in the next few months, and this type of initiative is typical of our niche marketing approach.'

Strategy and Management

The company intends to be within the top three of its peer group (in essence, the converted building societies) in terms of return on equity and aims to achieve this goal in the next three years. Another goal is to be within the top three in terms of cost/asset ratio. However, one ambition it definitely does not have is to be the lowest cost provider. Jeff Warren: 'Our policy is to be specialists, to be very competitive – in short, to be approachable experts. We offer value for money quality products, not cheap or cut-price solutions.'

The strategy is simply expressed: to focus on just three markets and ignore anything 'outside the box'. Those markets are mortgages, savings and investments. Rather than be tempted into 'off-message' products, the company has focused on developing its distribution channels – to good effect. Jeff Warren: 'Our range of distribution is as good as any in the market and better than most, relative to our size. For instance, although we don't have truly national coverage through our branch network, we do through intermediaries, our postal offers, and so on. Indeed, I believe our non-branch distribution is better developed than that of many of our competitors.'

The company now operates in a marketplace more competitive than ever before – and one which will be yet more competitive in the future, according to most observers. This increased competition has been largely from non-bank operators entering the market. The company admits that these new competitors have squeezed margins, to the benefit of customers. Not only will these competitors remain, but more are likely to arise as European market barriers fall. The challenge for Bristol & West therefore is, how will it sustain its success and its profitability in the new market? Jeff Warren has no doubts. 'I am convinced that our distinctive strategy will allow us to do this. It comes down to a fundamental judgement: does the average consumer want to buy all his or her financial services from one supplier, or pick and choose the best? We have opted clearly for the latter, and time will tell whether we or the generalists have got it right.'

Another strand of the company's strategy will come from its Bank of Ireland group affiliation. Most pundits believe that further consolidation is inevitable in the financial services industry. It is now part of a group with considerable free capital, and one which is keen to deploy that capital for acquisition purposes as the opportunity arises. Such an opening will surely appear over the next few years; and as the Bank of Ireland group sees Bristol & West as its most important UK company, expansion through merger or acquisition looks like a strong possibility.

The Future

The outlook looks good for Bristol & West. It has a distinctive strategy, a supportive, capital-rich parent which is happy to allow it to operate autonomously, strong management and supportive staff. Clearly positioned as a specialist happy and willing to develop new means of distribution and new niche products within its three product sectors, the company looks set to enjoy continued growth considerably above what its size would suggest.

John Burke: 'We had 146 years of mutuality. Undoubtedly the building society environment was somewhat easy-going. The move to plc status, coupled with Bank of Ireland membership, offers many exciting opportunities. Our staff have the opportunity to share in the growth of both Bristol & West and the group, and to continue to develop a first-class business into the next millennium.'

British Aerospace

British Aerospace is a world leader in aerospace and defence with annual sales exceeding £8.5 billion and an order book of nearly £24 billion. It is Europe's major proven systems integrator and one of the most successful prime contractors in the world. British Aerospace employs around 46,000 people in the design, development, manufacture and testing of civil and military aircraft, guided weapon systems, artillery and ammunition, together with other high-technology systems and equipment. Around 90% of British Aerospace sales are exported to over 72 countries.

Scorecard:

Flexibility	★★★★
Innovation	★★★★★
Human resources	★★★★
Growth markets	★★★★
Quality of management	★★★★
International orientation	★★★★

Biggest Plus:
Europe's leading systems integrator and prime contractor in aerospace and defence

Biggest Minus:
Competition from a rapidly consolidating US industry

Key Figures:
(to 31 December 1998)

Sales	£8,546 million
Pre-tax profit	£596 million
Order book*	£23.8 billion
Employees worldwide	46,500
Employees UK	41,000

*at end June 1998

British Aerospace plc
Warwick House
Farnborough Aerospace Centre
Farnborough, Hampshire GU14 6YU
Tel: 01252 373232
Fax: 01252 383000
website: www.bae.co.uk

British Aerospace

Company Background

British Aerospace is a proud company whose history dates back to the earliest days of aviation and defence engineering. The company has been established as a pioneering defence and aerospace innovator for more than 90 years.

British Aerospace is Europe's major proven systems integrator and one of the most successful prime contractors in the world, providing total land, air and sea solutions to the most demanding customers worldwide.

British Aerospace is the UK's largest exporter of manufactured goods and the fourth largest aerospace and defence company in the world.

Operations and Markets

While much of the manufacturing base of British Aerospace (BAe) lies within the UK, its markets are global, with customers in 72 countries. In addition to the major contribution BAe makes to national security at home, the defence businesses contribute to the security of many other nations friendly to the UK.

Some of the best known projects in which British Aerospace is involved include the Airbus family of commercial airliners; the Eurofighter, Tornado and Nimrod MRA4 aircraft; and Rapier, ASRAAM and Seawolf missiles.

BAe supports some 3,000 military aircraft in service with 23 air forces. Similarly in commercial aerospace, BAe supports airliners in service with airline customers worldwide. Its broad customer base includes 1,900 Airbus aircraft now in service with 160 operators. British Aerospace is a 20% partner in Airbus Industrie, which has established a strong market position with customers in 70 countries.

British Aerospace's business units are organised under Commercial Aerospace, Defence and Other Business Units.

Commercial Aerospace includes the management of BAe's interests and responsibilities within the Airbus Industrie consortium, Regional

Aircraft and asset management. Main activities include the design of wings and fuel systems for all Airbus airliners; the manufacture and assembly of the primary structure of all Airbus wings; building the fuselage and wings for the Hawker range of business aircraft; and Airbus maintenance and aircraft conversion. Airbus has been successful in capturing over 30% of the market but with Boeing still dominating 60%, there's a lot to go for.

Defence, by far the largest business area, includes BAe Military Aircraft and Aerostructures, BAe Systems and Services and BAe Defence Systems. The latter incorporates BAeSEMA, Battlefield Systems, BAe Royal Ordnance, BAe Systems and Equipment, the former Siemens Plessey Systems and the company's interests in Matra BAe Dynamics, STN ATLAS and Sika International, a joint venture with Lockheed Martin.

BAe Military Aircraft designs, develops, manufactures and supports advanced military combat and training aircraft which, allied to its technology and systems integration capabilities, have given British Aerospace a world-beating reputation for quality and reliability.

The prime contract for the Nimrod MRA4 has seen engineering work build up rapidly on the UK's replacement maritime patrol aircraft. Nimrod MRA4 is one of the world's most sophisticated airborne platforms and the integration of its multiple sensors and systems represents a massive application of systems integration.

A notable programme milestone was the four nation Eurofighter signature by the defence Ministers of the UK, Germany, Italy and Spain at the end of 1997. The agreement enabled funding of the production investment phase to be subsequently released, and launched the programme into production. Eurofighter will be Europe's largest defence programme and a cornerstone of the defence capability of the European partner nations, and their allies, well into the next century.

The Tornado combat aircraft remains a substantial industrial activity. The GR4 (a major upgrade to 142 early GR1 aircraft) is being delivered to the RAF, while deliveries of Tornados to Saudi Arabia under the government to government Al Yamamah programme have been completed. Tornado is likely to remain a core element of military aircraft workload for the foreseeable future.

Hawk continues to attract strong export interest, with the government of Australia recently placing a contract for a new Lead In Fighter variant of Hawk.

Under 'Other Businesses', BAe Aerostructures is the most important, but flight training, consultancy services and BAe's Sowerby Research Centre in Bristol fall under its wing.

British Aerospace's research and development activities, spread across the businesses but centred on Sowerby, represent a massive investment in the technologies of tomorrow. They cover a wide spectrum, from software development through composite materials to synthetic environments and some 170 highly qualified scientists and engineers are helping to turn science fiction into reality.

Strategy and Management

Many companies and organisations today talk about 'partnerships' but in few industries is it as evident, and as important, as in aviation and defence engineering. 'We at British Aerospace view our customers as partners, and we see partnership as the key to providing effective solutions. By working together we can more readily identify the real issues, agree on the optimum way forward and progress as a team towards achieving our mutual objectives,' says Sir Richard Evans, chairman. British Aerospace has no fewer than 29 major international collaborative partnerships.

BAe welcomed the trilateral agreement signed in 1998 by the governments of France, Germany and the UK, supporting the principles of consolidation of the aerospace and defence industries of those countries.

Sir Richard Evans says: 'Recognising the challenge posed from the US of a strong, consolidated industry operating in the world's largest aerospace and defence market, British Aerospace continues to pursue opportunities to create further value through a restructuring of our industry. In Europe we have a long history of collaboration on major programmes such as Tornado and now Eurofighter. As a leader in the industry in Europe we are well placed to pursue our strategy through a combination of high-level dialogue with others with whom we share a vision of a strong European aerospace and defence industry and also through the pursuit of opportunities to acquire complementary businesses and build partnerships.'

Recognising the importance of the US, BAe values its transatlantic relationships. Its relationship with Boeing on the Harrier and T45 activity has been supplemented by a partnership between BAe and Boeing on the Nimrod MRA4 programme. BAe is also forging a relationship with Lockheed Martin on the next generation Joint Strike Fighter in the US and the TRACER land system integration programme.

BAe has merged its Dynamics guided weapons business with the French Matra Defence business to form Matra BAe Dynamics in 1996, which in turn acquired 30% of German guided weapons business Lenkflugkörpersysteme. The German defence systems integration business STN Atlas Electronik was also acquired and in 1998 BAe bid successfully for the UK and Australia based Siemens Plessey businesses. The integration of these businesses with others has formed the core of a new defence systems business.

In Commercial Aerospace, BAe's strategy is to combine efficient operations with international partnerships. The partners in the Airbus consortium have agreed to structure the partnership into a single corporate entity with an integrated and focused management team responsible for the assets across the Airbus system.

Technology is a vital differentiator in the aerospace and defence industry. The complexity of high-performance aircraft such as Eurofighter demands the application of advanced technology in the design, engineering and manufacture of such systems. BAe recognises that today, systems must work with exacting efficiency, reliability and, above all, at a cost that is affordable to the customer and lower than the competition. The development of its advanced systems capability is being focused in BAe's new defence systems division based around the Siemens Plessey business.

British Aerospace refers to its 'Value Plan', an initiative coursing through the business aimed at continuing BAe's success story in the face of an aggressive competitive environment. BAe identifies five values on which it focuses its efforts and gives its priorities for action: making customers the highest priority; recognising that its people are its greatest strength; accepting that its future lies in successful partnerships and making them really work; understanding that innovation and technology will give it competitive edge; and a commitment to continuous performance improvement as the key to winning.

The Future

Airbus is a very profitable activity for BAe and so progress on Airbus will be a central focus, especially as it will continue to be under severe pressure from the competition. The evergreen Al Yamamah contract to provide military hardware and support services to Saudi Arabia will also remain important. In addition to delivery of the Tornados, the programme includes Hawk, Harrier, Eurofighter aircraft, Rapier and Seawolf missiles, ammunition, defence, naval and communications systems.

Consolidation of the defence industries in Europe is probably the most critical factor in British Aerospace's future. Fortunately, this is a trend gathering momentum. BAe will be looking to increase its overall presence on the Eurofighter programme. The defence systems business has been given critical mass and the BAe/Matra join venture should increase contract wins.

While it will continue to cut costs and raise margins and productivity, winning new business will remain the order of the day. Consolidation of the European defence industry and bigger, stronger commercial partnerships will hold the key. With firmly-held positions in its markets and a long order book, British Aerospace looks set to be one of the major players in this long-term industry.

British Airways

British Airways is one of the world's leading airlines. In its own right, British Airways mainline scheduled services reach 166 destinations in 85 countries. BA's global alliance, which also includes equity investments in Air Liberté, Deutsche BA and Quantas, and codeshare arrangements with airlines including Canadian Airlines, American West Japan Air Lines and Finnair, means that its network of flight services is one of the most extensive in the world. British Airways (BA) is also a member of the **one**world alliance covering global marketing and customer service.

Scorecard:

Flexibility	★★★★★
Innovation	★★★★
Human resources	★★★
Growth markets	★★★★
Quality of management	★★★★
International orientation	★★★★★

Biggest Plus:
Well positioned to fulfil its mission to be the leader in world travel

Biggest Minus:
Battles with regulatory authorities can slow down progress

Key Figures:
(to 31 March 1998)

Revenue	£8,642 million
Operating profit	£504 million
Pre-tax profit	£580 million
Annual investment	£2 billion (committed)
Passengers carried	41 million
Employees worldwide	58,210
Employees UK	47,686

British Airways Plc
PO Box 365
Waterside Harmondsworth
UB7 0GB
Tel: 0181 759 5511
website: www. british-airways.com

BRITISH AIRWAYS

British Airways

Company Background

British Airways is, rather obviously, a British airline – and proud of it – but at the same time it is extremely global. It has global obligations to its customers, to its staff in 85 countries, to its partners, to shareholders, and to the world itself.

British Airway's new corporate identity, which includes an array of dazzling aircraft tailfin liveries drawn from design and cultural influences around the world, attracted much attention. Well received around the world, sometimes criticised at home as spurning its 'British' identity, it gave British Airways (BA) the opportunity to reinforce its global airline positioning. And quite right too.

British Airways can trace its origins back to the birth of civil aviation, in the halcyon days following the end of World War One. In its later guise as BOAC, the airline was in government hands until 1987 when it was privatised and floated on the London Stock Exchange with the repositioning of 'The World's Favourite Airline'. BA still has some 235,000 shareholders today.

BA is the world's largest international passenger airline. More than 40.9 million passengers were carried by British Airways Group in 1997/98, with 34.3 million flying on mainline BA services. The airline operates an average of over one thousand flights a day and its fleet, at January 1999, comprised 226 aircraft. BA's main base is London Heathrow Airport, the largest international airport in the world, and it also operates an increasing number of services out of London Gatwick Airport.

Operations and Markets

Bob Ayling, chief executive, states: 'British Airways carries on an international business whose history is in state ownership and regulated markets, but which today is in private ownership in deregulating markets. In tomorrow's world, British Airways must compete in a global airline economy in deregulated markets. And we must prepare for that future.'

Air travel remains a large and growing industry. It facilitates economic growth, world trade, international investment and tourism and is therefore central to the globalisation taking place in many other industries. In the past decade air travel has grown by 7% each year so that scheduled airlines carry around 1.5 billion passengers annually. The International Air Transport Association (IATA) forecasts that international air travel will grow by more than five per cent a year from 2000 to 2010.

A number of factors are forcing airlines to become more efficient. The European Union has ruled that governments should not be allowed to subsidise their loss-making airlines. Elsewhere, governments' concerns over their own finances and a recognition of the benefits of privatisation have led to a gradual transfer of ownership of airlines from the state to the private sector. In order to appeal to prospective shareholders, airlines are having to become more efficient and competitive.

Deregulation is also stimulating competition from small, low-cost carriers, led by the US in 1978 with Europe following suit. 'Open skies' agreements are beginning to dismantle some of the regulations governing which carriers can fly on certain routes, and EU regulations now allow an airline from one member state to fly passengers within another's domestic market. Strong nationalist sentiments towards domestic 'flag carriers' still persist, however, and airlines continue to face limitations on where they can fly in many parts of the world.

A record 40,955,000 passengers flew with BA in 1997/98, and the airline achieved a mainline passenger load factor of 71.3%. Air cargo is also very important, and amounts currently to a £600 million business for BA.

In 1997/98, BA announced pre-tax profits of £580 million on revenues of £8,642 million. These have both been on an upward trend over recent years, although a 'blip' was registered in 1997/98 due, primarily, to a cabin crew dispute

Strategy and Management

BA has set itself a new mission: to be the undisputed leader in world travel. It breaks this down into a number of goals: *customers' choice* – the airline of first choice in key markets; *strong profitability* – meeting investors' expectations and securing the future; *truly global* – global network; global outlook: recognised everywhere for superior value on world travel; *inspired people* – building on success and delighting customers.

BA's established strategy to secure strong global presence and future profitability through international alliances continues. BA's global alliance, which is all about routes, flights and pricing, includes a number of bilateral relationships including Qantas, Deutsche BA, Air Liberté,

Japan Air Lines and Canadian Airlines International, and has been expanded to include Finnair and LOT Polish Airlines. A memorandum of understanding has been signed with the Spanish carrier, Iberia, and discussions are taking place with a number of other parties. The alliances are complemented by a portfolio of franchise operators, which effectively takes the British Airways brand and worldwide network into smaller but important markets in Britain and other countries.

There is also a multilateral alliance called **one**world, launched in January 1999. **One**world is a more broadly based alliance providing global coverage in areas of marketing and customer service, including information sharing, check-in processes, transfers and global travel products such as 'frequent flyer' schemes. BA's partners in the **one**world alliance are American Airlines, Canadian Airlines, Cathay Pacific and Quantas, and covers some 630 destinations in 138 countries.

The proposed alliance between BA and American Airlines continues to be stalled by the regulatory authorities in London, Washington and Brussels, much to BA's frustration (other competitive airline combines are up and running). Airport infrastructure, especially landing and take-off slots, lies at the centre of questions concerning this alliance. New runway capacity at key airports is rarely a viable option (on environmental grounds) and BA believes that a system of slot trading among airlines is the most satisfactory and transparent solution.

The strategy to develop Gatwick Airport as a network hub, working in tandem with Heathrow, continues to progress.

In 1998 British Airways launched 'go', a new airline to compete in the fast-growing, European low-cost, 'no frills' alternative air travel market. As a stand-alone subsidiary, and based at Stansted Airport, 'go' commenced Boeing 737 services to Milan, Rome and Copenhagen in 1998, and other destinations will follow.

BA is dedicated to investing relentlessly in the continuous upgrading of its business infrastructure. In 1998 it committed a further £2 billion, as part of a £6 billion programme over three years on new services, products, aircraft and training. Much of this has gone into replacing the older parts of its aircraft fleet with modern aircraft that have greater customer appeal.

A new £250 million World Cargocentre at Heathrow was opened at the beginning of 1999, which has doubled BA's capacity for freight and mail.

BA has an ongoing Business Efficiency Programme (BEP), which delivered £250 million of further cost reductions over 1997/98. BEP is aimed at saving £1 billion a year by the turn of the century. And while the cabin crew dispute resulted in a one-off cost of £125 million in 1997/98, its resolution did secure the £42 million a year saving which was required from the cabin crew budget.

BA reacted quickly to the economic crisis in the Asia-Pacific region by realigning capacity with an increase in some services and a reduction in others.

The headquarters moved to Waterside, a new custom-built £200 million combined business centre at Harmondsworth, close to Heathrow. Its design and layout is intended to improve the productivity and business efficiency of the 2,700 staff relocated there.

BA also invests heavily in technology, which continues to shape radical changes in the airline industry. Investment in electronic ticketing, self-service machines and online booking via the BA website has eased congestion at airports and made customers happier.

And investment in people is at the fore. Education, training and career progression for employees is a top priority, as is recruitment. BA expects to recruit 15,000 new employees by the end of 2001, from all parts of the world. 'British Airways is becoming a truly global company,' says Bob Ayling. 'More than 60% of our customers come from outside the UK, and we expect this soon to rise to 80%.'

The Future

BA's overall outlook is favourable, with the airline well positioned in a world industry that continues to promise growth in passenger and cargo levels. There is good growth in European markets, fuel prices have fallen and sterling has dropped back from recent peaks. These effects will help offset the impact of any slowdown in the UK and US domestic markets and the current difficulties in the Far East.

BA has long since recognised the implications of the so-called 'millennium bug' and, through its Year 2000 Project Board, has invested at least £100 million in preventative measures to ensure the safety of customers and employees, together with the continuity of business systems.

With bigger international global alliances really holding the key to global success, BA will want a successful resolution of its proposed alliance with American Airlines. For an international airline, international boundaries really do need to disappear. As Bob Ayling puts it: 'We are proud of our British heritage, but we must never forget that our customers and service belong to the world.'

British Steel

British Steel is one of the world's largest steel-makers, a public company which cast off its nationalised heritage many years ago. It is also one of Britain's most international companies, with around £4 billion of exports each year out of a £7 billion total, and sales offices in more than 40 countries. It already has manufacturing plants in the US and has ambitions to produce steel in Europe and Asia in due course.

Scorecard:

Flexibility	★★
Innovation	★★★★★
Human resources	★★★
Growth markets	★★★
Quality of management	★★★★★
International orientation	★★★★★

Biggest Plus:
A manufacturer with a thoroughly international outlook and a strong track record of innovation

Biggest Minus:
Operates in tough international markets where there is chronic overcapacity in manufacturing

Key Figures:
(to 28 March 1998)

Turnover	£6,947 million
Operating profit	£265 million
Pre-tax profit	£315 million
Annual investment	£404 million
Employees worldwide	47,000
Employees UK	37,600

British Steel plc
15 Marylebone Road
London NW1 5JD
Tel: 0171 314 5571
Fax: 0171 314 5633

British Steel

Company Background

British Steel was privatised in 1988. Even while it was owned by the government it had transformed productivity and since becoming a public company the transformation has continued, making it one of the world's most efficient steel-makers. That has involved many high-profile closures of plants such as Ravenscraig in Scotland, but the company's management has been resolute in pursuing a low-cost, high-innovation strategy which allows it to compete successfully in the very difficult global steel industry.

The strategy has included a determined push to internationalise the group. The clearest evidence of that is in two production sites in the US, plus interests in Germany, and a desire to make acquisitions in Eastern Europe as well as Asia once the region's economy is in good shape.

As well as aiming to manufacture closer to its markets, British Steel's strategy is to overcome the cyclical nature of the industry, the consequences of which can be seen in recent financial performance. Profits, which had risen rapidly in the mid 1990s, peaked in 1996 and fell back sharply as prices on the world market dropped and the high pound made life tough for exporters. The group's finances remain strong, however, and it continued to invest both in manufacturing plant and in research and development.

Operations and Markets

Most of the group's steel is made in the UK, with four major plants dominating output – Port Talbot and Llanwern in South Wales, plus Scunthorpe and Teesside. Manufacturing also takes place at 11 other sites in the UK, while British Steel has established a toehold in the US with two steelworks in Alabama. Output covers an extremely wide range of steel products, with stainless steel included in Avesta Sheffield, a joint venture with the Swedish group, Avesta.

Construction and the car industry are the largest UK markets for steel and they are also the top two customers for British Steel. Third comes packaging and these three end-users dominate both the company's and the industry's output. Imports have made steady inroads into the UK and now account for almost half the total domestic steel use, but that is matched by British Steel's strong export push, which means that just over half its production is now sold abroad.

'We want British Steel to be perceived as the world's best-performing steel company. Because customers are global we have to establish some kind of global relationship. But it is difficult to break down social and national boundaries,' says Geoff Hooker, director, product and market development.

The industry throughout Europe has suffered from overcapacity for decades, which has been difficult to reduce because of widespread state ownership and the political importance of steel in many countries. The extent of government involvement has been reducing, however, and there has recently been some encouraging consolidation among producers.

Overcapacity has made it difficult to sustain adequate price levels except at the peak of the steel cycle. Pricing pressures increased in 1998 because of the downturn in Asia. That region had become a large customer for European steel as the economies boomed, but the sudden slump, combined with the construction of new Asian manufacturing capacity, added to the global production surplus.

In the words of the chairman, Sir Brian Moffat: 'The economic crises in South-east Asia, Korea and Japan are bound to cause disruption to traditional world steel trade flows, particularly for export-based business. The outlook for steel demand in the UK will rest heavily on the effectiveness and efficiency of our export-driven customer base.'

As the world's fourth largest producer, and the second largest in Europe, British Steel benefits from economies of scale in manufacturing and marketing. It has also steadily pushed down costs so that 37,000 employees now produce more output than was manufactured by 166,000 in 1980. Success with important new products has also emphasised its skills in innovation and marketing

On the other hand the group faces enormous difficulties making strategic moves, both to encourage consolidation of the industry in Western Europe and to acquire capacity elsewhere. It could also be at a disadvantage compared to European competitors by remaining a sterling-based business, outside the recently formed euro zone.

Strategy and Management

With excess manufacturing capacity unlikely to go away in a hurry, British Steel's strategy is based on expanding the market for steel as well as maximising its market share against competitors. Internationalisation is another key leg of strategy, while a third leg is to move 'downstream' by moving further into processing basic steel products, for example to make 'blanks' for the car industry, taking over some of the metal forming traditionally carried out by the car makers. This approach is supported by a determination to build a strong environmental record and develop the skills and capabilities of employees.

'If you look to the long term the key thing that will determine the size of British Steel will be the competitiveness of steel against competing industries such as aluminium,' reckons Geoff Hooker. 'We have a very carefully thought out strategy to maintain or increase steel's market share in key sectors.'

There have been a number of significant product successes across the three key customer markets, illustrated in total by the fact that 80% of the steel the company sells today consists of products which have been developed over the past 10 years.

In construction, for example, British Steel has developed a new flooring system, called Slimdek. Because it is slimmer than traditional floor sections it reduces the height of buildings. Nine floors can be created in a building which would only accommodate eight using previous steel sections.

The group's construction specialists have also developed steel frames for domestic building, which are now in use in the UK. The company argues that these frames simplify construction and result in more efficient houses from an energy and sound point of view.

These specific products are continuing steel's advance in the construction sector, which has seen it steadily grab market share from reinforced concrete. That process has been driven by employing teams of structural engineers which have been able to sell the advantages of steel to specifiers who would otherwise have opted for concrete frames.

A similar approach has been taken in the car industry, where car designers have been recruited to work on ways of improving the attractiveness of steel compared with rival products. British Steel has been part of a global steel industry consortium which has rethought car design to arrive at a method of building stronger, lighter vehicles. A $20 million, two-year project came up with a solution which used steel innovatively to produce a car shell 25% lighter than traditional methods. The process will continue in a bid to ensure that car-makers continue to use steel in the world's vehicles.

These products, and others such as thinner cans for the food and drink industry, are a consequence of heavy investment in research and development – exceeding £50 million for the first time in 1997/8.

Investment in R&D and in capital equipment are long-standing traditions at British Steel. More recently the group has embarked upon a different kind of investment – building a brand to help differentiate the company from its competitors.

The 'brand proposition' focuses on performance – the best service and quality, best employers and most committed employees, combined with good financial and environmental performance. The brand image was encapsulated in the 'World Beaters' series of advertisements, featuring slogans such as 'Japanese airport, Italian architect, British Steel'.

These developments demonstrate the modern management approach taken under the chairmanship of Sir Brian Moffat. A long-serving British Steel executive, Sir Brian stepped down as chief executive in January 1999 after seven years, but continues as chairman – a post he has held since 1993.

Most of his fellow executive directors have had similarly long service with the company, but have demonstrated that they can drive change to meet the demands of this difficult market and are seen as having developed strong management throughout the business.

The Future

Internationalisation is the key challenge for British Steel over the next few years. It has already taken some faltering steps but further progress depends largely on factors beyond the company's control – such as the agreement of the Polish government to allow a takeover of a Polish steel company on terms acceptable to British Steel. Similarly, expansion in Asia is likely to await the recovery of the region's economy.

The group is well placed compared to most of its international rivals, however. It cast off the restraints of state ownership a long time ago, and already has a more international outlook than most competitors. Allied to a highly competitive cost base, this gives the group a head start in the development of the industry over the next few years.

British Sky Broadcasting Group

BSkyB is Britain's leading pay TV provider with approximately 3.5 million satellite subscribers, producing and packaging eleven channels with a total reach of 6.9 million subscribers. BSkyB is organised into Sky Entertainment (direct home-to-satellite business), Sky Networks (content) and Sky Sports (sports channels and interests). BSkyB also has a number of joint ventures managed under Sky Ventures. BSkyB's production and management offices are located at Isleworth in Middlesex, and its call centre operation in Livingston, Scotland.

Scorecard:

Flexibility	★★★★
Innovation	★★★★★
Human resources	★★★★
Growth markets	★★★★★
Quality of management	★★★★
International orientation	★★

Biggest Plus:
Market leader in the digital television revolution

Biggest Minus:
Due to the pioneering nature of the company, uncertainty always in attendance

Key Figures:
(to 30 June 1998)

Turnover	£1,434.1 million
Operating profit	£340.6 million
Pre-tax profit	£270.9 million
Employees UK	4,897 (full-time)

British Sky Broadcasting Group plc
Grant Way
Isleworth
Middlesex
TW7 5QD
Tel: 0171 705 3000
Fax: 0171 705 3030
website: www.sky.co.uk

British Sky Broadcasting Group

Company Background

BSkyB celebrated its tenth birthday in February 1999 after flirting, in its earliest days, with not making it to its first. Loss-making BSkyB came within a whisker of bringing down the entire News Corporation in the late 1980s, but it's all very different now. Turned around to profitability under previous chief executive Sam Chisholm, it has gone from strength to strength and now, under new chief executive Mark Booth, is poised to dominate the digital TV revolution in the UK.

News International still owns nearly 40% of BSkyB, Pathe has 17% and BSB Holdings 11%. Institutional investors hold the remainder, and the company has some 35,000 shareholders in all.

Sky started with four channels when there were two competing satellite TV providers. The two merged to form BSkyB. With Sky, third party and joint venture products, BSkyB provides some 40 analogue channels direct-to-home and now, through SkyDigital, up to an amazing 140 channels.

The company has effectively re-invented itself for digital, and has a major part of the market. SkyDigital was launched successfully on 1 October 1998 and everyone expects that digital will grow the market considerably. Sky is already in 7 million homes, approximately 30% of households in the British Isles. BSkyB's uninterrupted profit growth of 1993–97 did register a 'blip' in 1998, mostly due to the necessarily heavy cost of launching SkyDigital.

Operations and Markets

BSkyB's dual role of platform distributor and programme maker/content owner has been made more explicit by creating three divisions to optimise value and provide greater management accountability.

Sky Entertainment, the direct-to-home business, is responsible for driving subscriber numbers, distribution, striking deals with channel providers, new business and managing relationships with existing customers through the Subscriber Management Centre.

Sky Networks is the content business, responsible for the entertainment channels, including movies and documentaries, Sky One and Sky News (which is created internally) and joint venture channels. Networks also manages the distribution of these channels through the cable networks, and Sky Box Office, which was launched in December 1997.

Sky Sports consolidates all of BSkyB's sports channels and interests, and represents the leader in sports television in the UK. It also distributes its award-winning sports channels on cable – a task less onerous because the regulators demand it.

The 1990s saw a rapid growth of the direct-to-home platform, which slowed down in 1997/98 and is now perhaps even flat. Of 6.88 million paying subscribers in the UK and Ireland direct-to-home, or satellite, has 3.5 million (2.5 million subscribe to Sky Movies, 2.7 million to Sky Sports). The rest are through cable. BSkyB's approximate turnover split is: direct-to-home subscribers 67%, cable subscribers 16% and advertising 14%.

Expectations are that digital will increase subscriber numbers on the direct-to-home platform, although BSkyB is reluctant to make long-term predictions. In the first four months to 31 January 1999, BSkyB achieved over 350,000 digital sales, of which 120,000 were new customers. This greatly exceeded BSkyB's original target of 200,000 and a new target of 1 million sales by October has been set. The figures reveal the potential.

In programming, the most salient feature is the big increase (30%) in the budget devoted to original productions as opposed to bought-in shows. In 1997/98, BSkyB spent some £687 million making or buying programmes – 63% of total operating costs – underlining its commitment to having shows and content exclusive to Sky.

BSkyB has also started to produce its own films. Sky Pictures was launched in December 1998 to provide an alternative to bought-in Hollywood movies, and its $20 million budget aims to produce around 12 films in two years. One of these will be Ewan McGregor's directorial debut.

Sky Sports is an extremely successful business and has invested £1 billion in the FA Premier League since 1992 in what Sam Chisholm once described as 'one of the greatest corporate romances of the century'. There are three sports channels and, on digital only, Sky Sports News. Then there is MUTV (Manchester United TV), a joint-venture with MUFC and Granada.

BSkyB did what no-one else had ever done – charge separately for sports rights. Sports has been the driver of BSkyB's business, but bid prices had to increase as others eventually realised the value in (particularly) football. Knock-on price increases to subscribers probably adversely affected the image of the company, but a threshold (price freeze) was reached around 1997 and subscriber levels have been stable since.

Strategy and Management

Sky Entertainment has invested heavily to ensure that Sky satellite subscribers will receive a new digital television service that is superior to the competition. According to Mark Booth, 'The success of digital television is as inevitable as the successful introduction of colour television was 30 years ago. TV is constrained in the UK not by demand, but by analogue supply.' The onset of digital television is transforming what is possible through TV.

Important new services are available to SkyDigital subscribers, including the expansion of Sky Movies to eleven screens. Sky Movies will be 'multiplexed', ensuring that subscribers have a choice of up to five different movies starting every hour.

With other companies joining the digital revolution, BSkyB has set up a number of carriage deals to offer a wide range of independent channels to its own subscribers and, conversely, making its channels available through cable and digital operators. Many channels, however, have been secured on a satellite and cable exclusive basis, to differentiate clearly Sky's offer from terrestrial.

Digital television enhances programming options and opens up a world of interactive features. Sky Sports, for example, could show action replays or player information at the press of a button. It also provides greater capacity – viewers could opt to receive additional games over and above Sky's contractual fixtures and an experiment with the Nationwide League is in the pipeline.

British Interactive Broadcasting (BIB) is a joint venture between BSkyB (32.5%), BT, Midland and Matsushita, due to be launched in 1999. BSkyB believes that, by developing a range of services through interactive technology (under the brand name 'Open'), the television experience will be widened, allowing BSkyB to become a leader in transaction television. Expect home-delivery shopping, travel reservations, online banking, computer games and e-mail. Given the success of teletext with more limited technology, the possibilities for transaction revenues are enormous.

BSkyB is undertaking a major marketing campaign, which is described as 'on target', to drive higher subscriber numbers. People do not need a new digital television to receive digital service, only a new set-top box, to decode the digital signal to an analogue television, and a new, smaller satellite dish. BIB is subsidising the cost of digital satellite set-top decoders Sky offers, along with free installation, to existing subscribers.

BSkyB is well positioned in terms of content in its digital offer, and while it is in competition with OnDigital and Digital Cable, does receive 60% of their revenues if they succeed.

BSkyB, under chief executive Mark Booth, has evolved a different management style. The high-profile Sam Chisholm was credited with BSkyB's turnaround, but in an aggressive style which earned BSkyB the reputation of a bit of a maverick. Mark Booth has the same determination, but follows a more consensual approach. There is now a greater appreciation of the sensibilities of 'Middle England' and a strong desire to see Sky as an integral part of the broadcasting establishment.

Although there is, of course, one profit pool and one set of financial accounts, each of the three divisions is given autonomy and profit targets to hit, within their own structures.

The company is still certainly high profile. The current bid for Manchester United plc (owner of the football club) generated a huge amount of publicity and emotional outpouring. But this overstates its importance to BSkyB, although it is a sizeable investment. Digital is still the top priority.

The Future

BSkyB is driven by subscriber numbers, and future success will be measured by new subscribers and the successful conversion to digital of Sky's analogue customer base. SkyDigital is off to a flying start. It has also formed a strategic marketing alliance with Internet service provider AOL.

While 70% of BSkyB's revenues are non-sports, Sky Sports is very important to BSkyB, and Premier League rights are very important to Sky Sports. The OFT action against the Premier League, BSkyB and the BBC on whether individual clubs should be free to negotiate their own TV rights will be crucial. BSkyB paid the Premier League £690 million last time, which comes up for renegotiation in 2001.

Sky does face threats from digital terrestrial television and cable, and the key questions are which digital platform will succeed, and whether there is room for all the players. BSkyB is competing hard in this market, although it is not trying to put rivals out of business – BSkyB actually believes that there is room for everyone. ITV, which has not yet announced any plans for a digital service, might add to this competition. But whatever the competition, expect BSkyB to be among the winners.

Cable & Wireless Communications

Cable & Wireless Communications is by far the UK's leading provider of integrated communications, information and entertainment services. It is also the ninth largest carrier of international traffic in the world. The company is 53% owned by Cable & Wireless plc, one of the world's leading providers of international telecommunications services.

Scorecard:

Flexibility	★★★★
Innovation	★★★★
Human resources	★★★★
Growth markets	★★★★
Quality of management	★★★★
International orientation	★★★★

Biggest Plus:
A new company which has already made huge leaps forward

Biggest Minus:
Sailing in the uncharted waters of new technology

Key Figures:
(to year ended 31 March 1998)

Total revenue:	£2.2 billion
Operating profit:	£281 million
Pre-tax profit:	£151 million
Employees:	10,000

Cable & Wireless Communications plc
Watford Business Park
Caxton Way
Watford WD1 8XH
Tel: 0171 528 2000
website: www.cwcom.co.uk

CABLE & WIRELESS

Cable & Wireless Communications

Company Background

Cable & Wireless Communications came into existence in 1997 through a merger of Mercury with Nynex CableComms Group, Bell Cablemedia, and Videotron. It was the first UK company to offer multi-channel television and Internet services alongside the full range of telecommunications services. It is also strategically positioned to offer new products such as interactive digital services and multimedia products as they emerge.

The merger was widely hailed as a major move. The *Sunday Times* called Cable & Wireless Communications 'one of the biggest and most exciting companies to be formed in Britain for years'. The new company gave customers the best of telecommunications and the best of information and entertainment services from a single source. Cable & Wireless Communications is the only UK company to offer a combination of telecoms, broadband data transmission, video shopping and Internet access.

The company has over 33,000 Internet customers, making it probably the fastest-growing Internet service provider in the UK. Its corporate customers include Fiat, Dixons, Hewlett Packard, Tandem, Nortel and British Steel. Cable & Wireless Communications is currently spending £400 million on upgrading its national network. When complete, this will be one of the most advanced national telecommunications networks in the world.

The company's parent, Cable & Wireless plc, provides over 17 million customers in over 70 countries with a complete range of international, domestic and mobile communications. It is the world's third largest carrier of international traffic, provides mobile communications in 30 countries and operates the world's largest and most advanced cable ship fleet.

Operations and Markets

The company is organised into four business units: Consumer Markets, Business Markets, Corporate Markets and International & Partner Services. These are supported by a centrally managed operations unit, responsible for the network and customer service.

Each business unit addresses a distinct market with dedicated sales and marketing channels. They all use the company's continually expanding high-capacity local, national and international network. Cable & Wireless Communications is ideally placed to meet the growing demand for bandwidth-hungry applications right across the market.

Consumer Markets accounts for 24% of total revenues. It provides domestic users with cable television and telephony services, where it enjoys 20% and 25% shares of those markets. It also bundles such systems together for Internet and other uses, and markets products which relate to this marketplace: for example, Internet Life for less frequent Internet users.

Business Markets contributes 15% of the company's revenues. Declining before the merger, the latest figures show that revenues are now up 2% on the previous year's total. The introduction of new, innovative services such as a simple and affordable business mobile proposition, e-commerce, ISDN and others, have led to orders hitting record highs. The unit addresses the needs of smaller businesses which lack their own in-house IT experts, and provides technical support for such companies as well as marketing products to them.

Corporate Markets focuses on large corporates and governments, delivering tailored packages through dedicated project managers. Services of this unit include Call Management which uses Internet Protocol to allow customers to track telecom costs and customer service levels at each site; 'SecureDial', giving corporates the opportunity to provide their employees with secure, remote access to their own central IT network from anywhere in the world; and 'BranchConnect', which links remote sites to corporate HQs. This unit accounts for 25% of Cable & Wireless Communications' total revenues.

Contributing 36% of total revenues, International & Partner Services is the leading part of the company. It provides services for other company's carriers. For instance, it carries the majority of international traffic for Vodafone, the UK's largest mobile operator, and also for Germany's largest mobile operator.

Overall, the company has a vast product range, whose scope is ultimately limited only by what can be carried by cable. Cable & Wireless Communications is constantly developing new products in the fields of data, video, Internet and telephony: for instance, digital television, interactive education, information, enhanced entertainment services, and home shopping and banking, all of which it will launch in 1999. It is also building the most up-to-date network in the UK, called Network 2000. This will greatly increase capacity. Indeed, the company boasts that it will enable the entire population of the UK to speak at the same time!

Strategy and Management

Caroline Keppel-Palmer, the company's head of PR (Investor & Public Affairs): 'Demand in our area is rising hugely. We are ideally placed to cover all the key growth areas. Indeed, we are supply-constrained, not demand-constrained.'

Given this situation, part of the company's current strategy is to focus on investing in various programmes designed to overcome supply-side bottlenecks and enhance capacity. The first such investment is to improve customer services and rationalise the four units' systems and infrastructure. For instance, call centres of each unit can now deal with all enquiries, not just those relating to that unit.

Other recent investments include transferring the entire 1.2 million direct residential consumer base to ICMS, which was completed on schedule in September 1998. The Network 2000 initiative will raise the quality of services for existing customers and also meet future demand. Modern applications are capacity-hungry, but the new network will be more than capable of handling them. It will also include self-healing and remote provisioning.

Control of costs is seen as vital for the company's future. The merger which created Cable & Wireless Communications allowed the company to make savings of £136 million in its first year. The position now is that costs are being held while revenues are increasing by 14% and volumes are growing by 30% – a healthy picture.

Another aspect of the company's strategy is partnership. In September 1998, Cable & Wireless Communications announced an IT partnership with IBM: the largest of its kind between a major communications company and a leading IT services supplier. Under this ten-year, £1.8 billion agreement, IBM will provide the support needed by Cable & Wireless Communications to significantly improve business efficiency and service to customers. The company retains control of strategy while IBM handles delivery.

There are also a number of internal changes, designed to make everyone in the company work more effectively and improve productivity. This is already producing tangible results.

Also highly effective has been the company's branding. Prompted recognition of the Cable & Wireless brand was running at over 90% at the end of its high-impact £35 million marketing campaign in 1997, with unprompted recognition at over 35%. Cable & Wireless Communications won the Direct Marketing Campaign of the Year Award from *Campaign* magazine for this marketing initiative. Other wins recognising its effectiveness are the 1998 DMA/Royal Mail Direct Marketing Gold Award and the Strategic Use of Direct Marketing, Brand Building; and an array of other DMA awards.

Above all, the strategy is to focus on products which are seen as important for the UK's productivity. The company developed the digital cable network and also interactive television. This emphasis on leading-edge, vital products will help keep the company at the forefront of practical technology.

The Future

Although the marketplace in which Cable & Wireless Communications operates is increasingly competitive, the company has a unique advantage: it offers customers local, national, international and data telecommunications, allows them to access a wide range of information services and enjoy the latest in multi-channel television services from a single provider.

It also has a strong customer base. One million homes use its telecommunication services and 600,000 people are connected to its cable television services. It has 75,000 small to medium-sized corporate customers and around 6,000 large corporate customers.

Telecommunications is not a cyclical business. Even in a recession, telecommunications can still raise a company's productivity. Being able to deliver integrated communications is increasingly seen as the best way forward, and this is precisely the strength of Cable & Wireless Communications.

Planned future developments from the company include 'telebusiness', corporate Internet services, online Internet access services and number portability, digital television products such as impulse pay-per-view, near video-on-demand and, ultimately, video-on-demand.

All this would suggest that Cable & Wireless Communications is in a good position to maximise the enormous potential of its industry while being able to shrug off its competitive nature.

Cammell Laird

Cammell Laird is a fast-growing business providing ship repair and conversion facilities. The famous Cammell Laird shipbuilding business on the River Mersey had fallen into severe decline and had been put up for sale by VSEL when Coastline Industries stepped in to resurrect the name and provide the springboard for a successful new business at home and abroad.

Scorecard:

Flexibility	★★★★★
Innovation	★★★★
Human resources	★★★★
Growth markets	★★★★
Quality of management	★★★★
International orientation	★★★★

Biggest Plus:
Plenty of scope for business in an industry where building from scratch is very costly

Biggest Minus:
Still a young company, must prove itself in the long run

Key Figures:
(1997/98)

Turnover 97/98	£30.358 million
Operating profit	£4.065 million
Pre-tax profit	£4.184 million
Annual investment	£4.480 million
Employees worldwide	1,000
Employees UK	900

Cammell Laird Holdings plc
8 Princes Parade
Liverpool L3 1DL
Tel: 0151 236 5500
Fax: 0151 236 9094
website: www.lairds.merseyworld.co

Cammell Laird

Company Background

In Britain the name Cammell Laird was synonymous with shipbuilding for over 160 years. The forerunner of Cammell Laird, Birkenhead Iron Works, was first established by William Laird in 1824 on the River Mersey. A merger with the firm of Charles Cammell & Co in 1903 led to the establishment of the famous name.

From its earliest days the company established a reputation for technical excellence and innovation. Great vessels built at the Birkenhead yard ranged from the largest ever built for the Royal Navy, HMS *Ark Royal*, to cruise liners like the *Mauretania*. It was a pioneering, innovative facility that came to the fore during World War Two when no fewer than 106 warships were constructed at the yard.

The halcyon days of shipbuilding were receding by the 1960s and at Birkenhead the death rattle was sounded with the erosion of Ministry of Defence contracts. At its height 20,000 workers were employed at the Mersey powerhouse, but when owners VSEL closed the yard after failing to find a buyer in 1993, numbers had dwindled to a fraction of that level.

Even observers on Merseyside, so fond of the area's maritime tradition, imagined Cammell Laird was a once proud name that would be mothballed for ever. How wrong those perceptions turned out to be.

In 1995, after renting facilities for two years, Coastline Industries bought 50 acres of docks and land from VSEL – and heralded a remarkable renaissance. The company took over three dry docks, a non-tidal wet basin and, just as significant, the Cammell Laird name. Chief executive and majority shareholder John Stafford immediately decided that the future lay in ship repair and conversion.

In just three years, turnover trebled to over £30 million and profits in the year ending April 1998 stood at £4.184 million. A successful Stock Exchange flotation has taken place, docks in the north-east of England have been acquired and a 20-year lease has been won at the important international dockyard of Gibraltar.

Operations and Markets

From a standing start, Cammell Laird Holdings has evolved into the UK's leading ship repair company. Meteoric rises are not unfamiliar in business, neither are equally swift descents, but that surely does not apply here. The business has already established firm foundations, infrastructure, a motivated leadership and a flexible workforce.

The bedrock of the business is repair and conversion, offering customers fabrication, engineering, electrical and technical services. At Birkenhead the dry docks work alongside the non-tidal wet basin. Reconstruction work on these docks has totalled more than £3 million and involved the reclamation of land, removal of 100,000 tonnes of silt and in-house construction of new dock gates.

As a result of the increased capacity, man hours sold rose from 225,000 in the first half of 1997/98 to 625,000 in the second half. In July 1997 the company was successfully floated on the stock market. Shares opened at £1 to give a market capitalisation of £21 million, but the company's market value rose to over six times this. At the time of the flotation around 200 employees received a minimum of 1,000 share options.

Later in 1997 DG Electrical was bought with its skilled team of electrical engineers. Group financial controller Ged Gurney explained: 'We want to be able to provide all the principal services, from the design stage to the finished product. DG, for instance, enables us to cut out a further layer of subcontracted work.'

In February 1998 the board looked towards making an international impact and was successful in bidding to run the dockyard in Gibraltar on a 20-year renewable lease. This breakthrough has meant Cammell Laird being situated at the crossroads of the international shipping highway – over 70,000 shipping movements occur each year in the Straits of Gibraltar.

In September 1998, north-east rivals ALB and Tyne Dock Engineering were acquired in a significant industry move, one that executives say has put them in pole position in the UK. This has provided extensive facilities on the north-east coast where four dry docks are in operation at South Shields; a further three docks at Teesside; two at Tyneside, and further facilities at Wearside. In addition Wear Engineering currently operates from one of the largest fabrication and engineering shops in the UK. The acquisition places the company in an excellent position to offer a range of technical and engineering services.

Cammell Laird runs its own design team, offering technical support at offices in London, Merseyside, Newcastle and Oslo. The team includes naval architects, marine engineers and draughtsmen. All the different skills and personnel available are feeding into the overall philosophy of creating a 'one stop shop' of ship repair and conversion services.

Work undertaken by the group has included a host of vessels including cruise ships, 'ro-ro' ferries, jack-up rigs, semi-submersibles, supply ships and cable layers. Late in 1998 the Birkenhead yard undertook the overhaul of the mammoth semi-submersible Lolair which operates in the North Sea drilling fields, beating off strong European opposition to grab a key contract. An American contract worth over $40 million had earlier been clinched for the conversion of the drill ship Peregrine 7.

Chairman Juan Kelly explained: 'Most ship operators are seeing the potential of conversion as a cost-effective and time-saving alternative to new build.' When undertaking contracts, the company insists on supreme standards of workmanship, with every project monitored in accordance with ISO 9001/9002 Quality Assurance Systems.

Strategy and Management

As we have seen, Cammell Laird has made an extraordinarily successful debut as a new company, particularly now it has quoted stock. Chief executive John Stafford is well aware of the pitfalls of growing too fast with too little foundations and has made it clear that further expansion will only be carried out in a structured way.

Organic growth will be nurtured and while acquisitions are still a possibility, the board will not buy for buying's sake. The objective is to maintain and to strengthen the position of the UK's premier repair and conversion specialist.

Demand appears to remain strong and the business has already demonstrated its flexibility and capability. Indeed, with an ageing world shipping fleet, allied to the cost of new vessels, it seems inevitable that more operators will choose conversion. It is also thought the company can excel in other areas such as design and electrics.

The first-class facilities and a clear strategy combine with a highly motivated management. The different businesses are run as separate divisions but display tremendous synergy and to ensure that this runs smoothly, an operations board meets regularly.

Naturally managers cannot manage effectively without efficient employees and Cammell Laird believes it has the best, a workforce attuned to the requirements of the industry. All told, there are currently around 2,000 working on various projects compared with 200 just 18 months ago. Around 800 are based at the flagship Birkenhead yard. Ged Gurney further explained: 'We have a strong graduate and apprenticeship scheme with over 200 involved across the group.'

In financial terms, the operation has turned itself into a £100 million a year business from £11.5 million in 1995. Profits are expected to double in 1999 to £8 million and grow again to £15 million in 2000. Achieving these expectations will not only benefit institutional investors but also the company's employees as most have been given share options.

The Future

The future looks exceedingly bright for one of Britain's surprising success stories. There is little doubt that the very name Cammell Laird has played a massive role in the revival of a business which appeared to be dormant just a few years ago.

Projections that profits will increase substantially is indication enough that the company is confident of making continued progress.

In the coming years, the management team must strive to develop into a leading player in Europe as well as dominating the home market. Its growing reputation and base at Gibraltar make it a true company of the future in the ship repair and conversion market.

Card Protection Plan

CPP is the leading provider of card protection services in Europe with more than 4.5 million policyholders. The company is wholly owned by its chairman, Hamish Ogston, and had more than 6.3 million customer requests in 1998. Having expanded into Germany and Spain the group now has an aggressive overseas growth plan.

Scorecard:

Flexibility	★★★★
Innovation	★★★
Human resources	★★★★
Growth markets	★★★★
Quality of management	★★★★
International orientation	★★★★

Biggest Plus:
A rapidly growing market and helping hand from multinational business partners

Biggest Minus:
Ambitious overseas office openings will be a stern test for management

Key Figures:
(1998)

Revenue	£30.6 million
Pre-tax profit	£4.4 million
Policyholders	4.5 million
Employees	270

CPP Holdings Limited
Scorpio House
102 Sydney Street
London SW3 6NJ
Tel: 0171 352 7755
Fax: 0171 352 8776

CPP Card Protection Plan

Card Protection Plan

Company Background

After more than 15 years in the market, Card Protection Plan (CPP) is the largest provider of card protection services in the UK and Europe. The company works with blue-chip business partners such as NatWest Bank, Marks & Spencer, the Automobile Association and Abbey National.

With operating centres in London, Madrid and Frankfurt, CPP provides round the clock cover in 140 countries for its 4.5 million policy-holders. The company is about to open a second large call centre in York to underpin an expansion programme under which the company's staff should more than double in three years.

The key to the growth of CPP's business has been its success at distribution achieved by securing a daunting array of business partners which endorse its offering and provide the company with access to their large customer bases. Although CPP spent several years in the financial wilderness while it established the trust of would-be partners, this system of gaining access to potential customers is far more cost effective than other methods.

A heavy spend on the technology needed to provide a global service coupled with the very large growth in the European card market have helped propel CPP's sales and profits. Turnover has risen from just £2 million in 1988 to an estimated more than £30 million in 1998, while profits last year comfortably topped £4.4 million.

Operations and Markets

The growth in the volume of plastic payment cards is phenomenal. In the UK alone the number of cards in circulation has roughly doubled in the past decade, helped by the introduction of debit cards, store cards, affinity cards and more recently a whole range of cards offered by suppliers as diverse as British Gas and Ford.

Alongside this explosion, there has been an increased awareness not only of card fraud but also of crime. And the more plastic cards in a wallet or purse, the more ghastly becomes the prospect of loss. Industry figures suggest there are 8,000 card thefts every day in the UK, some 10% of which get reported to CPP.

CPP approaches potential customers through their card providers such as Barclays. It has probably twice as large a slice of the UK market as its nearest competitor, Sentinel, which is owned by US company Cendant.

Once a card issuer has provided access to its customer base, CPP will then devise a marketing strategy and will pay the business partner a commission based on the number of clients it attracts. This could simply involve sending mail shots. But as the relationship between CPP and its business partners is very close, marketing can mean that potential customers who ring their bank to inquire about payment cards are asked about card protection by a 'prompt' programmed into the call handler's computer system by CPP.

Although the commissions to partners, particularly in the UK, can be substantial this remains a cost-effective way for CPP to acquire distribution.

Figures from the company reveal that once it has attracted a customer, CPP is very good at keeping them on its books. In 1997 it reported a policyholder renewal rate of 97%. And one of the statistics which chairman Hamish Ogston likes to produce is that the company routinely beats its target of 10 compliments for every complaint.

Strategy and Management

Although CPP has operating centres in only three of the territories it covers, the group clearly has its eyes on developing a global presence expanding into regions such as the US, Latin America and the Far East. Partly this is prompted by the demands of the company's existing business partners which want to retain CPP as they move into new territories and partly it is the dynamics of the global card market where countries such as Brazil and Hong Kong already have massive card usage.

The advantage for CPP of having cultivated and nurtured its impressive gallery of business partners is that the first stages of expansion into new markets can theoretically be achieved on the coat tails of an existing relationship with an international bank such as Standard Chartered, for example.

Clearly there are difficulties for CPP in establishing a presence overseas. Quality management and ruthless enforcement of confidentiality standards are imperatives in addition to more mundane administrative skills.

Hamish Ogston also points out that acquiring new members is difficult and only when there is a substantial renewal income – probably four to five years after opening – will a foreign operation break into profit.

But the prize is immense. The company has spent heavily on its IT systems – it has 17.5 million cards on its database and is on its fourth in-house designed and modified computer system. CPP would benefit from being able to spread its investment across a wider base.

CPP is already established in Britain as an integral part of the card offering – many banks include a section on card protection cover on the card application form rather than supplying a leaflet separately. This means about one in four of each new card customers will purchase its services.

Long-term, that rate of business acquisition in international markets would give CPP an unrivalled base of customers to whom it could make direct approaches with other service offerings.

Any expansion will be achieved, however, without undue stress to the company's balance sheet position as Hamish Ogston says CPP's financial strength is critical to building the confidence of its business partners. The company's operations are also designed to be as 'disaster proof' as possible with identical computer systems in a secret location so almost no eventuality could force the company to stop operating for much longer than a couple of minutes.

CPP's ambitious expansion plans mean that it will be adding to its headcount rapidly in the coming three years as it moves towards a total staff of about 600, roughly 450 of whom will be based in the UK.

Most of the company's recruits in the UK tend to enter at school-leaver level, but Hamish Ogston says CPP looks for 'intelligent, com-passionate people' who have the composure and maturity to deal with often distressed people who are stranded thousands of miles away without a passport, airline ticket or credit card. CPP can deal with all of this and, in addition, will send £2,000 in cash to help customers.

The successes of staff are readily acknowledged in performance cer-tificates on office walls, alongside frequently changed corporate objec-tives and achievement targets.

The Future

Alongside the strategy of expanding overseas, CPP will benefit from the overall market rise in the number of cards in circulation. The company commands about two-thirds of the UK market's distribution and reckons that once individuals have more than four or five cards in their purse or wallet they are psychologically more predisposed to buy insurance protection.

But CPP also wants to raise the revenue it earns from each card customer beyond the current basic of £10.

The company clearly cannot provide financial services which might compete with anything offered by its business partners, but Hamish Ogston says the company already offers protection for cardholders' locks and keys for an additional £2 and this type of bolt-on service will be extended.

Hamish Ogston says there are 'a host of trade ups' which the company is about to introduce which might double the annual income from some classes of cardholder. This will not only increase turnover but, crucially, will benefit the bottom line as the cost of acquiring this additional revenue is comparatively cheap.

'Our hidden asset is our relationship with the card issuers. We can get straight through to them with new products such as insurance, peace of mind and convenience services,' he added. This will be important as CPP launches more stand-alone services. Being well known to and trusted by its business partners allows CPP immediately to introduce new products to a customer base of millions of people without having to spend time proving itself over again.

Although Hamish Ogston has only recently bought out his minority partner in the business, he admits the group might look for a stock market flotation towards the end of 2000. At today's multiples in the UK, the group would probably command a price tag of £55 million. In the US, however, the ratings are far fancier and this, coupled with the international profile, might tempt him to float the company in New York.

Cedar Group plc

Cedar Group plc provides combined software and consultancy service solutions to companies, allowing them to manage and link their customer communication systems to their core business activities.

Scorecard:

Flexibility	★★★★★
Innovation	★★★★
Human resources	★★★★
Growth markets	★★★★
Quality of management	★★★★
International orientation	★★★★

Biggest Plus:
An innovative company growing fast on sound strategy

Biggest Minus:
Yet to become a truly dominant player in its marketplace

Key Figures:
(year to 31 March 1998)

Turnover:	£12.5 million
Gross profit:	£8.6 million
Pre-tax profit:	£2.6 million
Net assets:	£6.7 million
Employees:	250

Cedar Group plc
Cedar House
78 Portsmouth Road
Cobham
Surrey KT11 1HY
Tel: 01932 584000
Fax: 01932 584001
website: www.cedargroup.co.uk

CEDAR

Cedar Group plc

Company Background

Cedar was founded in 1983 by Harry Menarche and Leon Fattal as a bureau business. It then developed into a company selling financial management software. Its first product was called cfacs, recently renamed Cedar Financials: a financial management tool built on the Oracle platform. More recent additions to the product line include QualTech, a tool to measure call centre performance qualitatively; Tele-Connect, a call centre scripting system; Cedar Time, a man-hour accounting system; PMPL, a data warehousing consultancy; and BusinessFlow, a document and workflow management system.

The company was floated on the stock market in 1994. Around this time, the original founders decided to draw back from full control of the company and began to put in place a succession plan. This came to fruition in 1997 when the current managing director, Mike Harrison, was appointed. As a former managing director of Oracle who had also worked with Infomix UK, Burroughs, Data General and IBM, he was an ideal choice to take the company forward into a new phase of strong growth.

Major clients of Cedar Group plc include Norwich Union, Lloyds Bank TSB, Virgin Direct, HM Treasury, BP Chemicals, the Scottish Office, Cellnet, Energis, Cranfield University, Great Ormond Street, the Ministry of Defence and Scottish Power. In addition, more than 200 government departments, local authorities, NHS Trusts and educational establishments have benefited from Cedar's assistance. It is increasingly seen as the partner of choice for Oracle-based financial accounting solutions.

Operations and Markets

The approach of Cedar Group plc can be summed up as follows. Every business survives on the competence of its core activity. Cedar provides a series of systems designed to make that activity more effective, by supporting the business's communication with its customers, monitoring and measuring key business processes, and acquiring and managing marketing knowledge generated by company contact. In doing all of these things Cedar is addressing the opportunity for enterprise systems. Its approach to this growing market is from the position of supplying complementary components to enable its customers to build towards enterprise solutions.

Cedar Financials comprises a suite of modules focused in and around full financial management for companies. These modules include purchasing and asset control combined with the ability to view financial organisation across companies which need to control multi-company and multi-site operations. Developed with the latest Oracle technology, Cedar Financials is fully supported on all the major UNIX hardware platforms.

The company has secured options to acquire businesses as well as intellectual property rights over several products. QualTech is one such example. Founded in 1994, QualTech was acquired by Cedar in 1997. It offers a special methodology for monitoring and measuring call centre value and quality on an ongoing basis.

As Paul Godfrey, Cedar's group marketing director says: 'Numerical measures of call centre behaviour are necessary but not sufficient. With QualTech's Reach service, calls are recorded, then sent to a trained analyst for evaluation across a series of criteria: politeness, key mentions, etc. This allows a company to plot the effectiveness of its current staff by identifying and migrating best practice. It can also help in identifying coaching opportunities to make its less efficient employees more effective. It may also be used to support performance-related payments.'

Another product offered by Cedar in the call centre marketplace is Tele-Connect. This is scripting and agent support software which allows a company to introduce best practice across its range of call centre operations.

PMPL is another company owned by Cedar. It works primarily for insurance companies, banks and building societies and is staffed by industry specialists. The skills of its employees enable PMPL to offer consultancy, data warehouse, data migration and data bureau products and services. In short, it allows companies to talk to their customers more effectively and improves their understanding of their needs through positive feedback loops.

BusinessFlow is a knowledge management system. Developed by COI, Cedar's partner in Germany, it is now used by over 300 international organisations as their basis for strategically managing disparate information. BusinessFlow captures all of the data and documents within an organisation whilst applying predetermined and ad hoc processes. This ensures that tasks key to that information and the organisation are performed in a procedural and timely fashion. The result is an interactive process for the production of knowledge sharing and knowledge management. COI's international partner the Cedar Group exclusively markets and supports the software as part of its global strategy.

Cedar Time (formerly 'Macris') was developed by GRAD Systems Limited, a company founded in 1993 and now owned by Cedar. This system provides a total man-hour accounting solution with the flexibility to suit every organisation's requirements across the entire man-hour-related set of application areas.

Cedar is expanding internationally. It now has a subsidiary in the US, having bought out its US distributor. It also distributes its products through partners in Australia and South Africa, and plans to establish a European presence in 1999.

Cedar's current structure is such that it derives 40% of its revenues from licence fees and 60% from services. Of that 60%, 25% is maintenance and 35% consultancy. In 1998, Cedar more than doubled the number of its consultants and plans to do so again in 1999 – growing from 20 to 100 consultants in the space of just two years.

Strategy and Management

The company's strategy is focused on the enterprise marketplace. Paul Godfrey: 'Our aim is to assemble a set of products and services which can be combined to deliver an enterprise solution. The customer can then address the application areas in the sequence which meets the priorities of the business as he sees them. This approach contrasts with that of the monolithic, single application methodology. By pursuing this strategy we intend to emerge as a key player in the ERM market space.'

Cedar is well placed to offer that type of modular package since its products are all attractive in their own right, but are also designed to talk to each other and work together seamlessly. Further products can also be added to the mix: for instance, the company is now looking at introducing an e-commerce product. The company's aspiration is to be in the right place at the right time with the right set of products – those which focus on areas where customers are set to increase their IT spend.

Mike Harrison expands the strategic picture: 'We perceived structural faults in the IT industry, which is vast and successful but has not, we believe, yet got it right in terms of selling solutions to the enterprise marketplace's problems. The IT industry also has an unusual structure, with a number of large, powerful companies and a huge number of small ones but with very little population in the middle.

'Big companies are slow moving, whereas the small ones are often successful niche players but lack the critical mass to expand rapidly.

Some big players will spin-off some activities while some smaller ones will cluster together and enter the mid-space – which is where Cedar wants to be. I believe there is a tremendous opportunity there for companies able to offer meaningful, flexible solutions to the enterprise marketplace, and I am confident that Cedar is well positioned to do so.'

In terms of management, the company is led by experienced corporate practitioners. Many have worked for such names as BT, IBM, Oracle and SAP. As a result, they understand the needs of Cedar's clients and speak their language. The company continues to recruit top-calibre people, and so far has had no problems doing so; its employees have grown by 100 in the last year. Cedar's rapid growth, its leading-edge technology and its impressive customer list no doubt are major aids here. All in all, the strategy and management look very well set to take the company through substantial future growth.

The Future

A main challenge for the company is moving from a proprietorial management style to that of a more corporate entity. Its August 1998 move from cramped offices in New Malden to a spacious new facility in Cobham has helped this change. The new office includes a well-equipped customer centre which allows Cedar to run in-house sales and support events for its customers and prospects.

The future looks bright for Cedar Group plc. It is a lively, young, energetic and dynamic company with a sound financial basis, a small but attractive set of products which sit well together, and many interesting opportunities. Growth has been rapid, not to say meteoric, over the last few years. The challenge will be to continue that growth and become a more dominant player, especially overseas. This will not be easy; but the evidence suggests that Cedar has all the right ingredients to make that transition.

Christian Salvesen plc

Christian Salvesen is a major logistics business specialising in the strategic management of the outsourced supply chain. Christian Salvesen works in partnership with manufacturing and retailing customers to optimise inventory levels while ensuring that goods are available for the consumer precisely when required. Christian Salvesen has particular expertise – and a broad and prestigious customer base – in the food, consumer products and industrial sectors. It also has a food services division specialising in frozen food processing. Christian Salvesen has 123 sites in the UK, Belgium, France, Germany, Holland, Italy, Portugal and Spain.

Scorecard:

Flexibility	★★★★
Innovation	★★★★
Human resources	★★★
Growth markets	★★★★★
Quality of management	★★★★
International orientation	★★★★

Biggest Plus:
Sharp focus on the growing business of supply chain logistics

Biggest Minus:
The fragmented nature of the European logistics industry

Key Figures:
(to 31 March 1998, continuing operations only)

Revenue	£544.9 million
Operating profit	£43.2 million
Pre-tax profit	£35.3 million
Annual investment	£41.6 million
Employees worldwide	14,000
Employees UK	12,000

Christian Salvesen plc
500 Pavilion Drive
Brackmills
Northampton NN4 7YJ
Tel: 01604 662600
Fax: 01604 662605
website: www.salvesen.com

Christian Salvesen plc

Company Background

Christian Salvesen has shown chameleon-like qualities over its 150-year history, changing direction many times. The journey has taken it through shipping, import/export, transport, even whaling at one time, into a 'mini Scottish conglomerate' in the 1980s.

Recent times have continued to be highly eventful for Christian Salvesen. In 1997 it de-merged Aggreko, its high-margin, mobile power generation business, which had tended to absorb much of the group's time and energy. Its corporate headquarters also departed from Edinburgh, a poignant moment after a long association with that city, and many employees (including the directors) chose to remain in Scotland.

The relocation to Northampton, however – 'the logistics capital of the UK' – was a sensible and practical move which fused together the corporate level with the management of the logistics business.

Christian Salvesen is now sharply focused, perhaps for the very first time, on the expansion of its logistics business, an area which is evolving rapidly.

Operations and Markets

In recent years, the UK logistics industry has responded positively to the challenges represented by pricing pressures on contracts. There has been a move away from basic transport into ever more complex areas of supply chain management. The focus of the industry has been narrowed; operating assets are now financed increasingly by third parties – a strategy Christian Salvesen itself adopted some time ago. This has freed logistics companies to concentrate on the development of sophisticated IT systems which add value, raise barriers to entry and enhance profitability.

The increasing trend in business worldwide towards outsourcing of logistics has played into Christian Salvesen's hands. In the UK, the industry is technologically advanced and Christian Salvesen is one of the top five players. Many countries in Europe are less developed, however, and industry forecasters predict a steady growth in outsourcing.

Christian Salvesen's core logistics business is organised into two divisions – Food and Consumer products, and Industrial. Both operations concentrate on the most complex areas of the supply chain, where Christian Salvesen can use its management expertise, organisational ability and its capacity to develop sophisticated IT and engineering systems to maximum advantage.

The Food Logistics business operates from 75 sites, with 7,500 staff and 1,150 vehicles and represents the bulk of Christian Salvesen's business at present. The numbers get even bigger – in 1997, Food and Consumer Logistics delivered 300 million product cases, washed 150 million product trays and delivered 40 million hanging garments across six miles of shelving in one warehouse and operated a total of 4.8 million square feet of warehouse space.

Christian Salvesen is very strong in this sector in the UK, and relatively so in Europe. In the UK, the company works primarily for food and consumer goods retailers, managing dedicated distribution centres for the likes of Marks & Spencer, Booker, Sainsbury's and House of Fraser, and has recently announced contracts with IKEA and with British Airways, to manage its fresh produce distribution at Heathrow. In Europe, Christian Salvesen has major relationships with Unilever, Danone and Auchon.

Christian Salvesen's Food Services business is more peripheral, but still related, and represents approximately 10% of group turnover. It is cash generative and has 35% of the UK frozen vegetable processing market. Its performance is inevitably affected by the fluctuations in price and the availability of raw vegetables, and consequently, profits can be volatile.

The Industrial Logistics business was accelerated in 1993 with the acquisition of Swift, the UK's leading shared-user industrial logistics network. Christian Salvesen has developed considerable business with the motor sector, delivering just-in-time parts from manufacturers to garages for Vauxhall, Mercedes and Ford, among others. Other customers served by Christian Salvesen's extensive network of depots and fleet of trucks include the *Daily Mail*, Dupont, Dunlop, Ronseal and Meyer Group.

Strategy and Management

'The main thrust of our growth strategy for the next four to five years is to further develop our logistics business across mainland Europe,' says Edward Roderick, chief executive. The opportunity is there – some

80% of Europe's population is on the mainland, but only 24% of the logistics market is currently outsourced to third parties, a much lower percentage than in the UK.

Christian Salvesen is zooming in on what it describes as 'a window of opportunity' before existing national customer relationships are replaced by regional and international ones. The company is actively reviewing opportunities for acquisitions and joint ventures in the major European markets in order to be able to offer full European coverage.

Specific countries and business areas are being targeted, to complement Christian Salvesen's strong frozen food distribution network in mainland Europe. The targets vary for each logistics sector but, broadly, the company will be concentrating on EU countries, on manufacturers in the industrial, food and consumer products sectors, and on retailers of food products.

The balance of power in Europe is more in favour of manufacturers than retailers (often the opposite in the UK), and it is the former who control distribution. The logistics industry is quite fragmented, and few have the breadth of experience and IT systems of UK companies. Christian Salvesen also intends to build its business further by developing quality relationships with manufacturers.

In Northern Europe, Christian Salvesen is already a very strong brand name. In Southern Europe there is more work to do, and Christian Salvesen has developed a joint venture with Danone, called Salvesen Logistica, to provide a network of chilled food distribution throughout Spain. A similar joint venture with Danone has been established in Italy.

'The joint venture route is interesting because it provides Christian Salvesen with a distribution network from day one without having to invest first and hope that business then follows,' says Chris Smith, corporate development director. 'We can then develop other third party business on the back of this infrastructure.' While such arrangements also mean sharing the profits, it is a very satisfactory way to get business moving in new areas.

The really exciting opportunities may lie in industrial logistics, where in Europe, outsourced logistics operations are developing faster there than in the foods business. Distribution as a percentage of total cost is much lower for industrial goods compared to food products, which explains the lag in development of industrial logistics. Motor manufacturers may prove to be a real engine room of growth in Europe for Christian Salvesen, especially when they 'walk the talk' of centralising, rather than localising, distribution and logistics decisions.

In the UK, the food and consumer products business is solid, but growth opportunities are not spectacular; the competition (especially in the UK) is strong, and retailers typically spread their business across a number of suppliers. Christian Salvesen's approach here will be to maintain and grow its strong position through service excellence and efficiency gains.

'Flexible, leading-edge technology underpins every part of the business – in particular the multi-user operations which are fundamental to our growth,' says Edward Roderick. 'In future we shall channel investment and management resources into these areas, while peripheral activities such as provision of property will be managed by us, but ownership will be relinquished to companies with more appropriate skills and resources.' Meeting time-critical deadlines and providing accurate service levels certainly depends on great technology, and Christian Salvesen has invested heavily in its SHARP and ULTIMA IT systems.

The new management team is nicely balanced, with extensive experience in the industry and broad-ranging international commercial skills. Chief executive Edward Roderick was previously managing director of Swift and was promoted on the de-merger. Formerly with Hays, he has a successful track record in the shipping and distribution business and is described by his colleagues as 'visionary'.

The Future

Christian Salvesen has embarked on a strategy which is rational, straightforward and clearly understood by managers. Edward Roderick says that it is 'ambitious in its targets for growth and value creation', but the trend towards outsourcing in supply-chain management, and the relatively under-developed infrastructure and logistics industry in continental Europe, offer real opportunity.

In the UK, Christian Salvesen provides an extremely high-quality service. If logistics services providers can demonstrate they add value, customers can justify paying a premium price. European customers can be less experienced in this regard and so Christian Salvesen will aim to demonstrate the value of a pan-European network.

'We're very excited about what we can do in Europe over the next three to four years,' says Chris Smith, 'but we're realistic – especially regarding managing the growth process.' Christian Salvesen is uniquely positioned and these could be exciting times as a new, energised management team sets about building a brand new business.

COLT Telecom Group plc

COLT Telecom is a provider of high-quality telecommunications services to business users in Europe's major business centres. COLT's fibre optic networks cover over 1,000 kilometres, double what it was a year before, and is growing all the time. COLT currently provides switched and non-switched services to nearly 2,000 directly connected customers in over 1,900 buildings. COLT is a rapidly growing company, having increased revenues by 133% in 1997, and by 160% in the first nine months of 1998.

Scorecard:

Flexibility	★★★★
Innovation	★★★★
Human resources	★★★★★
Growth markets	★★★★★
Quality of management	★★★★★
International orientation	★★★★

Biggest Plus:
Fast-growing, customer-driven telcoms company with a blueprint for success

Biggest Minus:
Highly competitive markets

Key Figures:
(nine months to 30 September 1998)

Turnover	£142.8 million
Gross profit	£26.8 million
Pre-tax profit	£37.5 million
Annual investment	£88 million
Employees worldwide	1,244
Employees UK	491

COLT Telecom Group plc
15 Marylebone Road
London NW1 5JD
Tel: 0171 390 3900
Fax: 0171 390 3701
website: www.colt-telecom.com

COLT Telecom Group plc

Company Background

COLT is a very young company, financed by seedcorn money from Fidelity Capital. Its genesis relates to the phenomenal success in Boston, USA, of telecommunications company Teleport, also founded by Fidelity as a joint venture with Merrill Lynch. Teleport was so successful that it was decided to repeat the venture in Europe. London was chosen. Paul Chisholm, the general manager of Teleport, was asked to repeat his success as chief executive of COLT. Fidelity still owns 57% of COLT and its original investment of $100 million is currently worth in excess of $5 billion.

COLT was established in 1992, when it was granted its UK operating licence. Its first major customer was signed up in 1993 after it had constructed its initial 15 km fibre optic 'backbone' in the heart of the City of London.

Operations and Markets

COLT is totally focused on providing telecommunications services to largely corporate and medium-sized businesses in Europe. Its fibre optic cable networks feature high availability services for both private wire and switched telephony services. The network is flexible enough to handle the higher bandwidth demands of businesses across Europe.

Knowing that everyone is looking for quality and value-for-money, COLT has sold itself on providing very high levels of service, but not the lowest price offering. A combination of high quality, reliability and reasonable prices seems like a winning formula. COLT's revenues have increased every year – by 133% in 1997 and by a massive 160% in the first nine months of 1998. Customers like big banks require sophisticated telecoms as an integral part of their business; reliability and quality become every bit as important as price.

COLT's core business is its own dedicated network. In London it has 200 route kilometres of fibre optic network, and the same template is applied to other major cities in Europe, including Frankfurt, Madrid and Paris. COLT owns all of its underlying infrastructure – an impor- tant differentiator against other re-sellers of telecoms services. Because COLT builds its own infrastructure, it can design networks specifically to meet the exacting needs of its big business customers.

The pace of COLT's growth is well illustrated by its European cover- age. In 1997, it had operations in six cities in three European countries; by 1998 this had reached 12 cities in eight countries.

COLT's revenues in the third quarter of 1998 were split 62% UK, 38% rest of Europe; the latter was only 15% in 1997, revealing the trend. The UK business is still growing strongly, but the company expects that by the millennium, non-UK activities will be the biggest contributor, with Germany the largest individual country.

COLT*Business Connect* is an advanced portfolio of intelligent network services such as Freephone 0800, Local Rate 0845, and National Rate 0870 services. COLT*Connect* is an indirect telecommunications service available to business users throughout the UK who are not on COLT's network, offering savings of up to 30% of the cost of their calls, includ- ing local, long distance, international and mobile calls.

COLT is an Internet service provider in its own right. COLT*Internet* offers a range of Internet access and value-added services for corporate users and other Internet service providers. Internet services include 'pure' telecommunications access, but web hosting is a fast-growing part of the business, serving customers like PA Newswire and Elec- tronic Arts. The latter hosts its European games on a COLT-facilitated website to allow customers to access its computer games. COLT offers its Internet services in just three countries, but it aims to roll out to all COLT-served cities.

The market opportunity for COLT is substantial. It estimates that in 1998, the total European telecommunications market was worth around £115 billion annually, and growing at about 5% each year. The business segment represents 50% of this total and perhaps COLT's addressable market is £30 billion a year. COLT's networks are concen- trated in selected city centres, although its network can be accessed by interconnecting with national carriers such as BT.

Strategy and Management

COLT revels in technical and engineering excellence, but the whole culture of the organisation, including the training of its people, is very customer focused. 'I know everyone says this, but we can back it up,' says John Doherty, director of investor relations. COLT endorsed its industry-leading reputation for service excellence by achieving a net- work availability exceeding 99.99% and a mean time to repair of only 68 minutes. This led to COLT being voted Best Telecoms Services Supplier in London by a decisive margin in the *FX Week/Syntegra Best*

Banks in FX Awards 1997 and 1998. For the same years, COLT has come first in the annual Quality of Service survey conducted by the Telecom Managers Association, which comprises over 400 members (all customers).

The major growth theme will be the rolling out of its fibre optic networks and accompanying telecommunications services to more European cities, and over time, creating an integrated broadband network across Europe.

'Our approach to new market entry has been refined to an almost scientific process,' says Paul Chisholm. 'We go in early, and with great urgency and drive, to serve our customers beyond all expectations.'

COLT plans by the end of 1999 to have built networks in 20–22 cities, and by the year 2000, maybe 26 cities. That might see some sort of levelling off, as these target 26 cities cover about 80% of COLT's addressable market, although the likelihood is that it will not stop at 26.

Another major growth push (for the whole industry) is the 'data explosion'. As more businesses become reliant on PCs and other computers sending information directly to each other, the demand for data carrying telecommunications is escalating. Customers like BMW, Siemens and Chrysler Daimler use COLT to interlink its factories and offices to send car designs, for example. But whatever material is sent is immaterial to COLT – it is what its customers are using its networks for that is important.

From the beginning, COLT highlighted superior service as its point of difference. 'Perhaps because we're a smaller company we have greater flexibility over how we can go about things,' says John Doherty. 'Our culture from day one has been to treat our customers as we ourselves want to be treated as customers.'

One London-based customer was in the process of moving offices. But one week before the move they got the call from their telecommunications supplier who said that they couldn't meet the agreed times for installing new lines. An irate customer called BT, which said that it couldn't handle the job at such short notice and actually recommended that the only company it thought could do it was COLT! It took COLT just one hour to review all the details and then say 'yes' – with only 2–3 days to go to the weekend of the office move. People worked 24 hours a day, pulling out all the stops, and the customer, RONIN, has since given COLT 100% of its business.

Of course, its people are absolutely fundamental to COLT's success. The whole approach that COLT adopts in each of its operations is to recruit locally. A simple rationale – local people providing local services to local businesses.

The sheer drive, initiative and devotion to customer care stems from the very top of the company. Chief executive Paul Chisholm spends 'a lot of time' on people issues. He regards it as crucial that the right people are employed, in the right positions. His personal style includes a phenomenal memory for individual faces and names, according to peers and colleagues. Few doubt that this is a wonderfully important attribute in a leader.

'In terms of recruiting, we realise there are many people out there with the right skills and technical qualities, but it's not just paper qualifications we're after,' says Ann Brown, HR director. 'It's what someone brings to the job, the positive attitude, a willingness to go the extra mile for the customer. This is the real skill we look for.'

A very high proportion of compensation at COLT is results oriented – probably more so than at other telecommunications companies – and approximately 90% of employees have an interest in COLT shares.

The Future

From a market perspective, the amount of data-related applications, as opposed to pure voice traffic, will be the real driver of the industry. Telecommunications companies may become, effectively, data carriers. From a technical standpoint, networks need to be designed to focus on data as well as voice and here COLT has a head start. Its own networks are new, modern, all fibre optic and digitised. COLT is extremely well positioned to benefit from the data explosion.

COLT will increasingly become a pan-European company rather than a collection of individual markets and countries. More importantly, its pan-European telecommunications network will be integrated. The telecommunications market is booming and, with its relatively new entrant status, COLT has a great opportunity to grow faster than the incumbents.

Davies Arnold Cooper

Davies Arnold Cooper (DAC) is a leading UK commercial law firm whose client base includes all sizes of British and international public and private companies in the manufacturing and service industries. It is particularly strong in insurance litigation, with a good reputation in the pharmaceutical, construction and commercial property sectors. Based in the City, DAC has other offices in Manchester, Newcastle and Madrid. DAC has 63 partners and a total staff of around 530.

Scorecard:

Flexibility	★★★★★
Innovation	★★★★★
Human resources	★★★★
Growth markets	★★★★
Quality of management	★★★★
International orientation	★★★

Biggest Plus:
Pioneering, innovative, more like a commercial business than a traditional firm of partners

Biggest Minus:
Needs to reduce dependence on insurance litigation into other sectors

Key Figures:
(to 30 June 1998)

Turnover	£39.091 million
Operating profit	£6.988 million
Pre-tax profit	£6.988 million
Annual investment	£1.126 million
Employees worldwide	530
Employees UK	518

Davies Arnold Cooper
8 Bouverie Street
London EC4Y 8DD
Tel: 0171 936 2222
Fax: 0171 936 2020
website: www.daclon@dac.co.uk

DAVIES
ARNOLD
COOPER

SOLICITORS

Davies Arnold Cooper

Company Background

Davies Arnold Cooper (DAC) has built its professional reputation on a practical and commercial approach, but it is also a pioneering firm, setting the pace for others in its profession. DAC distinguishes itself from its peers by its open culture, married to self-styled corporate values, in what is still largely a traditional profession.

Davies Arnold Cooper differs markedly in its determination to run itself like a business rather than a traditional firm of solicitors. It sticks to some of the standard rules of commercial enterprises including open and reasonable prices, restraint in expanding staff numbers, efficient procedures and preserving unity within the organisation. It encourages non-solicitors to progress to the highest levels in the firm. This approach is embedded in DAC's strong and unified culture that permeates through the whole organisation.

David McIntosh, who happens to be the longest-serving senior partner of any UK commercial law firm, believes that 'the legal profession is terrified of change. The biggest problem is seeing change as a threat.'

The formula is evidently successful. The firm has delivered strong organic growth throughout its 70-year history, and is very profitable. It has worked on many prominent cases including Lloyds litigation, Piper Alpha, Hillsborough, pensions mis-selling, Opren and the Channel Tunnel rolling stock claim.

Operations and Markets

Insurance litigation currently represents 75% of the practice in terms of income. DAC is market leader, and this area is forecast to grow at 25% per annum. The firm is also market leader in the pharmaceutical & healthcare and construction & property sectors, both forecast to grow at 20% annually. Financial services is becoming a core practice area with disputes here anticipated to grow by 50% annually. Retailing is another potential high-value sector for the future.

The London and Manchester offices have capabilities in all DAC's core dispute resolution sectors, while its Madrid and Newcastle offices (which were opened in response specifically to client demand) focus almost entirely on the insurance industry.

Davies Arnold Cooper is an international practice, and in addition to the Madrid office, its services are in demand outside the UK particularly for its construction expertise and its innovative use of Alternative Dispute Resolution (ADR) in a general trend towards mediation; a lot of work has been done with giant petro-chemical installations in the Caribbean.

Strategy and Management

DAC has undertaken thorough internal research to assess strengths and weaknesses of its clients to ensure that they could support continued profitable growth. The five sectors were identified as key to the firm – the insurance industry remains its predominant source of work; the others represent growth areas where DAC has significant business and expertise and where it foresees growth in their need for legal services, particularly dispute resolution. DAC aims to reduce its dependence on insurance litigation to 50% of total income by 2002.

In particular, it has looked for areas where 'brain surgery' service and advice was required (intensive in terms of high expertise time instead of high volume) and where high margin charges could be levied.

DAC has been quick to realise the potential for ADR mediation to create wealth and volume of work, in contrast to many UK law firms who view its coming with suspicion and fear. 'Clients like it too,' adds Kenneth McKenzie, partner. 'They used to send off their champions to fight positions but mediation will mean the clients win in the long run.'

DAC is using its structure to revolutionise its services. The firm is encouraging its staff and partners to consider themselves first as business people seeking to make a profit, second as lawyers. Client activities are being structured to maximise the understanding of what its clients really want and to encourage staff and partners to view the services they offer as products. This is wise, with products providing solutions whereas services often equate to no more than billable (or non-billable) time.

In 1997, DAC initiated a major change programme, covering three stages over five years, to challenge for the premier spot as the UK's number one legal services provider to the insurance sector and to prepare for long-term growth in clients, income and profitability that the insurance sector alone cannot bring. Key aspects of the programme are the focus on core skills, the firm's client base, and emerging markets.

The first two stages, both completed, saw DAC organise staff skills into a number of specialist resource groups and then identify the sectors for profitable growth. This dual focus has resulted in a new DAC account management system.

The third, ongoing stage of 'Action Focus' is a process of cultural change. In addition to the other commercial principles that the firm has embraced, Action Focus is intended to help DAC become better problem-solvers, listeners, and to give and execute commercial advice beyond the expectations of normal legal services. The programme requires teamwork, and its reward systems are geared towards assisting the selfless, not the selfish.

Key elements of DAC's Action Focus culture are support not blame; profit not income; collaboration internally and externally with clients; and accountability. The programme has been well received by staff and clients alike.

'Clients always said that everyone was the same and that it was difficult to be innovative,' says Nick Sinfield, head of insurance services partner. 'Therefore we've spawned two think tanks to concentrate on innovating with our brand and to develop a product depository.'

DAC has pioneered the use of case conferencing, a unique and streamlined way of case handling with clients' staff which reduces the number of 'touches', costing less as time needed is reduced. The process demands close collaboration, key tie-ups via technology and above all, trust. In this area, DAC has made, for a law firm, a vast investment in IT.

Revolutionary charging methods include fixed fees, a transparent charging basis agreed with the client. It's based on agreeing fees per individual and an acceptable profit margin, and calculating the average length of time to complete a case. And then sticking to it. Clients love it. And, as David McIntosh asserts, 'Hourly rates discourage the talented and encourage the grinder.'

At present, DAC has not forged any formal alliances and certainly has no intention of becoming the legal services arm of a multi-discipline consultancy. It is, however, in discussions with two 'top five' loss-adjusting companies to provide a joint 'one stop' service to insurers regarding employers' and public liability and public claims via out-sourcing. This would be a unique venture, the first of its kind.

Internationally, DAC is mindful of just opening offices everywhere and then swiftly making a loss. 'You have to ask yourselves what you want from an international presence,' says David McIntosh. 'It's better to talk to clients and say "do you need us there?"' Often that isn't necessary. Physical location does not prevent DAC working on international cases for international clients, and it avoids excluding itself from referrals by other firms overseas.

The DAC board consists of seven individuals, each with a specific, accountable responsibility in a top line process: brand enhancement, account management, management of resources, service delivery and fee earner support. There are also directors in specialist functional areas including HR, marketing, facilities and, uniquely in law, a project director.

The Future

DAC is not afraid to explore, experiment and develop the firm so that in 5–10 years' time it will be unrecognisable. By forecasting the way in which markets are evolving, by creating new and innovative products and selling via its revamped account management system, and by collaborating closely with clients, DAC is well on the right track.

Collaboration, and the increasing trend towards Alternative Dispute Resolution, offers a win–win situation in many disputes, as opposed to the win–lose so often typical of disputed litigation. This is a fantastic growth area for solicitors if not barristers. Solicitors have always been good negotiators and now have the opportunity to showcase their skills. The hero (or villain) is no longer the barrister in court. 'Bad lawyers can litigate well, but mediators must be good lawyers,' suggests Nick Sinfield. DAC saw this growing trend in ADR two years ago and trained every single fee-earner about its implications and workings. It's not alone in this, but is ahead of the game.

The firm has flexibility as a core currency and is a pioneer – to its own advantage – in what is often a very traditional profession. The culture and mechanics are almost in place. Time will reveal just how far this innovative law firm can go.

Diageo

Diageo is one of the world's leading consumer goods companies. Formed in December 1997 through the merger of GrandMet and Guinness, Diageo has an outstanding portfolio of world-famous food and drinks brands including Smirnoff, Johnnie Walker, J&B, Gordon's, Pilsbury, Häagen-Dazs, Guinness and Burger King. Diageo sells its products in more than 200 countries worldwide.

Scorecard:

Flexibility	★★★★★
Innovation	★★★★
Human resources	★★★★
Growth markets	★★★★
Quality of management	★★★★★
International orientation	★★★★

Biggest Plus:
Purposeful, well-managed, energised new company

Biggest Minus:
Early days, tough tests lie ahead

Key Figures:
(to 30 June 1998)

Turnover	£12.0 billion
Operating profit	£1,942 million*
Pre-tax profit	£1,850 million*
Employees worldwide	77,000
Employees UK	13,000

(*profits before exceptional items)

Diageo plc
8 Henrietta Place
London W1M 9AG
Tel: 0171 927 5200
Fax: 0171 927 4600
website: www.diageo.com

DIAGEO

Diageo

Company Background

The creation of Diageo was as close to a merger of equals as the corporate world has seen. Both GrandMet and Guinness had huge spirits businesses with some of the world's best-known brands, but in each case a combination of stagnating volumes and fierce competition was threatening to cause a serious hangover. As one wag put it, here were two good companies with a drink problem.

The creation of Diageo has taken them into the premier league, however. From GrandMet's perspective it was not a question of whether to merge with another company, but with whom. Guinness fitted the bill, and was receptive. The fit between the two spirits businesses, geographically and by product, was near perfect. And the merger was resolved with relative ease, with personalities proving no barrier to producing a balanced board.

'It's created a tremendous opportunity for Diageo to grow its brands faster and more profitably,' says Tony Greener, chairman. And it has a stunning portfolio – its top 30 brands all hold the number one or number two position in growing markets.

What's in a name? Classics students will quickly tell you that *dia* means 'day' in Latin and that *geo* means 'world' in Greek. Eyebrows were raised at the name, of course, but it reveals global purpose.

Operations and Markets

Diageo manages its brands in four businesses, which share the common purpose of creating value for shareholders through consumer enjoyment.

UDV, formed by the integration of IDV and UD (United Distillers), is the world's leading and most profitable spirits and wines company. It has annual sales of more than 100 million nine-litre cases and operating profits of £1.1 billion.

UDV's portfolio includes 18 of the world's top 100 premium spirits brands and brings a full product portfolio to the marketplace. Brand names literally trip off the tongue – Johnnie Walker, J&B, Smirnoff, Gordon's, Malibu, Cinzano and Baileys. Some 10 million measures of UDV spirits are enjoyed each day.

Pilsbury is one of the world's leading food companies, with a portfolio of dough-based products and international so-called 'mega-brands'. These include Green Giant, the world's largest marketer of branded vegetables; Old El Paso, the world's number one Mexican food brand outside Mexico; and Häagen-Dazs, the high-profile premium ice cream and frozen yoghurt brand.

Guinness stout is the world's leading stout brand, brewed in 50 countries and enjoyed in 150. Guinness stout is unique, distinctive and one of the world's truly great beers. The Guinness portfolio also includes international brands such as Harp lager, Kilkenny Irish beer and Kaliber alcohol-free lager, and local brands with international potential such as Jamaica's Red Stripe lager.

Burger King is the world's second largest hamburger restaurant chain, with over 10,000 restaurants in 53 countries; 90% of these are owned and managed by franchisees. In 1998 Burger King opened a record number of restaurants around the world and is growing its presence and market share in North America. There are 1,024 ways to order a Whopper, which is the most preferred hamburger in the USA.

Is Diageo a 'cup half-full' or 'half-empty' company? Its brands are highly successful. Yet they have enormous potential to grow internationally. UDV sells approximately 5% of total world spirits volumes and less than 1% of wines. Billions of the world's population have still to taste any packaged food, let alone Pilsbury's products. Guinness's 80% of the world stout market is less than 1% of the world's total beer consumption. And Diageo estimates that Americans will buy 70 billion meals and snacks outside the home during a year – but only 2.7 billion of those will be at Burger King.

Strategy and Management

Diageo's long-term goal is to be in the top five of a peer group of 20 of the world's leading consumer goods companies in terms of the total return generated for shareholders. This peer group includes its toughest competitors Heineken, Anheuser-Busch, Unilever, Nestlé, Seagrams and McDonald's, and other top-performing consumer goods companies like Coca-Cola, Gillette and Procter & Gamble.

Group chief executive John McGrath believes that his job description is simple: 'It's to make sure that everyone in this company is obsessed with delighting our consumers and creating value for our shareholders.' As a measure of progress, Diageo returned nearly £2.8 billion to shareholders in the 1997/98 financial year

A new structure was established for UDV, the spirits and wines business, which accounts for 55% of Diageo's operating profit. The 'new' portfolio was superbly balanced, and competed in many markets through its newly strengthened and extended relationship with Moët Hennessy and a trading and equity partnership with Jose Cuervo.

UDV has been redesigned to grow its brands. Although Diageo did not choose the lowest cost option, it anticipates that the merger will reduce UDV and Diageo's cost base by £290 million in the year ending 30 June 2001. The £630 million cost of achieving synergy is a major investment which includes headcount reductions, changing business locations, new systems and processes, and consequent asset write-offs.

Marketing is the key to making great brands greater. Diageo intends to grow its brands through a combination of unmatched consumer understanding, outstanding brand support and excellent sales and operations execution.

'Our strategy is to deliver profitable organic growth by investing marketing expenditure and capital behind our most powerful brands with the greatest value-creating opportunities,' says John McGrath. To help allocate priorities – and Diageo made a £1.7 billion marketing investment alone in the 1997/98 year – it uses measures of consumer perceptions of its brands and financial measures of investment returns.

The consumer lies at the heart of Diageo's business. Consumer measures ask what consumers think about Diageo's brands, how aware they are of the brands and the perceived value of these same brands – all tracked with the competition, year-on-year, to judge whether its investment in advertising and marketing is paying off and where the new opportunities lie.

Financial measures include the change in 'economic profit' (EP) and 'value creation' which investment brings about. EP is the income earned by a business after deducting a charge in the capital required to generate that income. It's an excellent measure because it brings together the profit and loss account and the balance sheet in one holistic measure to provide a true return on invested capital.

Ask John McGrath about shareholder value and economic profit and his eyes light up. These concepts, which were developed by US business schools some 30–40 years ago ('things sometimes take a while to travel across the Pond', suggests John McGrath) are sometimes referred to glibly by companies, but not Diageo. It has a real under-standing of their importance, and they are applied to each business, even to measure the opportunity cost of profitable individual brands – not just the corporation as a whole.

Diageo calls this process 'Managing for Value' and it is the company's core business philosophy. It helps Diageo develop strategies to build its brands looking some years ahead, covering strategic options, levels of investment and sales support, and discovering which route will generate the most value.

'Everyone in the company can help to create value,' says John McGrath. Marketing, production and finance can all use the same measures of efficiency in their own function. Managing for Value allows Diageo to reward each individual according to their contribution. A new incentive structure is being introduced to provide a direct link between the creation of value for shareholders and the way in which senior managers are rewarded.

Diageo recognises that the determining factor in performance is not just its brands and its business philosophy; it is ultimately the quality of its people who will drive the business forward. 'When you have great brands, you've got to have great people to manage and grow them,' says John McGrath. An innovative executive development programme has been launched to build Diageo's leadership and strategic insight.

The Future

A new culture of the merged business has been created quickly. There are no turf wars and all Diageo people seem to be aligned behind the new company's objectives and values. It is still early days and it will take some time for a newly planted culture to grow firm roots. But Diageo people will tell you that it feels different already.

Employees are being surveyed at all levels of the organisation. Do they feel they have the freedom to succeed and is the organisation harnessing their creativity? Are they proud of what they are doing in the company? Are they passionate about understanding what consumers want, and about using that insight to build Diageo's brands? Are they achieving the very best work of their lives?

If and when the answers are 'yes' then Diageo will have harnessed real momentum towards becoming one of the very best consumer goods companies. Its brands and financial measures are already top class. It is still a huge task, and the first three years' results after the merger will be the proof of the pudding. But the merger appears to be working, savings are ahead of timetable and everything seems to be going in the right direction.

Finelist Group plc

Finelist has five areas of activity within the vehicle parts, access-ories and consumer products market: motor factoring; warehouse distribution; retailing; cash and carry; packaging and manufactur-ing. The company was formed in 1989 when the present chair-man, Chris Swan, led a management buy-out of automotive products company Autela. Operating from 800 sites across the UK, the company employs 7,500 people and has annual sales approaching £500 million.

Scorecard:

Flexibility	★★★★
Innovation	★★★
Human resources	★★★★
Growth markets	★★★★
Quality of management	★★★★★
International orientation	★★★★

Biggest Plus:
Successful acquisitions are not hindering organic growth

Biggest Minus:
The company still has only 10% market share

Key Figures:
(to year ending 30 June 1998)

Annual turnover	£388.1 million
Operating profit	£37 million
Pre-tax profit	£30.3 million
Employees worldwide	7,500
Employees UK	7,500

Finelist Group plc
Regal House
Birmingham Road
Stratford-upon-Avon
Warwickshire CV37 0BN
Tel: 01789 414545
Fax: 01789 414580
website: www.finelist.co.uk

Finelist Group

Finelist Group plc

Company Background

Through a combination of acquisition and steady organic growth, Finelist has grown to dominate the vehicle parts after-market. The group encompasses a number of well-known brands, including Autela, Edmunds Walker, LSUK, Maccess, First Line, Autogem, Tuberex, Bancrofts, Ferraris, XL Components, Autostart and Motor World, and has operations that embrace a wide range of activities, from manufacturing through to high street retailing.

The Finelist brand itself is not promoted to end-customers, with each individual element of the group working to maintain its separate identity. That said, those who work for the organisation are encouraged to identify with the group's overall philosophies, culture and objectives.

Having been created through a management buy-out in 1989, Finelist achieved a full stock market listing in 1994, at which time it was valued at £28 million. Last year turnover stood at £388 million, up from £230 million the previous year. Further growth is expected as the most recent acquisitions bed down. The company claims 10% market share and is confident that there is significant opportunity for further profitable expansion.

Operations and Markets

Finelist has five main operating sectors, with a number of strong brands in each. The divisions are:

Motor Factoring – This division has over 300 branches and supplies 40,000 garages with parts on a 'just in time', one-hour delivery schedule. The principal brands are Autela Components (car and light commercial vehicle parts); Edmunds Walker (commercial vehicles, fleets and facilities management); LSUK (electrical, electronics and diesel); Bancrofts (vehicle body repair).
Warehouse Distribution – Over 30 sites operate under the Ferraris and Engine Express brands, servicing motor factors with same-day

delivery of parts. Finelist is looking at expansion of this division through greenfield sites.

Retailing – The main brands in this division are Motor World, RoadUser and Charlie Browns. Over 410 sites throughout the UK supply accessories and other consumables, including in-car entertainment systems. The stated objective is to expand further in Scotland, East Anglia and South-east England.

Cash and Carry – Finelist operates 23 cash-and-carry sites, primarily under the brand Maccess. These service retailers, installers and garage forecourts with accessories, parts, tools and other consumables.

Packaging and Manufacturing – This division boasts six brands: Autogem produces and distributes exhaust clamps and consumables for the fast-fit and parts distributor market; Autostart is a remanufacturer of rotating electrics and packager of ignition leads; Tuberex manufactures mild steel exhaust systems for supply to fitting stations and national retailers; XL Components remanufactures steering racks, brake callipers and distributors; Veco supplies a range of 6,500 parts; First Line distributes steering and suspension products.

Each operating company has an operating board that reports to a divisional director. In turn, these report to the main board based in Stratford-upon-Avon.

Strategy and Management

While Finelist, through its operating companies, is the major brand in most of its sectors, its overall share of the automotive after-market is only 10%. Its primary strategy is to boost this figure, both through organic growth (including opening greenfield sites where appropriate) and through acquisition. The range of brands under the Finelist umbrella is testimony to the aggressive acquisition activity of the group which has effectively given Finelist managing control of the supply routes to this sector.

Whilst it has absorbed many companies, Finelist has been careful to retain successful brands. If healthy relationships with customers have already been created, then the group sees no need to rock the boat. Equally, successful and enthusiastic managers and staff will always be retained if they are able to contribute to Finelist's success.

In pursuit of its ambitions to secure an ever-larger share of the market, Finelist is investing heavily. For example, it is cementing relationships with garages by installing a computer system called Concept 2000 on their premises. This delivers cost savings and administrative enhancements to the user and secures extra business for Finelist's Autela brand. Edmunds Walker has also invested heavily in servicing the commercial vehicle parts after-market and has launched a facilities management programme with BAA Heathrow. This is currently being rolled out to customers at other locations.

Finelist is particularly pleased to secure what it terms national accounts. This is where an agreement is signed with a major organisation to handle parts procurement and management. The Ministry of Defence, British Midland, British Telecom, Parcel Force and the Post Office are among the companies that have recently signed long-term contracts.

Customer service is of vital importance to Finelist's strategic vision. The fragmentation of the overall marketplace in which the group operates means that competition is intense, so there is a pressing need to satisfy and exceed customer expectations. For example, the warehouse distribution operation provides same-day delivery, whereas most of Finelist's rivals promise only next-day delivery.

In the retail market, Finelist has enhanced customer relationships with the launch of the Motor World Club Card, which provides cardholders with credit facilities in Motor World stores. As well as generating custom – average Club Card purchase values are 26 times higher than for other customers – the initiative provides Finelist with a customer database. There are plans to develop this further in future.

Another key element of Finelist's strategy is to become more successful by helping its customers to be more successful. In the case of the cash and carry division, Maccess Forecourt Distribution has been launched to provide a superior service to petrol stations and several blue-chip retailers such as Esso, Shell and Elf. The RoadUser franchise has been developed to support Maccess's independent retailer customers. With the motor factor division, the Autela franchise provides a tried and tested formula for the independent factor operation or the vehicle franchise dealer to enter the all-makes market. NAS, the Nationwide Auto Service programme, also utilises the franchise concept to provide the independent garage customer with a comprehensive marketing imaging package designed to focus on quality service and customer retention.

Further substantial investment in information technology is being made with a number of objectives in mind. First, a common system in use throughout the group will enable the various operating companies to communicate more effectively. This will assist stock management, ensuring that 'the right part is in the right place at the right time', and thereby increasing the return on capital employed. Furthermore, it will streamline internal reporting procedures, improving the quality of management information.

It will also enhance communication with customers, enabling Finelist companies to provide superior billing and accounting services. Thus a customer will be able to receive a single invoice covering a given period and including a range of orders. This should lead to a cleaner, more efficient process for all concerned. The group also boasts a corporate website and is scheduled to trial online ordering with its key corporate clients in the near future.

Although primarily a UK-oriented company, Finelist is aware of opportunities in Europe and is eyeing the potential of markets in the Netherlands and elsewhere. The main priority will remain in the UK, however; Chris Swan, chairman, feels it is well within the reach of the company to double its market share in the next five years.

While Chris Swan remains the dominant presence within Finelist's management, he has been careful to cultivate a strong senior management team to share his responsibilities, inject alternative thinking and deflect any suggestions that the welfare of the company rested too much on the shoulders of one individual. The consolidation of the 14 operating companies into the three divisions – trade, retail, and packaging and manufacturing, each of which has a divisional managing director – has further strengthened the group structure and should provide a platform for continued growth.

The Future

The automotive after-market remains fragmented, which means there is scope for consolidation. Finelist is not prepared to pay inflated prices for its acquisitions and is content to rely on organic growth if it cannot secure the right terms. The planned expansion of the Motor World retail chain to 500 branches from the current 410 will largely be through the development of greenfield sites.

In general terms, the market is relatively flat. The number of cars on the road is increasing and this together with the wider variety of vehicles, means more parts are required. However, parts themselves are lasting longer, which means the need for replacements is reduced. Overall, there may be 1% per annum growth in total demand.

Thus it will be Finelist's ability to further increase its penetration relative to its rivals which will determine its success. With its enviable track record of bringing successful companies under its wing and its determination to make its existing operations more successful, the future would seem to hold plenty of promise.

Fitch plc

Fitch is one of the world's largest business and design consultancies, with over 30 years of experience helping clients achieve competitive advantage. Fitch is a publicly listed company, with offices in London, Columbus, Boston, Detroit, San Francisco, Osaka and Singapore. It also owns the French international consumer style and trend forecasting agency Peclers Paris. Fitch plc generated total revenue of £22 million in 1997 and currently works with over 200 clients in 24 countries. There are 350 full-time Fitch associates worldwide, 120 of them in London.

Scorecard:

Flexibility	★★★★
Innovation	★★★★★
Human resources	★★★
Growth markets	★★★
Quality of management	★★★★
International orientation	★★★★

Biggest Plus:
Making the next generation of design consultancy a serious business

Biggest Minus:
Merging different cultures is never easy

Key Figures:
(to 31 December 1997)

Turnover	£21.745 million
Operating profit	£2.152 million
Pre-tax profit	£2.165 million
Employees worldwide	350
Employees UK	120

Fitch plc
10 Lindsey Street
Smithfield Market
London EC1A 9ZZ
Tel. 0171 509 5000
Fax 0171 509 0100
e-mail: zuilmahwallis@fitch.co.uk
website: www.fitch.com

 !

Fitch plc

Company Background

Fitch & Company was founded in 1972 in London, and quickly became one of Europe's largest and most visible design firms, specialising in communications, retail design and architecture. It floated on the London Stock Exchange in 1984.

In 1988, Fitch & Company combined forces with Richardson Smith, a successful US agency primarily focused on product design with offices in Columbus, Ohio and Boston. The company changed its name to Fitch. Further US offices were opened in San Francisco (1995) and Detroit (1996).

In 1989 the company formed a 50–50 joint venture, called Polymer Solutions Inc., with GE Plastics, a $5 billion division of General Electric and the world leader in thermoplastics. The joint venture is focused on product commercialisation. In May 1998, Fitch acquired the French firm Peclers SA, a leading international consumer style and trend forecasting agency. Fitch also has an office in Osaka, Japan, and works with a network of associates worldwide.

Fitch's growth has been pretty steady in recent years, and 1997 was the fifth successive year of improved results. Turnover increased from £16.426 million in 1995 to £21.745 million in 1997, while profit before tax rose to £2.165 million over the same period.

Operations and Markets

Fitch's stated business purpose is 'helping manufacturers, retailers and service providers achieve and sustain a long-term competitive advantage', according to Martin Beck, chairman and chief executive. Fitch provides the products, communication systems and environments that make up a brand, ensuring successful 'touchpoints' between its clients and their own customers.

Increasingly these products, communications and environments are digital in nature; accordingly, Fitch has shifted its business so that digital, online and electronic solutions form an increasing part of the offer. This has seen Fitch's 'core competencies' increase from three to four:

Brand development – focuses on developing new brands and rejuven-
    ating existing ones by integrating a diverse range of skills, including
    market research, brand strategy, graphic design, information design,
    interactive media design and production.
Consumer environments – Fitch's retail and leisure development work
    is internationally renowned for redefining and reshaping both the
    shopping and entertainment experiences. Having worked with more
    retailers and developers in more countries than any other design
    consultancy, Fitch's knowledge is extensive.
New media – Fitch adopts a user-centred approach to interaction design
    for new media, developing techniques such as user profiling and
    scenario projections to understand the problem from the user's point
    of view.
Product development – Fitch's offer includes market and user research,
    product planning, industrial design, ergonomics and engineering,
    from concept development through to market introduction.

Geographically, Fitch is on the move, pursuing joint ventures and
strategic alliances as well as acquisitions to enter key markets. It is
developing a long-term relationship with GE. In November 1998, Fitch
launched a Singapore office (51% GE, 49% Fitch), with the primary
focus of sourcing global materials for manufacturing. The office in
Osaka was established in conjunction with Duskin, one of the largest
industrial companies in Japan, which is happy for Fitch to use this as
a business development base.

   Since the acquisition of Peclers, which forecasts forthcoming consumer trends and is particularly active in the textiles, cosmetics, home
environment and consumer equipment industries, Fitch has opened
its own office in Paris. This will be used as a platform for further
expansion in Europe, with Scandinavia and Germany viewed as particularly important markets.

Strategy and Management

Understanding consumers lies at the heart of everything that Fitch
does. It believes that when people hear the word 'design', all too often
they think of appearance rather than function; of décor rather than
sales; of logos rather than business solutions.

   Fitch prefers to think of design as a problem-solving process that
combines creative thought with creative expression. By integrating
strategy and design skills, and utilising its understanding of diverse
industries and markets, Fitch aims to confront business problems with

an informed, fresh perspective, generating new ideas and transforming them into business success.

In corporate terms, Fitch aims to become the biggest design brand worldwide. It sees vast opportunity – globally, no design business has more than 1% market share. How does it intend to get there?

Fitch's business posture asks the question: 'What's Next?' It believes the answer lies in building a so-called 'Third-generation consultancy'. Fitch argues that the second wave (which it claims it pioneered) moved the designer from being a tactical implementer of ideas (the 'how') to a truly strategic partner (the 'what'). Fitch believes its path now lies in helping its clients to know the unknown and to support them in fulfilling the myriad of opportunities that lie ahead.

So Fitch is busy in the process of expanding its futurist knowledge base through acquisition, organic growth and collaboration so that it can better prepare its clients with a view of the styles, influences, trends and directions that will shape the future.

Clients have tended to view traditional management consultants and designers as being quite separate – a 'left' and 'right' way of thinking. Fitch aims to bridge the gap between the two and offer 'informed intuition' – a perspective on world markets drawing upon the traditional analytical skills of management consultants and the intuitive skills of the design business.

This has forced Fitch to restructure itself to deliver against this objective. The opportunities to integrate skills from Peclers in the rest of the business, for example, are already being pursued. People with different skill sets are being deliberately recruited, particularly in research, planning and business analysis.

That throws down the challenge of integrating two different but complementary sets of skills within the business, which in turn throws open the issue of culture. It is difficult to separate strategy and manifestation, so Fitch has had to develop processes and working methods which facilitate this integration, and in so doing, to change its culture. But as senior director Zuilmah Wallis puts it, 'it makes people at Fitch feel relatively unique'.

Fitch has already moved away from a 'how' culture to giving strategic advice to clients. The 'what's next?' emphasis is needed because many client companies have already gone as far as they can in rationalising logistics and cost efficiencies. The focus has shifted instead on to the need to innovate, playing into the hands of creatively-oriented businesses.

Technology is playing its part too. Fitch has developed a global trends database, the contents of which are pulled together from each of the company's offices. Perhaps more apparent are the so-called 'trends walls' – visual compilations of consumer trends, ideas and lateral thinking, collated on large boards which can be found around Fitch's stylish offices. Consumers remain the driving passion in the design business, and the most important interaction is still with 'soft' data; that's why trends databases and trends walls both play their part as changing consumer tastes and patterns are fed into the business on a continuous basis.

The management structure has chairman and chief executive Martin Beck heading up the Fitch plc board. As he is based in the US, there is also a European chief executive, Jean-François Bentz, who splits his time between London and Paris. Each office has its own management team consisting of five or six people representing the most important disciplines such as creative, marketing, operations and finance.

The London office has two joint managing directors, one concentrating on revenue-generating activities and marketing, the other on operations and finance. Because strategy formulation at Fitch is described as 'push and pull', ideas move up and down the management structure. Local management teams are locked in a constant process of changing methods and culture. London is structured into three 'hubs', composed of up to three multi-disciplinary teams, each with a slightly different emphasis.

The Future

The third-wave consultancy is intended to propel Fitch into a different league as a serious business partner of the future to clients. The biggest challenge will be blending two very complementary sets of skills to produce a successful formula. It will have to work very hard to achieve this. Getting the balance right between creating a culture for individuals to think creatively, and the need to rein in to achieve specific objectives is never easy, and there's no blueprint available.

Of course, some management consultancies are also pursuing the same goal, more likely acquiring their complementary skills by moving 'downstream'. That's serious competition, although the perceptions of the design industry have improved in recent years and it is seen increasingly as being 'grown-up'.

Grappling with technology is absolutely necessary, of course, but poses its own problems. 'Hard' information may drive many industries, but design remains a verbally and visually led business where 'anecdotal', 'interesting' and 'provocative' feature more prominently in the vocabulary.

Fitch obviously wants to make itself as recession-proof as possible. In the recession of the early 1990s, Fitch had a much greater exposure to the high street and suffered accordingly. It has since spread its business across different sectors, markets and countries. The high expectations it sets itself – 20% earnings growth year-on-year is pretty testing – indicate that Fitch is confident of its future success.

Gemini Consulting

Gemini Consulting is a global management consulting firm that seeks to put more emphasis than some of its rivals on the extent to which it helps clients implement – rather than just design – change. In doing this it sets great store by 'the power of people', stating that, 'We know that the best consulting solutions are those that the people of an organisation can wholeheartedly embrace.'

Scorecard:

Flexibility	★★★★
Innovation	★★★★★
Human resources	★★★★★
Growth markets	★★★
Quality of management	★★★★
International orientation	★★★

Biggest Plus:
Much more focused on the emotional and human side of clients than typical analytical consultants

Biggest Minus:
The firm is not as well known as its rivals

Key Figures:
(1997)

Revenue (Group):	$900 million
Profit:	n/a*
Employees worldwide:	2,300
Employees UK:	340

* (part of Cap Gemini Group)

Gemini Consulting
One Knightsbridge
London SW1X 7LX
Tel: 0171 340 3000
Fax: 0171 340 3400
website: www.gemcon.com

GEMINI CONSULTING
A Cap Gemini Group Company

Gemini Consulting

Company Background

Gemini Consulting was formed in 1991 as an independent, wholly-owned subsidiary of the Cap Gemini Group of France. Though it stresses that it is a new company, Gemini is built on a 35-year heritage of experience created by the integration of more than a dozen firms around the world.

Steve Beck, managing director for the Northern Europe region, explains that from the start there was 'a conscious attempt to create a different kind of consulting company'. This entailed changing the perception of consultancy from an expense to an investment and meant the firm staking its reputation – and, in some cases, fees – on delivering bottom-line results.

The founders also set out certain values for the consultancy. To deliver on its promise to clients Gemini's consultants need to role model particular behaviours: including teamwork, personal mastery, excellence and enthusiasm. Even now, teams are measured on values on a monthly basis.

'We talk about making a difference and leaving a legacy,' says Steve Beck, pointing out that the consultancy always thinks of results in terms of measurable improvement and sustainability.

This in turn leads to the emphasis upon people, within both Gemini and client companies. While the 'high-end' strategy consultancies with which it competes typically hire a standard sort of business school-qualified young recruit, Gemini goes for a wider range of people, taking them on from industry and other firms as well as straight from winning their MBAs.

With regard to clients, the firm has long recognised that transformations of the type it is charged with helping to deliver only succeed if the workforces embrace them. As a result, it attaches great importance to dealing with not just senior management, but employees at all levels of organisations. 'Sustainability comes through people – the way in which they think, act and feel in their work,' says Steve Beck.

Operations and Markets

Gemini employs 2,300 people in more than 30 offices around the world, spread between the east coast of the United States and Singapore, and between South Africa and Helsinki. Since being set up it has continually expanded and the recent integration of Bossard Consultants has strengthened its already powerful European base even further.

At the same time as broadening its geographic reach – both the South African and Singapore operations were established from the London office – the consultancy has added to its service offering. It now concentrates on nine key business sectors around the world:– telecommunications and media; consumer, retail and distribution; financial services; life sciences (healthcare and pharmaceutical); travel and transport; oil, gas and chemicals; manufacturing; automotive; and utilities. In addition, it works with the information technology arm of the Cap Gemini Group to target combined IT and business change services in four major industries – insurance, life sciences, telecommunications and utilities.

Though it boasts that one in three of *Fortune* magazine's Global Top 100 companies are among its clients, Steve Beck stresses that the firm wants to work with 'leading companies, not the biggest. Leading companies are those that are shaping their industry in the future,' he adds, pointing to new telecommunications operators as an example.

As with other firms of its type, Gemini emphasises that the client is central in its organisation and operations. It stresses that being organised by industry and geography enables it to provide the capabilities and cultural understanding required by clients. It says its structure, policies and practices are designed to deploy 'people, knowledge and capabilities rapidly around the globe; unhindered by organisational boundaries'.

What this amounts to is a multi-disciplinary approach that, regardless of the industry in which the client is operating, entails consultants working with people in what Gemini sees as the four main elements of a business – strategy, operations, people and information – with the intention of implementing solutions that will drive lasting change.

Strategy and Management

As a young company, Gemini is clearly set upon a growth path. However, Steve Beck is concerned that growth should not be so rapid that quality is threatened. Last year, Gemini in the UK grew by 15%, a figure that he believes is sufficient to provide employees with opportunities at the same time as maintaining the quality of the work and the people doing it.

Many consultancies, especially those with links with the large accounting organisations, have started extensive advertising campaigns. But Steve Beck does not see that as an appropriate way to raise awareness of his company. He is a firm believer in growing on the strength of Gemini's reputation. A good proportion of the organisation's assignments come as a result of referrals, leading him to point out: 'We really need to execute well on the proposition of delivering results – changing the motivation of people and leveraging technology. If we do this repeatedly, it drives a virtuous circle for our own people and our economics.'

Gemini believes that, although rivals increasingly talk about working alongside clients, it has long had a fundamentally different way of approaching projects. 'We work *with* their people rather than operate on them,' says Steve Beck. But such concepts are difficult to get over in advertising and ultimately new clients are urged to 'go and experience it'.

Having put so much emphasis on ensuring that clients' employees embrace the changes their organisations are going through, Steve Beck is conscious that Gemini exemplifies best practice in terms of human resources. As a consulting firm, the future is about attracting and retaining the right people.

Consequently, the firm has carried out extensive research into the issue known as the 'work/life balance' and is a member of the national forum devoted to the subject. On a practical level, Gemini was a pioneer in the area of offering employees flexible benefits and it has moved on to offer increasing flexibility in working arrangements. Some employees have become approved sub-contractors working on specific projects, while others have contracts to work a certain number of hours a year.

'We recognise that people have lives outside of work. People want to balance their work life with home life and other interests,' says Steve Beck, acknowledging that the firm must also accept that different employees will have different priorities at different stages of their careers. 'I want us to have the "moral right" to own the people issue in the marketplace. This means we must stay at the forefront with our own people policies and practices.'

The Future

A key challenge for Gemini is to build awareness of its brand. The increasingly wide geographical presence will help with that, but Steve Beck says the firm is also targeting key business sectors where it feels it can make a difference.

Moreover, increasing sophistication among buyers of consulting services should assist a firm that has set itself up to deliver sustainable results. At the same time, the trend towards increased specialisation among consultants favours an organisation that still keeps the functional disciplines of strategy, operations, people and information management separate rather than mixing them up. 'The art is being able to bring people from different disciplines together,' says Steve Beck.

That much is true of most broadly based consultancies. Where Gemini thinks it has something that will help it prosper in the years to come is in the notion that its projects genuinely seek to change the way in which organisations do things.

As it was a first mover in results-based consultancy, so Gemini sees itself as a first mover in helping clients to build capability. In a business environment characterised by an accelerating pace of change, agility will separate the winners from the losers. Gemini's explicit focus on developing its clients' capability, in addition to delivering bottom-line results, is unique. The benefits to Gemini and its clients will be clear and measurable.

The Go-Ahead Group

The Go-Ahead Group was formed in 1987 through a management buy-out of the state-run Northern Bus Company. It is now one of the UK's leading providers of public transport, with extensive bus operations in the North-east of England, Brighton, Oxford and London, and two railway franchises – Thames Trains and Thameslink. The company is active overseas and is developing ground-handling services for airlines. Go-Ahead achieved a stock market flotation in 1994, since when annual turnover has grown from £61 million to £415 million.

Scorecard:

Flexibility	★★★★
Innovation	★★★★
Human resources	★★★
Growth markets	★★★★★
Quality of management	★★★★
International orientation	★★★★

Biggest Plus:
Go-Ahead will benefit from the increased emphasis on public transport

Biggest Minus:
Competition and the need to 'go green' bring pressure

Key Figures:
(to 27 June 1998)

Annual turnover	£414.3 million
Operating profit	£35.5 million
Pre-tax profit	£36.9 million
Employees UK	11,000

The Go-Ahead Group plc
Cale Cross House
Pilgrim Street
Newcastle-upon-Tyne NE1 6SU
Tel: 0191 232 3123
Fax: 0191 221 0315
website: www.go-ahead.com

Go-Ahead

The Go-Ahead Group

Company Background

The Go-Ahead Group's roots are in the North-east of England. When the Conservative government moved to deregulate much of the UK bus industry in the mid 1980s, managers and employees at the Northern Bus Company engineered a buy-out. Expansion soon followed, and the company acquired the Oxford Bus Company and the Brighton & Hove Bus and Coach Company. In London, it acquired London Central and London General.

Diversification into railways came with the privatisation of British Rail in the mid 1990s. Go-Ahead's two rail franchises, Thames Trains and Thameslink, also serve London and the South-east. The company has a clear vision of integrated public transport and is working to develop a seamless network of trains, buses and underground systems.

Go-Ahead is also developing its ground-handling services at major airports in the UK and Europe and is working to develop transport systems in a number of foreign cities. In December 1998, Go-Ahead was awarded the contract, in partnership with the French group VIA-GTI and a local company, to operate the Stockholm commuter rail network. This operation commences in January 2000.

Expansion and diversification is being achieved without compromising profitability, which has improved steadily and reached £37 million for the year to 27 June 1998.

Operations and Markets

Half of the Go-Ahead Group's £400 million-plus turnover is generated from its bus operations, with half of that amount coming from regulated London bus operations and half from deregulated bus operations in the provinces (Oxford, Brighton and the North-east of England). The company operates 2,400 buses and carries over 310 million bus passengers a year.

London has the largest urban public transport system in Western Europe and is unique in the UK in that it remains regulated; a tendering regime applies which is geared to five-year contracts for each route. Go-Ahead has two subsidiaries in the capital – London General and London Central – which together operate 1,100 buses, including the world's largest fleet of the famous red open-backed 'Routemasters'. In total, the company has almost 20% of the London market, carrying 220 million passengers each year.

The bulk of the remaining turnover is accounted for by the rail franchises, Thameslink and Thames Trains, which carry 50 million passengers annually. Under the privatisation of the British railways industry, franchises for certain collections of routes are awarded for limited time-spans, at the end of which competing firms can tender for the business. The Thames Trains franchise was secured by Go-Ahead in October 1996 and runs for seven years six months; the Thameslink franchise started in March 1997 and runs for seven years one month.

Go-Ahead's developing areas of interest include partnerships with transportation providers overseas and the provision of ground-handling services, including check-in facilities, ticketing, baggage and ramp handling. The anticipated continued growth in airline traffic is expected to boost the company's interests in this area.

Strategy and Management

Go-Ahead's strategy has always been to diversify both in terms of the sectors of the public transport industry in which it is involved and the geographic areas in which it operates. Thus, although the corporate headquarters remain in Newcastle-upon-Tyne, the lion's share of the business comes from the South-east of England.

It is also worth noting that the group has a clear ethos of decentralis-ation, as Christopher Moyes, commercial director, explains: 'We are not really interested in building a national brand identity for Go-Ahead itself. Our aim is to motivate strong local teams in tune with their immediate market. This is why our operating companies retain their separate liveries. The approach also ensures we control those costs that can sometimes be associated with creating a corporate empire.'

Much of Go-Ahead's strategic thinking is determined by events on the political stage. The present government has voiced its determi-nation to reduce the number of journeys undertaken by car and has signalled that the private sector must be prepared to provide alternative transport services. This clearly bodes well for operators such as Go-Ahead and the company is optimistic about its prospects.

Sir Frederick Holliday, chairman, comments: 'The government is directing public opinion towards a more restrained use of the private car. This change in cultural attitude should lead people, particularly in the cities, to make considered decisions on whether to use the car, to walk or to find another means of transport. This change of culture will not happen overnight; it will take at least a generation for the ingrained domination of the car to be revised. In this climate, public transport should succeed in the medium to long term. Even a small percentage of private car users transferring to public transport would have an enormous impact on passenger revenue for transport operators.'

While policy at the macro level is encouraging for public transport operators, difficulties are often encountered locally because of road improvement schemes, town centre redevelopments and pedestrianisation. These are still conceived and implemented around the needs of cars and their drivers and frequently make it impossible for buses to run to a timetable.

To counter the problem, Go-Ahead is, wherever possible, working closely with local authorities to devise traffic management schemes which place greater emphasis on public transport. 'We need decision-makers to adopt a fresh, perhaps even revolutionary perspective,' says Christopher Moyes. 'That said, it would also be common sense. We simply need to evaluate traffic flow on the basis of the number of people, not the number of cars. You can move 50 people in a bus that takes up the same amount of road-space as three cars carrying, in all probability, just the three drivers.'

Go-Ahead argues that, for government transport policy to address the problem in any meaningful way, certain facts must be acknowledged, primarily that all modern building development is currently car-centric. Out-of-town shopping centres, for example, inevitably include vast car parks and make little allowance for public transport. Equally, greenbelt and edge-of-town housing projects assume car usage rather than buses. If progress is to be made, argues Go-Ahead, redevelopment of so-called 'brownfield' sites must begin in order to make the best use of existing urban areas.

Environmental issues are also at the forefront of Go-Ahead's deliberations. The company vociferously defends buses against the argument that they are primary causers of pollution, arguing that they carry proportionately more passengers than cars and demonstrating the cleanliness of modern engines. The company remains committed to the development of ever cleaner vehicles, including electric buses, buses using alternative fuels and conventional buses fitted with the latest 'green' technology.

Again, Go-Ahead believes that national and local government agencies must co-operate with the private sector to advance the environmental agenda.

The Future

Go-Ahead's future would seem assured, given the increasing importance being attached to public transportation systems, both at home and abroad. However, the battle against the dominance of the car will be long drawn out and difficult; the company is the first to acknowledge the power of the pro-car roads lobby. For this reason, it recognises the need to makes its services more attractive. It is therefore working hard to make buses and trains the first choice of commuters and travellers of all kinds.

This is being done in a number of ways, including improved vehicle presentation, easier access for the elderly, the disabled and parents with children and luggage, and the deployment of reliable, accurate information systems. These take the form of displays at bus stops and tell those waiting how long it will be before the next bus will arrive.

Go-Ahead was the first operator outside London to introduce wheelchair-accessible, low-floor vehicles into normal local bus service. This pilot project, which was jointly funded by Go-Ahead and the local Passenger Transport Executive and monitored by the Transport Research Laboratory, was an important influence in bringing about a national adoption of such vehicles.

Such innovations require significant investment and Go-Ahead is hoping for further co-operation with local authorities. For example, with regard to information systems, the company would adapt the buses if the authority would fund the necessary roadside equipment.

The integration of various public transport systems is seen as another important way in which the overall profile of public transport can be enhanced. An example of Go-Ahead's work in this sphere is the initiative which enables passengers in Oxford to buy a Travelcard which allows bus travel in Oxford, rail travel to London and unlimited use of the bus and underground networks in the capital. Further co-operation with local authorities and other transport providers will accelerate the development of this sort of scheme.

While its main areas of interest will remain bus and rail transportation networks in the UK, Go-Ahead's involvement in a number of projects overseas and its diversification into the air transport sector signifies a company that has broad horizons, high ambitions and the means of getting to them.

Homebase

Homebase is a market leader in DIY and garden centres, and is part of the J Sainsbury Group.

Scorecard:

Flexibility	★★★★★
Innovation	★★★★
Human resources	★★★★
Growth markets	★★★★
Quality of management	★★★★
International orientation	★

Biggest Plus:
A warm and friendly company in touch with market trends

Biggest Minus:
Operates in a market changing faster than ever before

Key Figures:
(to year end 1998)

Sales (including taxes):	£1.2 billion
Operating profit:	£55.5 million
Number of employees:	17,000

Homebase Limited
Beddington House
Railway Approach
Wallington
Surrey SM6 OHB
Tel: 0181 784 7200
Fax: 0181 784 7755
website: www.homebase.co.uk

Homebase

Company Background

Homebase was founded 17 years ago by J. Sainsbury plc, with the aim of applying the skills of supermarket retailing to DIY. From modest beginnings – one store in Croydon – Homebase expanded rapidly to hold the position of equal fourth in the DIY sector.

Four years ago, Homebase had the opportunity to buy Texas Homecare: an unusual opportunity, since Texas was the larger company. Homebase seized this opening, and for the last three years has focused on integrating the Texas business into its operations. Today, the combined organisation has a nationwide network of almost 300 stores from Truro to Elgin and holds a 27% share of the home improvement and garden products superstore market.

In recent years, the DIY market has changed dramatically, fuelled (or reflected) by TV programmes such as *Better Homes* and *Changing Rooms*. Home refurbishment is now a far more acceptable and widespread hobby than in the past. People are redecorating on average every three years instead of every eight years, as was the case when Homebase was founded. Fashions and trends are more apparent, and the pace of change is increasing all the time. Homebase, centred on the decorative end of the business, is well positioned to maximise the potential of these changes.

Operations and Markets

Although Homebase offers both DIY and garden centre products, DIY remains the core business. Decoration, home improvement and enhancement to indoor and outdoor areas are key areas for the company. It also sells bathrooms and offers an installation service, with a similar set of services for kitchens available in some stores.

The scale of its operations is impressive, to say the least. The number of garden chairs Homebase sells in a year could seat a capacity Wembley Stadium crowd 16 times over. To continue the football analogy, the number of tiles the company sells in a year would cover 190 football pitches.

Homebase continues to expand its operations where this is appropriate. It now has around 285 stores across the UK, ten of which were opened in 1998. For 1999, new stores are planned for East Grinstead, North Finchley, Dundee, Greenwich, Kidderminster, Chelmsford, Southend and Seven Kings amongst others. Originally strong in the South of England, Homebase can now be said to have a far wider national coverage – due in part to assimilating the Texas network, which was far larger than the original Homebase chain.

Homebase is also not afraid to introduce new types of offer. For instance, its new store in Finchley Road offers made-to-measure curtains. In conjunction with Dulux, this Homebase store is now able to provide an interior design service. Its store in Ewell is the largest new store in the Homebase chain and is one of an increasing number of stores which offer a new co-ordinated range of lighting, wall covering, fabrics and cookshops. There are also storage, houseplants and bathroom accessories in-store: anything required to enhance the look and functionality of the home. Indeed, the average store stocks more than 20,000 products.

The company has also expanded its garden design service. Another recent innovation is *Living* magazine which offers home enhancement ideas as well as information on DIY projects. It has the largest circulation of any home interest magazine and is free to Homebase customers.

Services in Homebase stores include board cutting and paint mixing, while some stores even offer gift-wrapping facilities. DIY is a booming business in the UK, as evidenced by the increasing number of magazines now available on this subject – the total presently stands at around 30. Homebase will continue to expand its services wherever they are required.

In terms of demographics, ABC1s predominate among Homebase's customers, although as a large company with a national base, demand for its products naturally includes the entire demographic spread.

Strategy and Management

In the last three years, strategy has focused on the integration of the Texas Homecare stores into the Homebase network. This is now complete and the company is turning towards looking at the future positioning of the business. This will focus on expanding its share of the home enhancement market, a growing sector and one that undoubtedly offers huge opportunities for Homebase.

Another element of the company's strategy is to build on its traditional strengths. Judith Evans, HR director: 'We are there for people undertaking projects in their home. They want to get everything they need to handle that project under one roof, and our aim is to provide exactly that. For instance, bathroom redecoration might fall into three phases. Phase one: choose a new bath and other fittings and have them installed. Phase two: pick out the wall and floor coverings. Phase three: add the accessories. At Homebase, a customer can do all that and more.'

One of the strengths of Homebase is undoubtedly the quality of its products. Its strategy is to provide the best shopping experience in the business, aided by an attractive environment, an excellent product range and efficient operating systems. Most of all, though, quality depends on its people: how helpful they are and how expert their advice is. Homebase invests considerable sums in a wide range of training programmes to ensure that this aspect of its operation is always satisfactory to the customer. These include a retail management training scheme, a garden centre management training scheme and the Homebase Certificate in Garden Retailing.

The company recognises that there is more fashion in gardening nowadays, just as there is in DIY. This is reflected in colours, types of plants, and even in presentation. To stay in touch with these changing trends, the company needs to plan ahead so as to be able to provide customers with what they need, when they want it.

The strategy above all comes down to turning dreams into reality. Chief executive David Bremner: 'We're interested in helping people with ideas and solutions. We do that through traditional retail approaches such as giving helpful customer advice, allowing people to shop when they want, and making products both available and easily accessible. But we also like to add to that by developing offers unique to Homebase. We need to innovate constantly to retain our cutting edge.'

Also central to the company's strategy is having the right people. It looks for self-starters, those able to work on their own initiative – and also those capable of working within and as part of a team. The average store employs fifty people, so teamwork is a must, both for personal development and to deliver customer satisfaction. Its people include many gardening and DIY enthusiasts, so they are typically able to answer questions with confidence. This natural enthusiasm is of course supplemented by a great deal of product knowledge training.

Customers require different levels of advice, since DIY fans range from complete beginners to semi-professionals. They also require reassurance that the product they have selected is right for their intended job. Stores have sufficient levels of expertise that there is always someone on hand to answer even the most difficult questions. The company's management will continue to ensure that this spread of expertise is always available across the Homebase network.

The Future

The future for Homebase is very much about reinforcing the style aspect of its market. DIY is now a hobby, not a necessity, and as such is geared more towards customers' creativity which they choose to express in their homes. Homebase will continue to orient itself to meet that change.

This is undoubtedly an exciting time to work for Homebase. The market is lively and there is a great deal happening on both the DIY and garden centre fronts. The challenge for the company is to be able to keep pace with the rapid changes in its marketplaces; however, its record to date, and especially over the last few years, suggests that it should be able to take this challenge in its stride.

Huxley Associates

Huxley Associates is a specialist IT recruitment consultancy with annual turnover in excess of £13 million. Huxley Associates employs highly experienced consultants working in teams covering specialist business and technical areas. It is particularly strong in banking and finance. The head office is in the City, but it is extending its UK coverage all the time and has recently opened offices in Manchester and Reading.

Scorecard:

Flexibility	★★★★★
Innovation	★★★★
Human resources	★★★★
Growth markets	★★★★★
Quality of management	★★★★
International orientation	★★

Biggest Plus:
Fast growth and high earning potential

Biggest Minus:
Demanding, frenetic pace

Key Figures:
(to 31 December 1998, unaudited)

Turnover	£13.48 million
Employees UK	125

Huxley Associates
America House
2 America Square
London EC3N 2AH
Tel: 0171 335 0005
Fax: 0171 335 0008
e-mail: jobs@huxley.co.uk

Huxley Associates

Company Background

Privately owned Huxley Associates is a very young company. It was established in 1995 by Gary Elden, a consultant working for a large IT-based recruitment group. Fighting against the recession in the early 1990s, he took the opportunity to build networks of contacts and clients and by the time the recession was over, he had fostered strong loyalties between consultant and client – a philosophy that has remained with Huxley Associates today.

Huxley Associates is extremely fast growing and the figures speak for themselves. Turnover in 1996 was £17 million; in 1997 it nearly tripled to £4.9 million. By 1998 this had surged to £13.4 million, and the curve looks upward.

Operations and Markets

Huxley Associates specialises only in IT recruitment. Given the explosion of demand for specialists in all areas of computing and infor-mation technology, that's a pretty good business to be in.

Huxley Associates provides its clients with either permanent or con-tract staff, as required. Its range of services includes consultancy, inter-view and selection, search, advertising and database.

In terms of technical specialisation, Huxley covers most technical areas of systems integration, development, computer programming and support. This includes most client server and mainframe environ-ments, PC, UNIX, RDBMS, LAN/WAN, Lotus Notes and Internet/Intranet.

The main market areas covered include international banking and finance, management consultancy, insurance, legal, pharmaceutical, media, retail, manufacturing, software houses and facilities man-agement.

In terms of permanent assignments, Huxley Associates separates its operations into banking and finance, and commercial. Within each of these business sectors are the different skill sets and technical specialists with dedicated teams assigned to each. Then to one side is the account management function, which pulls the whole process together, fronting client service and development.

The banking and finance industry is characterised by increasing consolidation and mergers. Clients are demanding – they want IT specialists, but they also want people who can work under pressure, put in long hours, work with 'big money' and often be client-facing. The City pays well, has the best technology and wants the best people. Communication skills are just as important as academic qualifications.

The trouble is, there just are not enough good people around to satisfy. While that might be an indictment of the education system and the number of people studying mathematics and computer science, no-one is going to stand around and wait for them to emerge. The shortage has spawned a dynamic, fast-moving industry that goes out to find the right people with IT skills for its clients.

That requires strong networks of contacts, sophisticated headhunting techniques, a commitment to sizeable advertising and high visibility of the consultancy. These are qualities that Huxley Associates has in abundance.

'It's also a matter of looking strategically, not only tactically,' says Gary Elden, Huxley's managing director. 'Sometimes we encourage clients to compromise – to drop some of the business skills requirements, to look at opportunities to train or even re-train from another technical skill set.' That's where Huxley's consultancy approach comes in. Huxley doesn't just fill vacancies at client companies; it works with them closely as partners, meeting regularly, planning ahead of requirements and finding achievable solutions.

The commercial sector, in Huxley's definition, is effectively anything outside banking and finance. The characteristics of this market are really no different – the same technical skills are needed, the same shortage of suitable people exists. From the candidate's perspective, things do vary. There will be less of a need to understand the business itself than there is in banking. Location will be different (there might be the chance to live locally!). There is less pressure, more flexi-hours, and generally less 'hustle bustle' than in the City; pay might be lower. These factors will vary between industry sectors: telecommunications, for example, is one of the fastest growing, with its own special culture.

Huxley Associates doesn't just provide technologists and engineers. It handles a lot of very senior appointments for clients at the highest level, including managers, team leaders, business analysts and supervisors.

Contract recruitment is probably the fastest-growing, most profitable sector of IT recruitment at the moment, and accounts for 60% of all Huxley placements. There may be many different reasons for clients to take experts on a contract basis.

The year 2000 problem, or 'millennium bug', for example. Cobol mainframe programmers are in great demand just now, because this is where many of the dormant problems lie. And IT experts are virtually naming their price to work over the turn of the new millennium. Obviously to hire staff on a contract basis is cost-effective, without long-term commitment and hopefully, in this particular context, they won't still be needed after 1 January 2000!

Sometimes it is just the realities of market circumstances. If there is a gap or delay in filing a full-time position just because of a lack of availability of suitable people, contractors fill such gaps, but at a premium. Using contractors even allows companies to get beyond budgetary controls such as maximum head count.

Strategy and Management

Huxley's mission is 'to become the UK's No. 1 IT recruitment consultancy by working as one company, harnessing our power and potential to increase the profitability of us all, creating opportunities and enjoying what we do, and providing our clients and candidates with a service that far exceeds their expectations'.

At the heart of Huxley Associates' strategy is strong client relationships. The company has an established client base which is very loyal – an endorsement of Huxley's client-focused, consultancy-led approach, and the fact that it always pulls out the stops to deliver results. The focus will therefore remain on serving clients' needs.

Huxley Associates' philosophy is to get the best of 100 clients rather than any of 500. Choosing your clients rather than them choosing you is a sign of confidence, maturity and success.

In a business which is renowned for its electrifying pace, high earnings potential and pressure deadlines, Huxley Associates wants to be number one – not only in terms of clients, profits and turnover, but in the type of work it does. 'I always believe that you should enjoy what you are doing,' says Gary Elden, 'and that inevitably has the consequence that people produce better quality work.'

Huxley Associates admits to being constrained only by the number of good people available. 'Out of say forty or fifty people who are interested in joining us, we perhaps only take two,' says Elden.

Huxley clearly could expand the number of clients it works for, but it resists the temptation. Its managers believe strongly that quality is all important. Clients rely on them, and 'trust' is an important word. The company recognises that when markets get tougher, those who have over-reached or over-promised will struggle. 'We almost welcome a recession,' says Elden, 'as quality will prevail in a tightened market.'

Huxley Associates maintains a sophisticated approach; they regard themselves as consultants, not as agents. Knowing the candidates, the clients and their requirements, and the industry trends is everything. 'Walking the talk' of IT sophistication, everything is handled on powerful databases and online media.

People are vital to Huxley Associates' success. It's all that they have, effectively, and their calibre, speed, professionalism and hunger have contributed to making Huxley Associates a leading IT recruitment consultancy.

'Essentially we encourage "intrapreneurs",' says Gary Elden. 'The way we are set up, people can effectively run their own business within a business.' Rob Tillett, for example, has just been handed the task of opening, building and developing Huxley Associates' new office in Manchester, covering the North of England.

No-one joins as a manager, only as a recruitment consultant. Everything is based on what you can deliver for Huxley Associates' clients as a recruitment consultant. The evidence is that they have delivered a lot.

The Future

Huxley Associates wants to continue creating enough opportunities for its people. That means expansion, initially in the UK, where potentially Huxley might open up to ten offices. Beyond that, perhaps Europe. Gary Elden says this is a market he wants to hit, but realises his company is not ready yet. Huxley Associates can also maximise the number of business sectors it provides IT recruitment services in, without ever compromising its determination to be the best and always serve its loyal client base with dedication.

Future growth will depend on good people coming through the system, on senior consultants and team leaders pushing the managers hard. In a dynamic, hungry company there seems little chance of this not happening, and Huxley Associates looks set to go from strength to strength.

INVESCO Global

INVESCO Global is part of AMVESCAP plc, the holding company for one of the world's largest independent investment managers with some US$275 billion of funds invested globally. AMVESCAP comprises AIM Investment Management, INVESCO and the recently acquired GT Global. London-based INVESCO Global unites all of the group's non-US businesses. AMVESCAP plc is quoted on the London, New York and Paris stock exchanges and is currently a constituent of the FTSE-100 index.

Scorecard:

Flexibility	★★★★
Innovation	★★★
Human resources	★★★★
Growth markets	★★★
Quality of management	★★★★
International orientation	★★★★★

Biggest Plus:
Global reach in both institutional and retail investment markets

Biggest Minus:
Lack of recognition as a rising force in fund management

Key Figures:
(at 31 December 1998, for AMVESCAP plc)

Turnover:	£802 million
Operating profit:	£187 million
Pre-tax profit:	£231 million
Employees worldwide:	4,900
Employees UK:	518

INVESCO Global
11 Devonshire Square
London EC2M 4YR
Tel: 0171 626 3434
Fax: 0171 454 3962

Your Global Investment Partner

INVESCO Global

Company Background

INVESCO Global is part of AMVESCAP plc, which was created by the merger of London-based fund manager INVESCO with US-based AIM Management Group in February 1997. The group extended its global reach when it acquired GT Global in June 1998 for some US$1.3 billion, bringing additional investment management services for pension funds and institutional clients, and a new range of funds for individual investors is now marketed under the INVESCO GT brand name.

Operations and Markets

AMVESCAP's total funds under management are split evenly between the group's institutional and retail activities. AMVESCAP's operations are divided into four key business groups:

Managed products – Through the AIM and INVESCO range of products, retail funds are marketed to individual investors in the US via intermediaries, with the support of one of the industry's broadest, most effective distribution networks of 146,000 financial consultants. Funds under management increased to $134.5 billion at 31 December 1998, having grown by $33.1 billion over the year.

US institutional – In North America INVESCO has built one of the largest fund management companies for tax-exempt funds, serving corporate pension funds, foundations, endowment and public pension funds of many well-known US organisations. The US institutional group produced record results in 1998. Revenue and operating profit improved by 43% and 21% compared with 1997. The group ranks among the largest active-only asset managers in the US.

Retirement benefit services – This is a new operating business which co-ordinates, develops and manages defined contribution services in related retirement products worldwide. The group generated over

$1.3 billion in net new business for various units of AMVESCAP during the year, and was responsible for over $6.2 billion in funds under management for all distribution channels. The group currently services over 340 separate retirement plans with approximately 260,000 plan participants.

INVESCO Global – accounts for the group's non-US business, managing assets for institutional and retail clients all over the world. Total funds invested in global and non-US equity and fixed-income products has doubled to around $40 billion since the acquisiton of GT Global. Operating profits increased to £31.7 million in 1998, and operating profit margin climbed to 21%.

Strategy and Management

Following a highly successful acquisition of GT Global, AMVESCAP believes it now has the geographic platform it needs for organic expansion. Any further acquisitions, according to INVESCO Global's chief executive Michael Benson, would most likely be of the 'infill' variety to expand reach in a particular marketplace.

INVESCO Global operates through regional profit centres, each with its own CEO reporting to Michael Benson. These regions are Europe, Japan, South-east Asia and North America (international investments flowing into and out of the US). Central to the group's investment approach is for assets to be managed as close as possible to their region of investment. The four divisions employ a common global macroeconomic view that is set by the central Global Asset Allocation Committee on input from the regions.

INVESCO Global identifies two major pools of investment demand still to be captured, in continental Europe and Japan. It believes that some of the biggest opportunities will be in Europe as a result of the euro currency zone and demographic changes and it is well-placed to meet these challenges with strong operations in France and Germany. In Japan, the company has ambitions to gain pension fund business, including state-run pension funds. It is also fully aware that there is some $6 trillion of retail business in Japan to be exploited and has planned accordingly. INVESCO Global is well placed in Asia, where it is the fifth largest fund manager and continues to attract large volumes of cash from Hong Kong, despite the recent East Asian economic crisis.

AMVESCAP manages its fund management affairs in a highly prudent way. It does not take positions in financial markets and has thus been able to weather periods of high stock market volatility.

The group believes in 'bottom–up' stock selection, focusing on fundamental value relative to similar types of securities. This philosophy supports a wide variety of investment styles at the individual portfolio level, although there is a bias towards growth. All portfolios share a common three-step approach to investing: quantitative screening, corporate analysis and portfolio design.

Portfolio managers undertake their own research, and tend to be generalists. The research process is unstructured, to encourage innovative thinking. While managers have overall country and sector responsibilities, they are encouraged to research companies that they find interesting. Approved stock lists are not used – a commonality of holdings results from the teams' shared investment philosophy and approach to stock selection.

Although the acquisiton of GT doubled the size of INVESCO Global's business, the focus on client service has remained the same. The company believes that everyone, from the highest executive down to the person who answers the telephone, has to be aware of the importance of the service chain. Seeking to maintain stability and continuity, INVESCO Global places strong emphasis on relationships with institutional clients and pays close attention to specific client objectives and needs.

AMVESCAP is investing heavily in information technology to serve the needs of its global business. It recognises the need for a consistent IT approach throughout the world to serve both the integrity of the investment business and the group's administrative needs. It has been particularly important to integrate the different cultures of the US retail arm AIM and INVESCO Global. The group is also looking carefully at how best it might use the Internet for distributing its products.

AMVESCAP is headed by Charles Brady, who holds the posts of chairman and chief executive. INVESCO Global is run by the Hon. Michael Benson, chief executive, and Tristan Hillgarth, who is deputy chief executive. The functional responsibility for investment management rests with the chief investment officer, Roger Yates; the chief financial officer is Jeremy Lambourne, and the chief operations officer is Anthony Myers.

As a service business AMVESCAP puts a great deal of emphasis on the quality of its human resources, recognising that people are the essence of the business. The group's professional staff includes portfolio managers, analysts, research specialists, traders, administrators and managers together with marketing staff and experts in product design. Development and training of staff is deemed crucial to expanding the intellectual capital of the firm. Rewards are excellent and INVESCO Global operates on the basis that well-rewarded employees will return better service to both company and clients.

The group takes financial management and controls very seriously. It operates a highly rigorous compliance operation to ensure that all legal responsibilities and regulations are fully adhered to and is very aware of the need to monitor and control risks throughout the group.

One of the group's financial goals is set in terms of Return on Revenue (ROR). The company has dramatically improved its ROR over recent years and has now reached the industry benchmark of around 35%. Revenues and cash flows throughout the business have been improved, the corporate structure has been reshaped and the company has managed to draw together very different cultures in the effort to produce a higher ROR. City analysts believe that synergies among AMVESCAP businesses will, over time, produce substantial enhancement of earnings.

The Future

The fund management industry has a dynamic future, driven by a number of key industry changes. Governments will be relinquishing management and control of savings, moving them from the public to the private sector. INVESCO Global expects the sheer weight of money through pensions and savings provision, as governments recognise the need to provide for the future of their people, to drive this expansion. It sees particular opportunities in continental Europe where the pensions system is greatly underfunded and it also regards Japan as a relatively untapped market for independent fund managers.

AMVESCAP also recognises there is a need to improve communication with investors of all kinds, particularly when markets have become exceedingly volatile. The Internet may have an important role to play, allowing faster access to investors and cutting through the paper chain. Beyond that, e-commerce may play a leading role in the fund management industry, particularly in serving the retail sector.

AMVESCAP looks set to maintain its financial record and produce a good return for shareholders on both sides of the Atlantic by prudent financial management of ROR and a constant focus on the all-important customer/client relationship.

INVESCO Global is ambitious, but takes the view that to succeed in the fund management industry you don't necessarily have to be the biggest. It is more interested in being the best in both delivery and performance. It is not necessary to have a huge headcount, simply good systems and a well-motivated workforce. That said, the infrastructure is now in place to support a much larger global organisation and INVESCO Global will be looking to secure above-average performance records on larger capitalisation mandates to achieve its ambitious growth objectives.

ISE Group

The ISE Group is a retailing operation whose principal brand, Poundland, operates from 49 locations throughout the UK. It also runs a buying operation, the ISE Group Far East, which is based in Hong Kong; a software company, M&O Business Systems; and it is developing a new retail concept, Homes & More. The group is also involved in negotiations with retailers in Europe, South Africa, South America and the Middle East. Since it was launched in 1990 the company has grown rapidly, with turnover expected to reach around £79 million in 1998.

Scorecard:

Flexibility	★★★★
Innovation	★★★★
Human resources	★★★
Growth markets	★★★★
Quality of management	★★★★★
International orientation	★★★★

Biggest Plus:
The Poundland brand is reinvigorating the high street

Biggest Minus:
Retailing remains competitive in a low-inflation economy

Key Figures:
(to end 1998)

Annual turnover	£79 million ex VAT
Operating profit	n/a
Pre-tax profit	£2.6 million
Annual investment	£3.5 million
Employees worldwide	1,710
Employees UK	1,700

The ISE Group plc
The Meadows
Cannock Road
Wolverhampton WV10 0RD
Tel: 01902 306306
Fax: 01902 306090
website: www.poundland.com

ISE Group

Company Background

The ISE Group encompasses the Poundland retail brand, which was launched in 1990 at a pilot store in Burton-on-Trent and which has since grown into a national network of 49 retail outlets based in some of the UK's most prestigious shopping centres and high streets. The concept is as simple as the name suggests: everything in the stores, from toiletries to stationery to confectionery, costs £1. Over 3,000 items are stocked.

The success of the Poundland initiative – more store openings are planned for the future – prompted the group to establish its own buying and shipping operation, the ISE Group Far East. The amount of merchandise sourced via the Hong Kong office is expected to increase by 40 per cent in the next three years.

From its inception, Poundland used bespoke software supplied by M&O Business Systems and Software (Oxford). In 1997 the decision was taken to acquire a controlling interest in the firm so that it could enjoy greater control of development and reap the benefits of marketing the company's products to other retail operations.

It was in 1997 that the decision was taken to change the name from Poundland plc to the ISE Group plc, in order to allow the separate companies within the organisation to develop their own identities. The group now employs 1,800 staff and expects to recruit more to support its planned branch openings. In 1998, it reported a pre-tax profit of £2.6 million.

Operations and Markets

From the outset, Poundland has enjoyed a very clear vision of the place it wishes to occupy in the retailing universe. Its single price approach means that it makes a straightforward offer to the consumer, with household name brands such as Walker's Crisps, Mars, Radox and Panasonic being used to underline the perception of genuine value for money.

The success of the concept has demonstrated that manufacturers are keen to work in partnership with Poundland, either supplying their normal range of goods under their own brand or providing products that retail under Poundland's own branding. In the Far East, many suppliers manufacture bespoke products to meet the company's specifications. The Hong Kong buying operation has proved particularly successful at sourcing original items for sale exclusively through Poundland.

The group's profitable growth has been further facilitated through the use of bespoke software to control stock management and ensure that top-selling brands are always available to meet demand. While head office determines overall product supply tactics, the system is sufficiently flexible to recognise the different experiences of individual stores and react accordingly. The group hopes to generate increasing revenues from sales of its software to other retailers; in fact, the group achieved a sale of the system to another retail organisation in early 1999.

Distribution costs are another important element in the equation. To increase efficiency, the group operates from a purpose-built distribution facility called The Meadows in Wolverhampton. Operating 24 hours a day and servicing a large fleet of lorries, it ensures that, if items are ordered by noon, they will be delivered the same day. And to further enhance cost-effectiveness, the journeys undertaken by the lorries are carefully planned so that they can collect stock from suppliers on the way back and thus avoid returning empty to base.

Strategy and Management

Ever since opening its first store in the Octagon Centre in Burton-upon-Trent in April 1990, Poundland has placed great emphasis on providing great value for money without compromising the quality of the shopping experience. Thus its stores are located in fashionable and popular shopping areas and are fitted out to high standards. This strategy has been pursued relentlessly in order to put further clear blue water between the company and its rivals, who still suffer from the perception that they only stock end-of-line items in dingy, cramped and down-market surroundings. According to Gerry Loughran, Poundland's marketing manager, the intention is to make people proud to shop at the store. 'What is wrong with saving money and getting quality? We are appealing to shrewd customers who want to get maximum value for their spend. This crosses all lifestyles because everyone wants to get value for money.'

Gerry Loughran is an enthusiastic advocate of aggressive and innovative in-store marketing and has worked with merchandise suppliers to develop eye-catching promotional initiatives that have led to increases in sales of up to 250%. He is also working on television and radio facilities which will broadcast exclusively to the branch network, carrying information on special offers and seasonal promotions: 'The physical presentation is all-important in developing a quality feel. We are talking about retail theatre. We want Poundland to be a pleasurable experience, a fun place to come and shop.'

Poundland's strategic thinking also places great emphasis on the contribution made by staff and considerable effort is made to build a group feel, despite the fact there are different brands within the group operating from remote locations. The group-wide TV and radio channels help serve this purpose when used outside retailing hours. Feedback from staff is actively encouraged.

The group's energetic strategy of opening new outlets – 12 Poundland stores alone in 1999 – is in part a response to the activity of other retailers. For example, supermarkets are increasingly diversifying away from food retailing and competing with other high street outlets; by stocking such a wide variety of products in as many locations as possible, Poundland wants to be seen as a viable alternative to the dominance of a few mega-chains. 'We have the muscle of a national brand but we strive to retain a high degree of intimacy with the customer,' says Gerry Loughran. 'We are at the forefront of the rebirth of the high street.'

So meteoric has been the successful growth of the Poundland concept that the group is confident of success in its new markets, including its overseas ventures such as Dix Francs in France. Gerry Loughran comments: 'Wherever you are in the world and whatever product you are talking about, people want value for money. If you can demonstrate that you have the quality and the keenness of price, you will succeed. It is a recipe for global success.'

Many outsiders visit Poundland and instinctively feel suspicious about the availability of such products at such prices. Where's the catch? they wonder. The answer is simple: there is no catch. By sourcing its own high-quality merchandise, negotiating attractive deals with outside suppliers and running a superb distribution operation, the company is able to keep a secure lid on its costs and pass on its savings to its customers.

Proof of its success, if it were needed, comes with the fact that other retailers often make bulk purchases from Poundland so that they can re-price the goods for sale in their own shops. That alone speaks volumes about the merits of the ISE Group's strategy – and that of others in the retail marketplace.

The Future

The ISE Group's aggressive plans for Poundland store openings in the UK should reinforce the brand, strengthen its image and thus help widen its appeal to those who may retain some suspicions of low-cost, single-price retailing. The mantra of 'value plus variety', together with the promotion of well-known brands across a wide product range, will prove persuasive to all consumers interested in getting the most for their money. Aggressive in-store marketing campaigns should also encourage consumers to spend higher amounts on their visits to branches.

The strength of the purchasing, distribution and stock control systems will help manage costs, increase efficiency and boost the potential for profitability. The group's international collaborations will also provide new theatres of operation, with joint ventures and supply agreements extending the management's skill base.

Poundland is also exploring how it can exploit the Internet and what is termed 'e-tailing'. It has set up a work study group to analyse the best way to attract custom using the latest communications technology. The project will address a number of issues, such as the required information systems, order fulfilment, delivery and service.

The group's vision is simple: 'We intend to build upon our strengths of operational excellence, product leadership and customer intimacy and make the group a truly global organisation. What is certain is that we will make sure that the experience of growing our business is never boring, for either our customers or ourselves.'

Kewill Systems plc

Kewill Systems plc is a business software group specialising in support, development, implementation, consultancy and support services. Specialist divisions deliver ERP (Enterprise Resource Planning), Logistics and Electronic Commerce solutions to over 20,000 customers worldwide.

Scorecard:

Flexibility	★★★★★
Innovation	★★★★★
Human resources	★★★★
Growth markets	★★★★★
Quality of management	★★★★
International orientation	★★★★

Biggest Plus:
An international company at the forefront of technology, expanding rapidly without compromising its standards

Biggest Minus:
Wide range of complex products requiring a great level of resource commitment, application and expertise

Key Figures:
(1998)

Pre-tax profit:	£8.4 million
Turnover (expected, 1999)	£70 million
Employees worldwide	650

Kewill Systems plc
Case House
85–89 High Street
Walton-on-Thames
Surrey KT12 1DL
Tel: 01932 233200
Fax: 01932 233222

Kewill Systems plc

Company Background

Kewill has been delivering supply-chain software and services for over a quarter of a century. Chief executive Geoffrey Finlay attributes this to the company's steadily growing base of satisfied customers, which has ensured the company's consistent and profitable growth.

When Geoffrey Finlay joined the company in February 1998, he immediately began streamlining the company and says, 'An important cornerstone in the growth and expansion we intend is the reorganisation of the group into three key operating divisions – Electronic Commerce, ERP (Enterprise Resource Planning) and Logistics – each of which is an aggregation of our existing products and companies and each of which represents quite a significant business opportunity in its own right.' The group had previously consisted of 15 small to medium-sized divisions.

Chairman Andy Roberts cites the Electronic Commerce division as one that has experienced particularly strong growth in sales. 'This division's outstanding achievements stem from its principal focus of linking large numbers of suppliers to their major trading partners in the food, home-shopping, stores and public sector markets.' He claims that the company's trading position was further strengthened by the entry into the group of ElectricMail Ltd, a company specialising in Internet connectivity.

Kewill describes itself as a 'one stop shop solutions provider' and trading community management vendor. It provides companies with EDI, e-mail, Internet, Intranet, or Extranet services as well as ERP, warehouse management and shipping systems.

Kewill has over 8,000 ERP installations to its credit, more than 7,000 electronic commerce customers, 300 warehousing systems and 6,000 shipping systems for a total installed base well in excess of 20,000 worldwide.

Based in Walton-on-Thames, Kewill has seven UK offices plus bases in 20 countries globally. American operations are based in Boston and

San Francisco, while German-speaking Europe is serviced from bases in Munich and Vienna.

Operations and Markets

Kewill has expanded its electronic commerce and ERP business by increasing market share in the US through acquisition. Chief executive Geoffrey Finlay says the group is in a constant acquisitive mode, having taken over an additional four companies within the past year. 'The Supply Chain Logistics Division was expanded by acquisition and also returned excellent results, whilst the thriving E-Commerce Division expanded its user base to over 7,000 corporate clients, growing at some 40%.'

The group currently operates across the UK, USA, Germany and Austria and in 1998 made record pre-tax profits of £8.4 million sterling, up by 13.3%. Kewill Systems plc is a publicly quoted company employing over 650 highly skilled and professional people worldwide.

More recently Kewill has completed successful initiatives with both Sainsbury's and Bentalls. Chairman Andy Roberts says it has illustrated the possibility of combining the benefits of electronic data interchange technology with low-cost, two-way Web access to a large proportion of their suppliers.

Clients include BP, Cable and Wireless, Intel, IBM, Hewlett-Packard, Canon, Dunlop Tyres, Ford, Gillette, J Sainsbury, Marks & Spencer, Mobil, Nationwide, Nokia, Rolls-Royce, Royal Doulton, Siemens, SmithKline Beecham and Zeneca.

The firm's success is built on a foundation of reliable products with a dedicated and highly skilled workforce who have a strong commitment to customer service. It is this high level of customer orientation and service which Kewill markets as the main attraction for customers, priding itself on delivering both quality and value for money. The emphasis is on long-term results as opposed to short-term opportunism.

A graduate induction programme is due to start in early 1999, taking on board several of the brightest candidates available. Kewill currently is rapidly expanding its professional staff, taking on specialists in all supply-chain related applications, electronic commerce and software development.

Strategy and Management

Kewill specialises in the rapidly expanding supply-chain software sector, providing both stand-alone and integrated solutions. It pays particular focus to the small to mid-sized enterprise (SME) market so often overlooked by the very largest software companies – those selling extremely expensive solutions that most 'real world enterprises' simply cannot afford. Kewill's success stems largely from providing mission-critical systems with world-class functionality in a manner that allows smaller companies to implement them cost effectively and to achieve a timely, tangible return on investment. Its business is split nearly evenly between its three operating divisions and nearly half its revenue comes from outside the UK.

Kewill's mission statement sums up the company's proactive approach to business. 'Who will? Deliver the next generation of world-class supply-chain software solutions, in a manner that provides clients with optimal results in the fastest time frame, and at costs that are reasonable and justified. We will! Kewill. The Results People.'

Kewill's philosophy of bringing best-of-breed solutions quickly to market is enabled by its long-proven financial strength, thereby allowing it to buy established products and companies and merge them into the group's superstructure. Key talents from the acquired companies are most often retained and encouraged to follow their original vision, helped along by the management expertise and credibility that the group provides.

The Future

The unprecedented growth of e-mail and the Internet will ensure that electronic commerce is the key enabling technology which transforms the way business is done beyond the turn of the century.

Whereas many companies are now waking up to the fact that they face the risk of potential computer chaos next year, Kewill claims that it will escape the predicted computer chaos in the year 2000. Geoffrey Finlay says the company first identified the problem in 1991, which means the company is now not currently strained in trying to sort out the Y2K issues.

Company loyalty is highly evident at Kewill, despite the fact that it's a relatively new company. Chief executive Geoffrey Finlay believes that the company's continuing success is due to two major factors: Firstly, the commitment of highly qualified and skilled specialist staff with knowledge in a particular area, many of whom have remained with the company for over ten years. Secondly, he cites the company's 'corporate-wide commitment' to products, development and service provision. Some 80% of the company's 650 employees are directly involved in bringing best-practice support services to customers.

The company provides customer service charters and uses the latest 'HelpDesk' technology including Internet pages and bulletin boards to deliver a fast service to the community.

The continuing commitment to maintaining standards and testing all products is of great importance to the company. Kewill feels that having achieved this level of customer trust, it can enable clients to exploit the latest industry developments without jeopardising previous or future investments.

Kewill aims to double the company's size over the next two years. Expansion is planned in three major areas: consumer/supplier trading applications, shipping management systems and consolidating its dominant position in 'tier three' of the Enterprise Resource Planning global market. Expansion plans across Asia are currently under negotiation, including moving into China, Thailand, Taiwan and Singapore.

'Future prospects include building a secure Intranet system and expanding productive use of web-based application systems to handle both volume and deliver security for major businesses,' says Geoffrey Finlay.

The Lombard Risk Group

Founded in 1988, the Lombard Risk Group is a world leader in both software and training for the financial markets, with a special focus on derivatives and enterprise-wide risk management.

Scorecard:

Flexibility	★★★★
Innovation	★★★★★
Human resources	★★★★
Growth markets	★★★★★
Quality of management	★★★★
International orientation	★★★★

Biggest Plus:
A fast-growing, dynamic company with a prestigious client list

Biggest Minus:
Perhaps too understated about its own success

Key Figures:
(to year end 31 March 1998)

Turnover:	£7 million
Pre-tax profit	£2,369.00
Annual investment	£2.7 million
Employees worldwide	94
Employees UK	90

The Lombard Risk Group
21 New Fetter Lane
London EC4A 1AJ
Tel: 020 7353 5330
Fax: 020 7353 2280
website: www.lombardrisk.com

The Lombard Risk Group

Company Background

The Lombard Risk Group was founded in 1988 by former merchant banker John M. Wisbey. From his experience at Kleinwort Benson (eight years with its banking division, four years in trading), he had come to realise that the needs of the options trading area were not well met by existing systems.

The group has expanded rapidly. Over the last ten years, it has grown from employing two people to its current position of employing around one hundred. In 1998, it did business in some form with 43 of the top 100 banks in the world: and with 30 of the top 50 banks. It also has a number of local authorities among its clients. John Wisbey believes that this rapid growth will continue, especially given the group's involvement in risk management, particularly credit risk; with recent scenarios of banks losing money in Asia and Eastern Europe due to lack of adequate credit risk protection, events look likely to bear him out.

The group should not be seen as a pure IT business, although it is skilled in this area. What it prides itself on is its business knowledge – and its ability to capture business knowledge in a systematic way into business designs. Around twelve of its senior people have high-calibre banking backgrounds, so the group certainly understands the needs of its clients inside out. The challenge is to maintain its balance between business and technical experts. This could be a problem during times of programmer shortages; however, the group offers such people interesting and challenging technology to work on, which is always a recruitment incentive.

The group's systems have been installed in the Far East and Europe as well as in the UK. Indeed, only around 40% of its sales derive from the UK: this, together with its rapid export growth, led to its winning the Queen's Award for Export Achievement in both 1994 and 1996. Lombard Risk Systems has offices in London, New York and Hong Kong, and agents in Sydney, Seoul and other world centres.

Operations and Markets

The group's three main businesses are Lombard Risk Systems Limited, Lombard Risk Consultants Limited, and Lombard Document Systems Limited.

Lombard Risk Systems Limited was the first company to be founded, set up to develop Oberon, an advanced integrated trading system for managing major interest rate and foreign exchange instruments and associated hedges. Oberon handles the complete life-cycle of a deal, from pricing and deal capture to everyday risk management.

Lombard Risk Consultants Limited provides training courses in all aspects of the derivatives market and associated areas. It also offers consultancy facilities, advising on matters such as the installation of trading systems, the efficiency of risk management, and analysis of highly structured products.

Lombard Document Systems Limited provides global document management solutions. Banks use LDS solutions for local and global management of confirmations, while local authorities can benefit from its access to data and documents through the Internet, allowing them to manage access to planning decision databases.

The group has built on its earlier success with its software designed for the derivatives market, which has been a large and growing market over the last ten years. This marketplace has now extended itself world-wide, whereas it was previously a feature of only a few countries. As a result, any bank working at a strategic level is a potential user (if not an existing user) of the group's products.

Training has good synergy with the systems side of banking. Training people on derivatives also helps to get the systems right. If training leads to consulting, long-term relationships can be fostered – which is the group's aim, so as to grow with its clients.

The group's latest product to be launched is called Firmament: a strategic solution for integrated credit and market risk management and the optimisation of capital usage. John Wisbey: 'Market risk and credit risk are so closely aligned that we believe they deserve to be under the same initiative. Firmament takes a top–down approach to banks: we ask them, how does the process work in your bank? In effect, we create building blocks which allow us to structure solutions tailored to the needs of our clients, without having to reinvent the system every time.'

The group is not hierarchical in structure: indeed, not all key decisions are initiated by the board. At the same time, it is quite disciplined in terms of its financial controls. The company is structured in business areas which are organised around the product areas, and are made up of small, closely-knit teams. John Wisbey: 'I believe that this structure is highly effective. It allows control without excessive red tape: allowing the maximum in flexibility, speed of response and initiative.'

Strategy and Management

For the next generation of systems, the group's approach is: the bigger the system, the greater the need for business design over programming. Taking an analogy from architecture, the Lombard philosophy is to provide a plan – otherwise, lack of design can be a problem. Business design is essential, the group believes, when it comes to large products such as risk management systems, and these are the systems it intends to focus on in the future.

The group's growth has been so rapid and marked that one of the biggest challenges for it is to build on this for the future. John Wisbey: 'Fortunately, we have a huge asset in our customer base, and our strategy flows from that. Banks who use our trading systems can move into our risk management systems and so on. Our aim is to gradually expand our product range, and here the Firmament product with its credit risk protection is very important.'

Diversification is also a valued trend for the group. Although its banking products are highly successful, its local authority product is also a winner. The group intends to build on this dual strand over the future.

Over the next five years, the group intends to build on its central idea: that software can be written far more effectively when it has really good business architecture. Markets are changing constantly, as the introduction of the euro underlines. Good architecture allows products to be rebuilt instead of junked and rewritten from scratch. As a result, the group sees change as a positive advantage for itself.

As well as a customer and a product strategy, Lombard has a people strategy. Its aim here is to employ outstanding people and retain them. The goal is to employ fewer people, keep the numbers down and thereby raise turnover and reward staff better. John Wisbey foresees a scenario in five years' time whereby employee numbers have doubled, turnover has increased sevenfold and productivity is far higher – a distinct possibility, in his view.

Lombard also intends to go public when the time is right. As John Wisbey says, 'A flotation will give us more flexibility and allow us to buy more companies and reward staff more effectively. But we definitely intend to retain our independence.'

The Future

Risk management will be a very large and expanding area for the next two years for banks. They will be plagued, Lombard believes, by alliances in the market whereby consultants make a series of recommendations – which may not in some cases be the best solutions. The challenge for the group is to differentiate its products from these inferior solutions.

The trend in banking is towards more and more mergers. This raises the size of customers and the opportunities within those organisations. It also reduces the number of potential customers, but with 10,000 banks in the USA today, the group feels sanguine about this situation!

The banking market is also unstable, with managers moving between organisations more frequently than before. This gives the group introductions to new clients but also means it has to reinvent its relationships when existing people are replaced.

Above all, Lombard has a key advantage in having expert business knowledge which it harnesses in business architecture and modelling tools in a form which software programmers can understand – a combination which most of its competitors cannot match. This distinctive strategy looks set to help the Lombard Risk Group go from strength to strength in the years ahead.

M&G Group plc

M&G is a large, independent investment management company with more than £19 billion of funds under management. It was the first group to offer unit trusts in the UK market and has an established and well-regarded name in retail financial services. The company also provides investment management services for institutions such as corporate pension funds and charities.

Scorecard:

Flexibility	★★★★
Innovation	★★★
Human resources	★★★★
Growth markets	★★★★★
Quality of management	★★★★
International orientation	n/a

Biggest Plus:
A leading light in a rapidly growing market

Biggest Minus:
Having to deal with incessant takeover speculation

Key Figures:

Revenues (1997)	£152.2 million
Pre-tax profit (1997)	£67.4 million
Funds under management (31/3/98)	£19.4 billion
Employees (31/3/98)	£1,112

M&G Group plc
3, Minster Court
Great Tower Street
London EC3R 7XH
Tel: 0171 626 4588
Fax: 0171 623 8615

M&G

M&G Group plc

Company Background

M&G was established in 1931 as an investment management company and is now one of the best known and trusted retail service brands in the UK. The group offers a range of investment products including unit trusts, personal equity plans, investment trusts and unit-linked life and pension policies. It also acts for some institutional clients such as pension funds.

The company has about 725,000 customers, roughly 55% of which are direct with the rest being referred through independent financial advisers. The large direct customer base is one of M&G's strengths; it holds down the costs of attracting business as new products can be offered directly to clients.

Over the past decade M&G's funds under management have quadrupled and profits have risen from £23 million to £67 million. A third of the company's shares are owned by the Esmee Fairbairn Charitable Trust.

Operations and Markets

M&G's business is entirely focused on the UK where the growth in savings, spurred by tax incentive vehicles, is expected to continue for the foreseeable future. The company expects new products such as the government's Individual Savings Accounts to emphasise the climate in which saving is regarded as interesting and desirable.

The company is, however, not alone in the realisation that the personal finance market in Britain is likely to grow rapidly as the population increasingly accepts that state benefits such as pensions and healthcare are unlikely to endure and that individual savings will have to bridge the gap.

The competition faced by M&G is intense. Traditional players such as investment groups Perpetual and Fidelity have more recently been joined by the mighty supermarkets including Tesco and Sainsbury's, which have been aggressively marketing bank accounts and other savings products. In addition, quality retailers such as Marks & Spencer are in the field alongside 'trendy' newcomers such as Virgin.

The group has recently conducted a complete review of its product offering to ensure it is keeping pace with and anticipating consumer tastes. Although M&G recently launched an index tracker fund the company's chief executive, Michael McLintock, says active management, rather than tracking, will remain the backbone of M&G's business.

Strategy and Management

M&G has a young management which prides itself on its ability to attract and retain able people and to exploit one of the most powerful brands in the domestic financial market.

Chief executive Michael McLintock says the brand is at the heart of everything the company does. The overall market for investment products is expanding fast – a double digit annual growth rate – stimulated by high-profile marketing and advertising campaigns from new competitors such as Virgin.

The strength of the M&G brand means the company can usually rely on getting more than its share of this overall growth. And its performance track record has helped it retain most of that, although sales did suffer a couple of years back following an investment performance wobble.

Although M&G is an established player, the company prefers to continue to concentrate on the UK market where the investment to expand its business is manageable rather than stretch itself to expand overseas.

Michael McLintock stresses the importance of nurturing the large – 700,000-plus – customer base which has an unusually high proportion of direct clients rather than those who are referred by intermediaries. In a sector where winning new business is costly, the ability to 'speak' directly to so many savers enhances M&G's cost effectiveness.

City analysts have given the group credit for improving its investment performance and the quality of its customer service, while accepting that the full benefit of these might take time to flow through to the profits.

A significant contributor to the group's customer service reputation is its impressively low rate of staff turnover – less than 12% a year. Michael McLintock says employees 'have a real affection for M&G' and that culture is a major protection against staff defections.

M&G prides itself on a 'can do' ethos for staff who are empowered by the company's clear belief in meritocracy and its habit of directing employees into project-based work which brings them into contact with all levels of people and all types of business within the group.

Executives say there is also a spirit of integrity which informs the attitude of employees – a stress that the customer's interests should come first means the rather 'spivvy' tactics often associated with financial service sales find no succour in the organisation.

The company's staff are based in two main locations: the City of London, where the intake is increasingly at graduate level, and Chelmsford, which tends to be staffed locally and mainly by school-leavers to provide support and back-office functions for the business.

The group launched an index tracker fund in February 1998 to ensure a strategic presence in this market even though M&G is committed to 'active' investment and has stakes in some 250 companies. Importantly, in an era when the role of institutional investors is increasingly under the spotlight and when matters of corporate governance are at the centre of the industrial stage, M&G says it believes strongly in maintaining a constructive dialogue with the management of those companies in which it holds substantial interests. It votes its shares on all major issues.

The company prides itself on having the courage to buck the investment trend in an effort to achieve above average performance in the long term. It carries out much corporate analysis itself and will typically visit 2,500 companies a year to decide where to invest.

It is impossible to discuss M&G's operations or its strategy without raising the issue of a takeover. Fund management is regarded as one of the most attractive businesses in financial services and notably big American banks are now paying extremely high prices to buy a slice of the UK market.

As a top-notch independent, M&G is a potential takeover jewel. But Michael McLintock fiercely argues for the group's independence. 'Being shareholder-owned helps our business focus,' he states, citing the rigorous approach the group adopts towards technology investment. 'This is a people business and I don't think the industry's experience of big daddies is very happy.' He also points out that the economies of scale which come from takeovers are not necessarily realisable in the world of fund management, adding that any gains could easily be outweighed if investment professionals were to leave because of a change of ownership.

The Future

Demographics and wider political issues, such as ISAs and stakeholder pensions regulations, will be major factors influencing M&G's business which, however innovative the management, is at root a savings operation significantly dependent on the growth in the wider financial markets.

Macroeconomic issues such as continued low inflation – which tends to encourage savers to look for alternatives to building society accounts – will be crucial as will social imperatives such as the growing awareness that a 'job for life' is probably a thing of the past for much of the working population.

The increasing number of women in the workforce and the growing longevity of the population will also determine longer-term business growth. Recent worries that house prices will rise less spectacularly are also encouraging people to look for alternative ways to provide wealth for their old age.

M&G has been trying to reshape its customer base, which was centred on older males. Products for the future are being aimed at younger people – in the 40 to 45 year bracket rather than 50 to 55 year olds. And women, who are reckoned to account for some 30 per cent of total new savings, are coming very much into focus.

There is, of course, the threat that the big high street banks will become more effective at marketing to their enormous customer bases and that this will pull business away from independents. In addition, new methods of selling such as the Internet might start to attract custom. But M&G appears convinced that strong brands will stand out from the crowd on the Internet and that the company has a trustworthy, solid and reliable image which will stand it in good stead in a sea of newer, less well-recognised competitors.

Marks & Spencer

Marks & Spencer is one of the world's most successful retail groups. Though best known for its department stores in the UK, it is also prominent in continental Europe, the Far East and North America. It has also been a pioneer in taking retailers into financial services.

Scorecard:

Flexibility	★★★
Innovation	★★★★
Human resources	★★★★
Growth markets	★★★
Quality of management	★★★★
International orientation	★★★

Biggest Plus:
Commitment to developing flexible workforce

Biggest Minus:
Intense competition from other retailers, mail order and Internet

Key Figures:
(to 31 March 1998)

Revenue:	£8.24 billion
Pre-tax profit:	£1.17 billion
Employees worldwide:	71,300
Employees UK:	59,300

Marks & Spencer
Michael House
Baker Street
London W1A 1DN
Tel: 0171 935 4422
Fax: 0171 487 2679
website: www.marks-and-spencer.co.uk

MARKS & SPENCER

Marks & Spencer

Company Background

Marks & Spencer has its origins in a market stall hired by Russian refugee Michael Marks in Leeds in 1884. A decade later he formed a partnership with Tom Spencer, a cashier with I J Dewhirst, the wholesale company with which the company continues to trade.

By the time the company became public in 1926 it had already adopted the then revolutionary policy of buying direct from manufacturers and two years later registered its symbol of value and reliability, the St Michael trademark. In 1930, it opened its Marble Arch store in London's Oxford Street, to this day the company's flagship and not long afterwards another plank in the Marks & Spencer reputation – the staff welfare department – was opened.

It is indicative of the extent to which Marks & Spencer is regarded as a socially responsible company that during the Second World War it helped the UK government set up a scheme for ensuring that clothing of dependable quality was within the reach of everybody.

Since branching out of the UK in 1975, with the opening of stores in Paris and Brussels, the company has been keen to establish itself as an international brand. It now has operations in most European Union countries, in Eastern Europe, the Far and Middle East and North America, where it owns Brooks Brothers, the well-known clothing company, and the grocery chain Kings Super Markets.

Though reliability and value for money have long been watchwords at what British shoppers have come to call 'Marks and Sparks', the company is keen to stress its record in innovation. It has constantly sought fresh markets, expanding in recent years into home furnishings and, more significantly, financial services as well as spreading geographically.

Moreover, the company and its suppliers are always working to use technology to enhance what they can offer customers. By pioneering the 'cold chain' – which enables food to be kept chilled throughout its journey from the producer to the shop – the company has helped to define Britain's eating habits. 'We were the first people to sell grape-fruit. We had to explain how to eat it,' says one manager.

In clothing, too, the company has led the way, working with sup-pliers to introduce, first, machine-washable lambswool knitwear and, more recently, what it says is the first lambswool garment that can be tumble dried. Meanwhile, teaming up with DuPont has enabled that company's Lycra material to be used to, for example, help keep the creases in Marks & Spencer's highly popular men's suits. According to a senior executive, keeping the customer at the forefront in terms of product development is 'absolutely key'.

Operations and Markets

Having seemingly been content to remain a national institution for nearly a century, Marks & Spencer has over the past two to three decades set about transforming itself into an international force with many different facets to it. The UK remains the dominant market, accounting for nearly £7 billion of its 1998 sales of £8.2 billion, but both the Americas and Europe amount to substantial businesses, with turnover of more than £500 million each.

Since the 1930s, Marks & Spencer has been renowned for selling high-quality food alongside its clothing ranges. Indeed, it is widely credited with introducing ready-prepared meals to the British home. But in the 1980s, it introduced a third strand – furniture – and the company is now developing a comprehensive range of items for the home. The late 1990s have seen the launch of mail-order clothing catalogues, and executives are looking at trading via the Internet – though there are concerns about the practicalities and environmental ramifications of moving towards extensive home deliveries.

Meanwhile the financial services business, that effectively began with the launch of the company chargecard in 1985 and came of age 10 years later when life and pension products were introduced, continues to be a profitable area of high growth. In 1998, operating profit rose by nearly a fifth, to £89.4 million, meaning that the oper-ation employing more than 1,200 people contributed more than 8 per cent of group profits. The company believes that its 'strong name, high-quality products and excellent service' put it in a good position to benefit from opportunities being created by the UK government's increasing focus on personal savings and pensions.

Strategy and Management

The end of 1998 saw Europe's most profitable retailer in the unusual position of warning of a sharp fall in profits for 1999. However, it says a good deal for the popular perception of Marks & Spencer that, once

Peter Salsbury was chosen to succeed Sir Richard Greenbury as chief executive, the company was widely expected to recover its momentum. After all, observers pointed to the fact that it still held nearly a fifth of the women's clothing market and was Britain's leading supplier of underwear and socks.

Moreover, having won the British Quality of Management Award four years running, the company has enormous confidence in its ability to achieve sustainable growth. Sir Richard, who continues as chairman of the group, says that the loyalty and commitment of the staff is the company's most valuable asset and adds that all are encouraged to develop as individuals with the aim of making as full a contribution to the business as possible.

Another executive points out that the company's 'strength in depth' should stand it in good stead as the trading environment becomes more competitive. One of the outcomes of the strategic review carried out at the end of 1998 is a greater emphasis on management autonomy. 'Decision-making is devolved to the level at which it ought to be taken,' he says.

Meanwhile, great management opportunities are being created through an ambitious expansion programme. In the company's 1998 annual report Sir Richard said the company was adding 2.4 million sq. ft of store space around the world. At the same time, the company has begun rolling out a new generation of highly sophisticated tills. The programme, costing £100 million, will allow customers to pay using a variety of currencies, including the euro.

Sir Richard has acknowledged that such a 'period of bold investment' would inevitably affect profits. But since the company had always been prudent about managing cash and taken the long-term view about developing the business, he was confident that Marks & Spencer would remain Europe's most profitable retailer.

The Future

Executives are adamant that they are not allowing a long run of success to make them complacent. Rather, they see that success as founded on the company's ability to continually re-invent itself and the constant desire to innovate in terms of products and service to the customer.

The latter is expected to become even more important in the coming years. In particular, the company is keen to stress that it is adapting its offering to suit different needs, not just in different parts of the world, but also within national markets. As Sir Richard says, 'there is no longer a typical Marks & Spencer store', even within Britain. Outlets vary in size and layout from a 150,000 sq. ft department store in a regional city to a specialist sandwich shop in central London, while there are even out-of-town stores.

The company is conscious that, in the clothing field in particular, it is facing increasing competition from international groups. Accordingly, with all of these formats, the company is working on improving the presentation of merchandise and providing the appropriate ambience, whether customers are buying sweaters or making financial transactions.

As with other retailers that are well-established in their domestic markets, Marks & Spencer will continue to focus on international expansion. There, one executive says, the challenge is 'adapting the offer to suit local needs'.

But with its long-held sense of community and commitment to the longer term, Marks & Spencer is confident that it can prosper in an intensely competitive market.

McKinsey & Company

McKinsey & Company is arguably the leading management consulting firm in the world. Founded in 1926, McKinsey has enjoyed continued growth since that time and is now a truly international firm serving many of the world's most prominent organisations. McKinsey has worldwide revenues of around $18 billion, over 550 partners and some 4,000 consultants working in 76 offices in 38 countries. The London office is one of McKinsey's largest, employing around 275 consultants and 210 support staff, representing 30 nationalities.

Scorecard:

Flexibility	★★★★★
Innovation	★★★★
Human resources	★★★★★
Growth markets	★★★★
Quality of management	★★★★
International orientation	★★★★★

Biggest Plus:
The blue-chip consulting firm with blue-chip clients worldwide

Biggest Minus:
As the leading firm, always there 'to be shot at'

Key Figures:
(1998)

Revenue	approx. $18 billion
Operating profit	not disclosed
Pre-tax profit	not disclosed
Employees worldwide	7,000
Employees UK	485

McKinsey & Company
1 Jermyn Street
London SW1Y 4UH
Tel: 0171 839 8040
Fax: 0171 873 9777
website: www.mckinsey.co.uk

McKinsey&Company

McKinsey & Company

Company Background

Founded in the US in 1926 by James O. McKinsey, it was not the first management consulting firm but, in the words of *Business Week*, 'McKinsey is by far the most influential consulting firm in the world.'

McKinsey focuses on business issues of most importance to senior management, advising on strategy and organisation, and how to improve operations such as sales or manufacturing.

McKinsey's pre-eminence stems from the reputation it has earned for objectivity and independence, and for bringing the highest intellectual and analytical skills to bear on the major challenges confronting the world's leading businesses and institutions. For this, McKinsey – or 'The Firm' as its members have long since called it – relies on the professionalism and dedication of its consultants worldwide.

Other firms may have the same brainpower, but they lack the same reputation. Rajat Gupta, McKinsey's managing director, says: 'All I know is that every consulting firm anybody talks to always says they're second to McKinsey.'

Operations and Markets

McKinsey's (confidential) client list is impressive – virtually a 'Who's Who' of the world's major organisations including multinational companies, national governments and charities, as well as fast-growing smaller firms.

McKinsey's advisory work cuts across all business sectors from investment banking to retailing, from television to oil companies – and the firm is proud that many of its clients are leaders in their sectors. In the UK and Ireland offices, financial institutions, energy and consumer goods have recently accounted for the lion's share of hours worked by McKinsey consultants.

In the 1990s, McKinsey has been at the forefront of management thinking worldwide, covering such issues as technological innovation, logistics, alliances and acquisitions, vertical integration, organisation design and the role of the corporate centre.

McKinsey findings often find their way into leading business publications such as the *Harvard Business Review*, the *Financial Times*, *The Economist*, the *Wall Street Journal*, or into its own journal, the *McKinsey Quarterly*, which is sent out to about 60,000 top managers around the world. Sometimes its research leads to books and, in all, McKinsey consultants have published close to 100 titles.

McKinsey's success with clients has led to the firm growing at an average annual rate of 10%. Today, McKinsey has established 76 offices in 38 countries around the world. Many of its offices are long established; others, like Bogota, Dublin, Istanbul, Johannesburg, Moscow, Prague and Shanghai, have been opened more recently.

The London office is one of McKinsey's longer-established offices. Opened in 1959, it is based at No. 1 Jermyn Street in the heart of London's bustling West End.

Strategy and Management

McKinsey's stated mission is 'To help our clients make distinctive, lasting and substantial improvements in their performance, and to build a great firm that is able to attract, develop, excite and retain exceptional people.'

McKinsey consultants really do think that they are the best. They certainly inspire awe in many people, reflecting the premium placed within the McKinsey culture on very 'bright' people.

McKinsey operates a 'one-firm principle'. While each office is strongly rooted in its national culture, all consultants share a common working approach and the same high standards of client service. Consulting teams are often pulled together from all over the world as some of the firm's work crosses national boundaries.

The impetus for opening a new office comes not from some central directive, but from individual consultants who take the initiative and succeed in establishing a client base in a new country or region. McKinsey never expands into a new market through affiliations or buying local firms.

Smaller offices do still depend on experts from other offices, but the very supportive team culture makes this link almost seamless. Use of voicemail and e-mail is central. Invariably, a multi-discipline, multi-cultural team 'clicks into gear' almost within minutes of sharing an assignment. McKinsey consultants share the latest management ideas and techniques (where client confidentiality permits), enabling it to apply the best thinking of 4,000 smart people.

There are several reasons that make McKinsey a special management consulting firm. It only accepts assignments where it believes that it can make a positive, lasting impact. McKinsey works *with* its clients, not *for* them, so that it can make solutions stick. The firm only works on issues that are really important to senior management. It considers the problem from all angles, but always puts together an integrated view of the way forward from a top management perspective.

Each year, McKinsey spends $50–100 million on original research through the independently established (in 1990) McKinsey Global Institute. Much of this research takes place in 50-plus interest groups or 'practices' – informal networks of consultants who are interested in, and knowledgeable about, a particular field of management. Practices are focused either on a management function, on a particular industry, or on specific key issues of concern to clients. Consultants disseminate their knowledge within McKinsey via regional or worldwide meetings and conferences, as well as through one-page bulletins and longer documents.

Outsiders have never regarded McKinsey as an open organisation, and the company tends to shun publicity. This all adds to its mystique. It tends to deal with things internally. McKinsey accommodates a broad diversity of opinions, fostering rigorous debate to get the right answer. Yet it tries to achieve things collectively and the McKinsey culture probably functions so well because it hires the same people over and over.

Teamworking is absolutely fundamental. A team's success hinges on the ability of its members to work together in gathering information and performing the analysis that will prove or disprove their hypotheses. The McKinsey environment is therefore a mutually supportive one, with clients the primary focus. Ian Davis, head of the London office, says, 'Although now managing partner, I still see myself primarily as a consultant and strive to spend about half my time working with clients.'

Human resources is an absolutely critical function in McKinsey. Necessarily, a major priority is placed on hiring exceptional individuals. The recruitment process can be a gruelling one, but this makes sure that the candidate is right for the firm, and vice versa.

Strategy consulting is all about solving problems and influencing people. McKinsey therefore seeks individuals with outstanding intellectual ability and interpersonal skills. The qualities it looks for in candidates are problem-solving ability, personal impact, leadership and drive.

McKinsey believes that developing its people is just as crucial as serving its clients, although of course this is a virtuous circle. The firm invests heavily in each consultant's personal learning, through both formal training and on-the-job coaching.

A demanding environment is maintained – rigorously. If at any stage in the career path a consultant ceases to progress, he or she is asked to leave McKinsey. This 'up or out' policy applies throughout the firm, from associates to senior partners, and ensures that the firm continues to motivate exceptional people and provide superior client service.

The McKinsey alumni are found all over the business world, many at the head of very large companies and corporations. Alumni of the London office include Sir John Banham, chairman of Kingfisher; Howard Davies, deputy governor of the Bank of England; Nick Kirkbride, managing director of Virgin Cola; and William Hague, leader of the Conservative Party.

The Future

In troubled global markets, several financial and manufacturing firms are said to have curtailed their use of management consultants. But McKinsey, along with other leading firms, says it expects to continue to hire people and to continue to grow revenues.

In a world seemingly overpopulated with consultants, the question remains whether McKinsey can endure as one of the ultimate worldwide brand names. Or are the others catching up?

Other consultancies may claim that McKinsey's consultants are no brighter than their own, probably with some justification. But McKinsey has the reputation, aura and credibility that appears to be unquestionable and unstoppable. No chief executive ever lost his job by hiring McKinsey. The Firm just goes from strength to strength.

The nature of its clients' businesses is continually changing, however, and this raises a genuine debate whether McKinsey needs to shift with it. As a 'top management' strategy consultancy, McKinsey has been less inclined to venture into areas such as implementation and information technology-based consultancy, which it leaves to others. With the increasing importance of technology in just about every industry and business, this may have to change.

And there is the question whether management consultancy can and should be sold as 'products' rather than services. McKinsey has always eschewed 'flavour of the month' consulting ideas, preferring instead to market intelligent thinking to strategic issues. But The Firm may have to consider shifting this stance and try to sell the next big idea.

These may only be distractions. McKinsey's core consulting service rests on deep relationships with senior managers in business, who return to the firm time and time again. McKinsey remains the consulting firm others would like to emulate.

The National Grid Group plc

The National Grid Group is the world's largest independent transmission operator. It owns, operates and maintains the UK high-voltage network which connects generators with major customers and regional electricity companies. It also balances supply and demand across the network and facilitates the trading of power through the daily bidding system whereby generators compete in providing power. It has a growing international operation, uses its expertise to provide design, construction, maintenance and metering services, and has a major holding in its former subsidiary Energis, a UK-based advanced business telecommunications company.

Scorecard:

Flexibility	★★★★
Innovation	★★★★★
Human resources	★★★★
Growth markets	★★★★
Quality of management	★★★★
International orientation	★★★

Biggest Plus:
An innovative and forward-looking company which knows where it wants to be

Biggest Minus:
Operates in a highly regulated home environment

Key Figures:
(to year ending 31 March 1998)

Turnover	£1.6 billion
Operating profit	£543 million
Pre-tax profit	£574 million
Profit after tax	£441 million
Number of employees	3,500

The National Grid Group plc
National Grid House
Kirby Corner Road
Coventry, CV4 8JY
Tel: 01203 423268
Fax: 01203 423249
website: www.nationalgrid.co.uk

The National Grid Group plc

Company Background

For much of its life, it would be fair to say that electricity transmission was the Cinderella of the industry. Although the grid has been in place for over 60 years, it was merely a system of wires and pylons. A fundamental change came when it was decided to take the electricity supply industry into the private sector, thus separating transmission from energy production and facilitating competition among the generators.

The company was privatised in 1990, making it the first privately owned transmission operator in the world. It took its current name of the National Grid Company at that time. For the next five years the company remained in the shadows, being owned by the regional electricity companies. However, all this changed when it was floated in December 1995 and the National Grid Group was formed, giving it overnight more than a million shareholders instead of 12 – and considerable extra freedom to expand its operations, including the ability to look outside the UK.

Today, the group is a FTSE-100 company with a £7 billion capitalisation. In a few short years it has used its core skills to expand into new growth areas. It has also had a major success story with its former telecommunications subsidiary Energis, which it floated in December 1997, retaining 74% of the shares. In January 1999 the group sold around 25% of its remaining shares, and the City was so keen to snap these up that the books were closed in just three days. Energis is expected to become a FTSE All-Share company in its own right.

Operations and Markets

The National Grid Company has three main roles in the UK: transporting power, balancing supply and demand, and facilitating the trading of power. It also has a growing number of overseas operations, works in contracting, and, as stated above, has a major holding in Energis.

To transport power, the company owns, operates and maintains the high-voltage network in England and Wales. The system comprises 7,000 route kms of overhead lines, 650 kms of underground cable and over 300 substations. National Grid also owns and operates interconnectors which enable it to transfer electricity between the England and Wales market and Scotland and France.

Balancing supply and demand calls for experience and expertise. Surges in demand (such as major England football matches being shown on TV!) must be forecast and planned for. This is a complex role which requires innumerable calculations and second-by-second adjustments to ensure frequency and voltage remain stable.

National Grid provides services which underpin the operation of the wholesale electricity market, known as the Pool. This involves managing the daily bidding system for generators competing in providing power – and this in turn requires the group to evaluate 48 bids from each of 260 generating units. Two subsidiaries calculate the payments due from each day's trading and transfer funds accordingly.

Turning to its international operations, the base of its overseas business is in Argentina, where it owns and operates the transmission system. In Zambia, the group and its partner CINenergy Global each invested around £15 million to buy 80% of the Power Division of Zambia Consolidated Copper Mines. The resultant new company, the Copperbelt Energy Corporation, supplies electricity to mines in the Zambian copperbelt. The group is also building 400 km of new high voltage lines between Mangalore and Bangalore in India.

In December 1998, National Grid paid £2 billion to acquire NEES (North Eastern Electricity System, a substantial North American business. This both builds on existing skills and takes the group into new areas, since NEES is a distribution as well as a transmission operator. David Jones, group chief executive: 'North America is an exciting market which is opening up to competition. NEES is a bridgehead for our expansion there. It is a very well-run company with lots of experience, and will help us develop both geographically and in terms of business skills.' This acquisition was followed in February 1999 by an agreement whereby NEES will acquire all the outstanding shares of Eastern Utilities Associates (EUA). This company's principal activities are the distribution and transmission of electricity in Rhode Island and South-eastern Massachusetts, adjacent to NEES's service territories.

The other two areas of operation are contracting and Energis. In contracting, National Grid uses its expertise to offer design, construction, maintenance and metering services. Energis was the first nationwide telecoms network to be built from scratch using advanced fibre optic technology, and is well placed to exploit the potential of the UK business telecoms market. Enhanced voice and data services are especial strengths.

Strategy and Management

A clear strategy of National Grid is to increase to over 20% of its total earnings those which come from non-regulated business – which effectively means those from outside the UK. It is well-equipped for overseas expansion since it has a strong reputation internationally. As the first to privatise its grid operator, the UK is seen as a role model overseas. This has already led to earnings growth: the NEES acquisition is immediately earnings-enhancing, as well as building up the group's core skills.

This strategy will almost certainly mean further overseas ventures: but only where the opportunities are right. The National Grid Group has a well-deserved reputation for caution and for developing only where its core skills can be most effective. For instance, it considered a move into Kazakhstan, but rejected it after careful consideration because it deemed the risk not worth the reward and the deal not in the best interests of its customers and shareholders.

Another strand to overseas expansion will be in the telecoms area. The group learned a great deal from its experience with Energis, and is now expert at creating telecommunications infrastructures. This bore fruit recently when a consortium in which National Grid has a 50% interest won the licence to provide a competitive telecommunications network in Brazil. The licence provides a 40-year concession in a market where demand is expected to increase rapidly over the coming years.

The strategy for the future may well include building on National Grid's sophisticated realtime software skills. An example could be the much-mooted privatisation of the air traffic control system. David Jones: 'Such a move would make use of our experience in running technologically advanced, real-time, nationally vital service. We also have plenty of experience of running a monopoly in a regulated environment – so this type of opening, if it arises, may be of interest to us in the future.'

Two other important aspects of strategy for the group are concern for the environment and its people. David Jones: 'We are acutely aware of the importance of the environment and are conscious of the need to demonstrate our care for it. For instance, we plant several hundred thousand trees every year; we have used helicopters to bring in heavy equipment and materials in special areas such as Snowdonia; and as part of the first tranche of our Community 21 Awards we gave over £30,000 to seven local authorities for the best sustainable development projects to improve the social, economic and environmental quality of life in communities.'

On the people issue, National Grid remains a people business and is committed to recruiting, retaining and motivating the best men and women. This includes hiring from the best skill pools. The group's business development director is Dutch and has played a major role in Brazilian, Argentinean and Zambian projects. National Grid's finance director is a former senior employee of Coopers and Lybrand's, and the group's executive directors include two former chief executives of UK electricity companies.

The final strategic goal is to use its money effectively, meeting the needs of its customers and its shareholders (in terms of both capital and dividend growth and the solidity of the share base). In both areas the group has been very successful.

The Future

The future for the company will undoubtedly be to build on current strategy and be seen as an increasingly important international player. David Jones: 'We want to be seen as a global utility, not just a successful English and Welsh player.'

Growth will surely be at a steady pace, building on core skills and taking advantage of only the most appropriate opportunities. Carefully thought out and highly focused moves will remain the watchword of National Grid.

In terms of overseas expansion, the Americas are likely to be the most important area. However, as David Jones says, 'Eastern Europe offers a number of interesting possibilities. We are also exploring the Australian market, and our offices in the Pacific Rim monitor the region carefully.'

National Grid has a well set out strategy. This will undoubtedly evolve as the company develops; it is, after all, a very young company. However, it has stood National Grid in good stead so far, and would appear to provide the basis for further growth, expansion and development.

Nortel Networks

Nortel Networks works with customers to design, build, and deliver telephony and IP-optimised networks. Customers include public and private enterprises and institutions; Internet service providers; local, long-distance, cellular and PCS communications companies; cable television carriers; and utilities. Nortel Networks' common shares are listed on the New York, Toronto, Montreal, Vancouver and London stock exchanges.

Scorecard:

Flexibility	★★★★
Innovation	★★★★★
Human resources	★★★★
Growth markets	★★★★★
Quality of management	★★★★
International orientation	★★★★★

Biggest Plus:
At the centre of change in the telecommunications market

Biggest Minus:
Continually attracting the best people in a fast-growth, competitive industry

Key Figures:
(to year ending 30 December 1998)

Worldwide revenues:	$17.6 billion
Worldwide net earnings:	$1.07 billion
Number of employees:	75,000

Nortel Networks
Maidenhead Office Park
Westacott Way
Maidenhead
Berkshire SL6 3QH
Tel: 01628 437494
Fax: 01628 437479
website: www.nortelnetworks.com

NØRTEL
NETWORKS™

How the world shares ideas.

Nortel Networks

Company Background

Nortel Networks has emerged as a world leader in the provision of data-rich networks. Its range of technology includes every major digital standard of wireless, as well as broadband, high-speed optical transport, SONET/SDH, Internet/Intranets, Multimedia, and software architectures.

Its roots go back to the very beginning of data transfer – the telephone. Alexander Graham Bell invented this instrument at his parents' home in Ontario in 1874. He patented his invention in the USA in 1876 and in Canada in 1877, where 75% of the Canadian telephone patent was assigned to his father, Melville. He in turn sold his share to National Bell, the predecessor of AT&T. In 1880, the Bell Telephone Company of Canada (Bell Canada) was formed, with the manufacturing branch incorporated as a separate company, Northern Electric and Manufacturing Company Limited, in 1895.

In 1899, Bell Canada bought a cable and wire company. In 1914, the two manufacturing companies merged to form the Northern Electric Company Limited. For its first fifty years, Northern Electric made products mainly for Bell Canada's use. In 1978, it changed its name to Northern Telecom Limited, and in 1995 changed again to Nortel. The recent merger between Nortel and Bay Networks gave the company its new identity of Nortel Networks.

The company was the first to successfully pioneer GSM technology in a moving car; it invented fibre optics transmission; it created the first switch to handle one terabit per second of information; and it is currently perfecting the method of sending and receiving the Internet through powerlines, at speeds of up to ten times the pace of ISDNs. It was also the first major electronics company to eliminate ozone-depleting CFCs from its manufacturing operations. Today, it employs 75,000 people worldwide, 19,000 of whom work in Europe with 8,500 of those in the UK. Its revenues exceed $17 billion, and it operates in over 150 countries.

Operations and Markets

The company's key strength is its focus on continual innovation, allowing it to frequently anticipate market trends. Maurice Duffy, European resourcing director: 'This puts us at the centre of change in the telecommunications market. Furthermore, our corporate structure is loosely organised – so we are quick to adapt. Our capacity is vital; we're able to deliver ahead of our competitors what customers need for tomorrow.'

The company's customer base has globalised rapidly, and Nortel Networks has had to react accordingly. It has achieved that through acquisition, organic growth, and a series of joint ventures. It also works wherever possible with the local workforce – something it does in over 100 countries. Nortel Networks has played a pivotal role in the liberalisation of the marketplace in the UK, Europe, USA and Asia. As a result, over three-quarters of corporate customers choose the company as its primary provider.

The merger has added to the company's strength. Nortel brought to the equation lots of history and a global presence. Bay Networks added knowledge and skills in the data marketplace. The new company has significantly stepped up the ability to add value to anything either partner had before the merger.

Three forces of change are evident for the company: the convergence of computer and telecommunications; globalisation, permitting easy flow of information; and deregulation worldwide.

To take advantage of these trends, Nortel Networks is organised along five business lines: enterprise networks, enterprise data networks, wireless networks, broadband networks and public carrier networks. These work together to meet customer needs, allowing the company to offer genuine network solutions rather than simply sell products.

The company today is recognised as a world leader in technology and innovation. It is not too much to say that it has laid the foundation for tomorrow's economies in its work on optical networks, leading to a radical shift in the perception of what telephones and computers should be able to do.

Europe accounts for 22% of the company's global business. It has a presence in 30 countries, and has both independent and joint venture operations (including five major joint ventures in Germany, Austria, France, Turkey and Israel). Of its 19,000 European employees, 25% work in R&D – helping to maintain the company's innovative cutting edge into the future. It also has 23 major distribution partners in Europe.

Over half of the European PTTs choose Nortel Networks. European deregulation is a major force behind a growth rate which is rapid even by Nortel Networks' global standards. National boundaries are disappearing, technologies are emerging and converging at an increasingly rapid rate. However, the company has the people and the products to keep pace with this change and use it as an opportunity for growth.

Strategy and Management

The company has a business planning process which follows closely what external markets are doing. It then develops an overall strategic plan on a five-year basis. Maurice Duffy: 'This plan is driven by our customers to some extent, and also what we want to achieve. We are focused on customer solutions, not on selling off-the-peg products. Staying in partnership with our clients is a mainstay of our long-term strategy.'

The whole telecommunications market is evolving. Businesses are now looking for a more integrated approach. In effect, they increasingly demand end-to-end solutions. Nortel Networks has the size, the resources and the sophistication to partner even the most demanding customer and meet its future needs to its satisfaction. And while some new players and alternative suppliers have local or niche knowledge, Nortel Networks has technical solutions they cannot offer. Most of all, it has the expertise of a highly experienced workforce. Its strategy is certainly to recruit even more of those highly skilled people, and retain them by offering them exciting, leading-edge work and excellent remuneration packages.

Strategically, four types of product have been driving innovation. Webtone carries Internet and data traffic with the reliability, integrity, security and capacity of dialtone; Power Networks are able to transform a company's disparate networks into integrated multimedia networks; Fixed Wireless Access provides enhanced telephony services over wireless access infrastructure; and PowerLine permits data transfer over electric power lines.

The business will continue to grow, through acquisition and organic growth. As it does so, the strategy will be to move the company into a new way of operating. The marketplace has huge opportunities; Nortel Networks has a record of innovation, an enthusiastic and skilled workforce, and the level of expertise to be highly successful in that marketplace.

Another strand of corporate strategy has to do with globalisation. The company is now truly global. It is also more knowledge-based than at any time in its past history, with more entrepreneurial people working for it. In the final analysis, the growth potential is huge; everyone needs telephones. The Chinese market alone offers a vast market here. The company's strategy is to realise that potential by maximising its undoubted skills and strengths, and by continuing to offer complete and effective solutions to customer needs.

Above all, the strategy for Nortel Networks is to deliver what it calls Unified Networks solutions. Its aim is to empower people through the effortless exchange of ideas, whenever those people wish it, and wherever they happen to be. Unified Networks solutions will deliver new levels of performance, scalability and reliability. Using this concept, virtual teams will be able to work and collaborate across geographies, freed from the limits of today's lower-speed access technologies. As a result, companies will be able to reduce costs by shifting workers elsewhere or allowing them to work from home, the cost and environmental impact of commuting will be reduced, and productivity will rise.

The Future

The future for the company looks remarkably good. Maurice Duffy: 'We have the right technology and the best people. This combination has allowed us to win substantial amounts of business relative to our competitors. We also look at our positioning continually. This focuses on the type of organisation we want to be.'

This means that the face of the company is changing. It is now moving from a technical to a knowledge-based company, built around self-organising teams and flatter structures. Increasingly, the culture will be dynamic and unique, global and diverse, open and candid. It will offer its people multiple roles while being ever more focused on the customer.

The market will undoubtedly see more use of data networks as customers move towards e-commerce, real-time and Internet-time. All this places Nortel Networks in an enviable position of strength.

Oracle

Oracle Corporation is the largest supplier of database software and the second largest supplier of business applications in the world. Its products include the Oracle8i database, server-based development tools, and business applications for the front and back office. Services, including education, consulting and support, are increasingly important. Oracle Corporation UK Limited is the largest subsidiary outside of the USA. Tremendously successful, Oracle's revenues trebled over 1995–98 and have continued rising since.

Scorecard:

Flexibility	★★★★
Innovation	★★★★★
Human resources	★★★★
Growth markets	★★★★★
Quality of management	★★★★★
International orientation	★★★★★

Biggest Plus:
The Internet should make Oracle one of the big winners in the industry

Biggest Minus:
How quickly will customers switch from PCs to Internet computing?

Key Figures:
(fiscal year to 31 May 1998)

Revenues	$7,144 million
Operating income	$1,244 million
Net income	$955 million
Employees worldwide	38,000
Employees UK	4,500

Oracle Corporation UK Limited
Oracle Parkway
Thames Valley Park, Reading
Berkshire RG6 1RA
Tel: 0118 924 0000
Fax: 0118 924 3000
website: www.oracle.com

ORACLE®

Oracle

Company Background

Oracle is a big organisation – its annual revenues currently exceed $8 billion and it has offices in 145 countries – but it's a young company, having been formed in San Francisco only in 1977. Oracle's 45,000 dedicated professionals provide clients with innovative products, consulting, education and support services.

The company has enjoyed extremely fast growth over the last decade. For many years it doubled revenues each year. Oracle has reached sufficient size now that such 'repeat business' is not feasible, but in fiscal 1998 earnings before acquisition charges grew to almost $1 billion on revenue up 26% at $7.1 billion.

These figures strengthen Oracle's position as the world's largest supplier of information software. As chairman and chief executive Larry Ellison puts it: 'At the dawn of the Information Age, that's a pretty good place to be.'

A powerful combination of business expertise and technical innovation continues to deliver phenomenal growth across Oracle's global operations. While Oracle's strapline 'Enabling the Information Age' suggests a graduation of timelines from dawn, one wonders whether this age will ever have a dusk.

Operations and Markets

In 1998 Oracle continued to increase its share of the world market for database software, where it has been number one for some time. Oracle also developed the most important set of enhancements to its database technology since its introduction nearly 20 years ago. Oracle8i, the Internet version of its database, is due for delivery by March 1999.

The Oracle database is already a key building block of the Internet. Eighty per cent of the Web's most popular sites, from Amazon.com to Yahoo!, depend on Oracle's ability to handle huge numbers of users and enormous quantities of information: text, images, audio, video –

everything. Oracle8i goes even further, designed specifically for corporate Internets and the World Wide Web.

The standard Internet programming language, Java, is built into Oracle8i, defining a powerful new platform for developing corporate Internet and Web applications. Oracle also added an Internet File System (iFS) to Oracle8i. Simply drag-and-drop any Windows file into iFS, and instantly you get the power of a database combined with the ease-of-use of a file system. Java will attract more programmers to Oracle and iFS will attract more data. Both are good for business.

Database is Oracle's largest business, but applications represents its fastest-growing business. In 1999 Oracle delivered Release 11 (R11) of its sales and service, manufacturing and supply chain, and finance and human resources applications. R11 has a comprehensive set of self-service transactions, plus an integrated business intelligence system.

Oracle R11 is the only suite of business applications that runs entirely on corporate Internets and the World Wide Web. Every R11 application is accessed using a standard Internet browser, which enables self-service data entry. For example, salespeople can enter their own sales forecast data. In turn, self-service business intelligence lets executives see every change to the worldwide sales forecast. Information moves instantly, from the people who have it, to the people who need it.

And soon businesses that use Oracle's application software will have the option of running on servers they own and manage, or on servers Oracle owns and manages for them. In other words, businesses that cannot economically justify buying and managing their own networks, servers, operating systems, databases and business applications will be able to use Oracle's – via the Internet.

Oracle's service businesses – consulting, education and support – are growing even more rapidly than its software businesses. All of Oracle's service businesses operate in an environment where demand outstrips supply, allowing Oracle to grow these services rapidly while simultaneously improving margins.

Oracle Services recognises that the power to implement technology efficiently is as important as the technology itself. With attention to service at the heart of its strategy from the outset, Oracle Services focuses on helping its customers make the most of their investments in Oracle products. With three constituent operations, it now represents around half of Oracle's annual revenue.

Oracle Education delivers top-quality training in 260 education centres in 64 countries around the world, with hundreds of course offerings and opportunities for customised classroom or media-based training.

Oracle Consulting delivers solutions to the information management issues of target industry sectors, with experienced consultants focusing on the unique needs of companies and managing the essential information that drives their respective businesses.

Realising that when class is dismissed, customers around the world may still be hard at work, Oracle Support Services delivers time-sensitive support from three global support centres and more than 90 local support sites throughout the world.

Name an industry sector and Oracle is there. In media and entertainment, telecommunications, energy, financial services, government, transportation, manufacturing, pharmaceutical, consumer goods and, of course, the computer and IT industry.

Customers include NBC, Sony, Dreamworks SKG, Yahoo!, France Telecom, Chevron, Union Bank of Switzerland, the US Ministry of Defense, Air Canada, General Electric and many, many more. Oracle databases have been so successful in making shared access to information easy, fast, economical, reliable and secure, that virtually every major company around the globe uses the Oracle database.

Strategy and Management

The Internet has changed everything and really opened the door for Oracle. It could prove to be the single decisive factor in Oracle's battle with Microsoft. Larry Ellison says: 'The Internet is an "organic revolution" in the industry and my prediction is that the PC will become a peripheral product.'

The Internet means businesses can deploy information securely and economically to wherever it needs to go, within or outside the enterprise boundaries. It means connecting to the supply chain, developing customer relationships and putting systems right in the front office where they make a difference.

Technology is no longer about controlling or reducing costs, or automating processes. It's about doing things differently in order to gain competitive advantage. The limitations of IT are disappearing. The complexities of client/server computing, the difficulties of managing individual PCs, the non-standardised world, are now in the past.

'Connected' enterprises use the economic levers of the Internet to their advantage. Using the Internet as the connection means that they have no or very low start-up costs. 'Connecting' their core business ensures direct channels to both suppliers and customers, and access to a global marketplace 24 hours a day, 365 days a year. They have leapfrogged 30 years of technology problems to take market share from traditional businesses.

Any business can do this, because buying in standardised IT services means off-loading the complexities of managing skilled IT workers and bespoke specialised systems. Internet computing leaves the enterprise free to concentrate on the parts of their business that actually make a difference competitively and financially.

Oracle understands these issues, and Oracle's entire strategy is to help its customers who share this common vision. It is the reason why the top ten global business-to-consumer electronic commerce websites and nine of the top ten global business-to-business electronic commerce websites are all powered by Oracle technology.

Oracle has invested thousands of man-years developing dozens of application products like these to run on Windows PCs in a client-server network. Within a few weeks of its Internet tools becoming available, it could move every single one of these large, complex applications from PC clients to an application server, enabling them to run on a corporate Internet – and it didn't have to change a single line of application code to do it.

Since it was so easy to move its applications to Internet technology, Oracle has been able to invest the bulk of its efforts elsewhere – such as lowering business costs through efficient process automation. All of its supply chain management software was enhanced, but special attention was paid to the most important piece – the customer. Oracle's new front office/customer care applications automate companies' customer service centres; its Internet store allows customers to serve themselves online.

Raymond Lane, president and chief operating officer, reckons, 'As we prepare for the new millennium, business, government and educational services will become more available at lower cost through Oracle's technology and applications.'

The Future

With the right products and a 'big idea', the task now is to get the message across and convert customers. Oracle does have a certain reputation for being an aggressive company. But as Vance Kearney, vice president for human resources, puts it, 'Oracle has not grown from nothing into an $8 billion company by being shy and retiring. If our sales effort is forceful, we are still delivering outstanding value and outstanding products to our customers.'

Oracle's meteoric rise looks set to continue for a good while yet. That in itself presents a challenge in recruiting the right people – people who can learn quickly and match the rate of change in the business.

But perhaps the single most important feature of Oracle is the sheer scale of its ambitions. Oracle has positioned itself in direct competition with Microsoft and, having embraced the potential of the Internet earlier than many others, has a very powerful friend.

PowerGen

PowerGen is a UK leader in power generation and energy supply with global interests stretching from Europe to Asia-Pacific. A publicly listed company, it was privatised by the British government in 1990. With the acquisition and subsequent absorption of East Midlands Electricity (EME) in July 1998, the company refocused its business on being an end-to-end electricity and gas company with 2.3 million customers. The group employs some 8,000 people (including EME) of whom over 680 are based overseas.

Scorecard:

Flexibility	★★★★
Innovation	★★★
Human resources	★★★★
Growth markets	★★★
Quality of management	★★★★
International orientation	★★★

Biggest Plus:
Strategic vision to be a leading integrated energy business

Biggest Minus:
Regulatory constraints on power businesses

Key Figures:
(to year ending 29 March 1998, before acquisition of EME.
Staff figures include EME.)

Turnover	£2,932 million
Operating profit	£591 million
Pre-tax profit	£580 million
Capital Investment	£188 million
Employees worldwide	7,898
Employees UK	7,211

PowerGen plc
Westwood Way
Westwood Business Park
Coventry, CV4 8LG
Tel: 01203 424000
Fax: 01203 425432
website: www.pgen.com

PowerGen

Company Background

PowerGen is one of the power generating companies carved out of the old Central Electricity Generating Board when the electricity industry was privatised in 1990. Since then it has built a private sector culture, increasing the efficiency and flexibility of operations and in particular improving the performance of its generating plant to world class standards in order to compete effectively in the energy marketplace.

The company operates in a highly regulated marketplace which to some extent has limited the scope of its activities in the United Kingdom. This has encouraged PowerGen to diversify its sources of earnings in a number of ways. It has expanded internationally and would eventually like to make a major acquisition in the United States. In the UK the group is focusing on developing enduring supply relationships with large corporate customers under which it provides all their energy needs. It has moved into the rapidly deregulating gas market and is able to provide customers and clients with bundled electricity and gas services. Most importantly, it has sought to broaden its supply and distribution base.

Its major breakthrough came in July 1998 when the group paid £1.9 billion to buy East Midland Electricity (EME), a regional electricity company (REC) based close to PowerGen's own head office at Westwood Business Park, near Coventry. As part of this deal the group agreed to dispose of 4,000 megawatts of power plant, thus turning a business which has been focused on generation into a more broadly based electricity and gas supply company with some 2.3 million customers.

The merger creates a number of synergies for the enlarged company. It enables PowerGen to bring together the industrial and commercial supply businesses; integrate information technology systems; improve its risk management; and lower overheads throughout the group.

Since privatisation in 1990 the group's growth record has been impressive with profits before tax climbing from £327 million in 1991 to £580 million in the year to March 29 1998 (the last financial year before the absorption of EME).

Operations and Markets

PowerGen generates 56 TWh and purchases 24 TWh of electricity per annum, giving it a total capacity of 80TWh. This is supplied to 2.1 million domestic customers who consume 40 TWh and industrial and wholesale users, who similarly consume 40 TWh of electricity per year. The company distributes 25 TWh of electricity. PowerGen also has a gas portfolio of 3.5 billion therms, and is the UK's largest user of gas (in its gas-fired power stations) as well as a leading gas trader. It has a profitable gas transportation business, and a gas shipping business for the RECs. It currently supplies 30,000 industrial sites and 500,000 households with gas.

PowerGen believes that the UK power industry will eventually consolidate into an industry of five to six national players and aims to be one of these. It has undertaken to reduce its share of the power generation market from close to 20% to around 15% as part of the process of increasing competition, following the EME acquisition.

But its objectives are not confined to the UK. Chairman Ed Wallis argues that it is the company's objective: 'To continue to use the experience we have gained in the UK liberalisation process as a basis from which to exploit opportunities in other liberalising markets. In this way, we can create new growth platforms from which to drive success.'

The company would like to attain similar market shares overseas to those it has achieved in the UK. The principal targets include India and Australia where it already has operations, but it would also like to become a significant player in the United States' liberalising energy market, and in Europe, where it has existing operations in Portugal, Germany and Hungary. PowerGen has invested £700 million to date in overseas operations.

In addition to its core generation, distribution and supply businesses in the UK PowerGen is a leading developer and operator of Combined Heat and Power (CHP) plants for commercial customers like Brunner Mond. Having already committed £150 million to this business, PowerGen announced in January 1999 that it had acquired Yorkshire CoGen Limited from the Yorkshire Electricity Group for £94.9 million. The company also developed an upstream gas and oil business to support its gas-fired power station programme and gain knowledge of the gas business. It has since sold this business to Centrica for £248 million, having achieved these objectives:

Brand development – PowerGen was among the first companies in the privatised UK electricity sector to recognise the importance of

branding in the deregulating UK energy market. Research by MORI
shows that PowerGen is the leading national electricity brand, with
higher recognition than other power suppliers. In 1989, the group
became the first company to sign a long-term national television
sponsorship and celebrated ten years as the sponsor of ITV National
Weather Bulletin this year (1999). PowerGen also launched a £7
million brand advertising campaign in 1998.

Customer interface – The company has pioneered a cultural change
in its relationship with customers based upon developing strong
partnerships. With an expanded presence in the smaller business
and domestic market, PowerGen has recognised the need to build
strong retail skills.

Product/project development – PowerGen has developed innovative
new products for its industrial and commercial customers, such as
its 'Profiler' software that helps clients improve their energy efficiency. The company's combined heat and power business has eight
schemes commercially operational and others under construction.
The group is marketing its project management skills internationally
and has plants under construction at Paguthan, India, Tapada Do
Outeiro, Portugal and Paiton II in Indonesia. New projects underway
include Csepel II, Hungary and Bina, India.

The company conducts its research and development through Power
Technology, which employs 200 skilled staff. It is involved in work for
operational power plants and new developments and provides advice
to a wide range of other generating companies and international organisations including the World Bank and European Commission.

Strategy and Management

The company recognises that the opportunities for organic growth in
the UK are limited because of the maturity of the marketplace and
the limits on demand. It is nevertheless determined to make the most
of the opportunities it has within this market by offering the best
energy packages available. Chairman Ed Wallis recognises that the
company needs 'further acquisitions' to maintain its momentum but
recognises that there may be significant regulatory hurdles. Ideally,
the company would like to develop a strong national supply business
to give it critical mass in Britain.

The limitations on UK growth mean that the company is keeping a
close eye on the opportunities arising from deregulation of the United
States energy markets. It has already engaged in detailed negotiations
with US energy groups about potential future alliances and is carefully
monitoring legislation, passing through US Congress, which would
ease the restrictions on foreign ownership of US utilities.

PowerGen's UK strategy is based on the integration of electricity and gas supplies. In this regard it is focusing on creating 'bundled' energy packages, supported by a great deal of innovation in sales and marketing. The company also believes that there is a real opportunity for the big UK power companies to make a bigger impact on the UK gas market where British Gas still controls the lion's share.

As a result of the EME acquisition the company's gearing (the ratio of its debt to its equity) has risen to 155%. A key objective of management is to bring this down over time, while making the most effective use of its capital resources. Nevertheless, if the opportunities arise, PowerGen believes it can raise the necessary debt and equity finance to press ahead with its merger and acquisition programme.

The detailed financial management of the group is the responsibility of the group finance director Peter Hickson, who takes his lead from the strategy set by the chairman Ed Wallis. Operational responsibility for the management of the UK electricity and gas business is under the control of Nick Baldwin, executive director, UK operations. With the transition from nationalised industry to pioneering private sector energy group, PowerGen has recruited a new group of young managers, creating an open and flat management structure which offers opportunities for rapid advancement for those with ability.

The Future

PowerGen has set itself the target of becoming a 'one stop shop' of electricity, gas and total energy management services and in the process become the UK's leading electricity and gas business. As part of this strategy for the future it would like to win control of another regional electricity company.

It is also looking abroad for its future. Among its targets is to become a major presence in the United States market by the year 2005. The company also believes that it can leverage its expertise in electricity production and supply to achieve the 15% market share it will have in generation in the UK, in four or five other countries in which it operates, with Australia among the more promising markets.

Rolls-Royce

Rolls-Royce is one of the most famous names in engineering, leading the world in gas turbine technology. Rolls-Royce plc serves customers in the civil aerospace, defence and energy sectors of international markets and has facilities in 14 countries. The gas turbine technology of Rolls-Royce generates 95% of the group's sales and has created one of the broadest product ranges of aero engines in the world. Civil represents 50% of Rolls-Royce's business, defence and marine 30% and energy 20%. There are some 53,000 engines in service with 300 airlines, 2,400 corporate and utility operators and more than 100 armed forces, powering both fixed-wing and rotary aircraft.

Scorecard:

Flexibility	★★★★
Innovation	★★★★★
Human resources	★★★★
Growth markets	★★★★
Quality of management	★★★★
International orientation	★★★★★

Biggest Plus:
Excellence combined with efficiency in gas turbine engine technology

Biggest Minus:
Powerful competition

Key Figures:
(to 31 December 1997)

Turnover	£4,33 million
Operating profit	£276 million
Pre-tax profit	£276 million
Research and development (net)	£216 million
Employees worldwide	42,300
Employees UK	11,000

Rolls-Royce plc
65 Buckingham Gate
London SW1 6AT
Tel: 0171 222 9020
Fax: 0171 227 9170
website: www.Rolls-Royce.com

Rolls-Royce

Company Background

Rolls-Royce is a class act with a proud 93-year history. Founded by Henry Royce and Charles Rolls in 1906 to sell exclusive motor cars, the company has nearly always made aero engines. Although still the owner of the Rolls-Royce marque, the pioneering achievements of Rolls-Royce have been in aero engines, where it has repeatedly furthered the cause of aviation.

Rolls-Royce Eagle engines powered the first non-stop transatlantic flight in 1919 by Alcock and Brown in a Vickers Vimy. The Merlin engine found fame in the Hawker Hurricane and Supermarine Spitfire during the Battle of Britain. The unique Pegasus engine powers the Short Vertical Take off and Landing Harrier 'jump jet'. The Dart-powered Vickers Viscount was the first gas turbine airliner to fly. And today, there is the Trent – the most modern and powerful three-shaft engine and the first to be certificated at 90,000lb of thrust.

Rolls-Royce aero engines have always been a bigger business than the luxury motor cars sharing the same name – despite some perceptions to the contrary. Fifteen times larger in fact – and even five times larger when Rolls-Royce parted company with its motors business upon its original flotation in 1973.

Rolls-Royce's core values of reliability, integrity and innovation have belonged to the company since it was formed, and quality is synonymous with the name. Great pride is taken in the name, and Rolls-Royce has always made clear provisions to protect its use, emphasising that the Rolls-Royce name belongs to the aero engine business. Now with the transfer of the use of the name on motor cars from Vickers to BMW there is a satisfactory outcome – BMW is a joint-venture partner with a neater, more symmetrical fit with Rolls-Royce's business.

Between 1971 (when it went into receivership) and 1987, Rolls-Royce was government-owned, though not nationalised. Today, the company has been transformed by following clear, consistent strategies. These are now bearing fruit, but they have taken time and needed investment and patience.

Operations and Markets

In 1998 Rolls-Royce introduced a new market-facing organisation that recognised that both strategy and structure begin with the customers' requirements.

In the civil sector, Airline Business covers the Trent family of engines, the RB211 family and the V2500. The Corporate and Regional Aircraft sector is served by the BR700 series, AE2100, AE3007 and Tay.

Defence markets are served by, among others, the EJ200, RB199, Pegasus and Adour engines for fixed-wing aircraft, and the RTM322, MTR390, Gem and Gnome engines for helicopters. Marine products are in service with 30 navies worldwide.

Civil applications range from the 1,900lb thrust FJ44 for small business jets up to the 100,000lb-plus thrust of the Trent family. Military aircraft using Rolls-Royce engines range from front-line combat aircraft and large military transports to combat and light helicopters. Rolls-Royce will provide at least 1,500 engines for the Eurofighter 2000. It is also participating in the US Joint Strike Fighter (JSF) programme, to develop a new multi-role fighter, an eventual requirement of some 3,000 planes.

Rolls-Royce's activities in energy markets include the oil and gas industry, and electrical power generation.

Over the next 20 years, the market for aero engines for airline customers is estimated to be worth around $280 billion, while the market in regional airlines and for corporate aircraft operators will be perhaps $70 billion. Additionally, spare parts are expected to add $150 billion. The defence market is estimated to be worth $300 billion.

In 1997, the group's profit increased by 17%, while turnover and orders reached record levels. Rolls-Royce also achieved its best-ever year for civil engine orders, capturing a market share of 34%.

Strategy and Management

Rolls-Royce's strategy has three main strands. First, it has invested to secure leading positions in the growing markets of civil aviation, defence (including marine) and energy.

In doing this, Rolls-Royce has focused almost exclusively on its strong foundation in gas turbine technology. 'We are a market leader, and our task is to take this technology to our target market sectors, gain market value and retain competitive advantage,' says John Rose, chief executive.

Thirdly, it has established a comprehensive product range. In 1987, Rolls-Royce had engines to power six types of civil aircraft; now it powers 32. It has achieved this through its own development programmes, through partnerships, and through acquisition – the purchase of Indianapolis-based Allison in 1995 is a recent highlight.

Rolls-Royce is currently enjoying the success of developments born of tenacity. In the early 1990s the end of the Cold War (the West's military business halved in size) and the Gulf War (an adverse effect on civil aviation) formed the backdrop to Rolls-Royce's highest level of investment in engines, especially the Trent family.

This inevitably put pressure on financial performance, but Rolls-Royce has pulled out the stops and still increased R&D spend at the gross level. An increasing number of partners has helped to share the risk, willing to invest in future programmes because of Rolls-Royce's demonstrable success. In the case of the Trent 500 project, partner share covers 30% of R&D costs.

Profits take time to catch-up with market share. Spares are more profitable than new engines, but reliable new engines produce a 'lag' of 6–7 years for the spares business. The mix of equipment also has an impact. Winning market share inevitably puts prices under pressure and sales growth has been driven by 'launch' engines; as these programmes mature, pricing is expected to become 'easier'.

Rolls-Royce identifies **four constituents** in the 'financial success equation'. Shareholders have financed much of the company's expansion and have taken a long-term view of the business.

And Rolls-Royce's customers have put tremendous faith in the company. Airbus Industrie for example has become a major customer. The V2500 engine powers the narrow-bodied Airbus range, and more recently the Trent 700 has been chosen for the Airbus A330. The next series of Airbus A340–500/600 will use only Rolls-Royce engines; the Trent 500. Other new customers include American Airlines, the world's largest airline. From nothing in service or on order in 1987, Rolls-Royce is now its leading supplier and the two are joint venture partners in a repair and overhaul business.

The Trent family of engines has established a 40% world market share for the new generation of wide-bodied, high-capacity aircraft. Ranging in thrust from 53,000lb to over 100,000lb, the Trent is the only engine family to power every large airliner, existing or planned. This offers clear advantages to the customer through commonality of product and support arrangements.

Suppliers are increasingly forming partnerships too, while employees are inextricably linked to the future and longevity of the company.

This virtuous circle costs money – some £750 million was spent on training, IT, financing and product development in 1997. Rolls-Royce faces two decisions: 'Is it a sound investment with a good business case, and can we afford it?' according to Peter Barnes-Wallis, director, corporate communications. Being strong financially gives the company this choice.

With two major competitors in the form of GE and Pratt & Whitney,

Rolls-Royce started 'a very small third'. Now in certain segments it is first, and is no longer third anywhere. The scale of the company is much larger, it has better market coverage than anyone, with products that live up to Rolls-Royce's values of technical excellence. It is now in a growing phase, creating lifetime relationships with customers and opening up a whole range of opportunities, including after-market and service. Recently, Rolls-Royce has taken one third of all civil aviation engine orders placed. Achieved effectively in the space of a decade, this is a quick turnaround.

The Future

Managing technical risk remains top of Rolls-Royce's agenda. Its product development will continue to build on existing technologies rather than 'step in the dark' research. The Trent series illustrates how technology is fed across the family and other family members often learn from each other, adding up to low-risk development.

Rolls-Royce has set itself the financial challenge of producing double-digit earnings growth over five years. Rolls-Royce is fortunate enough in that its order book is worth £12 billion with a high visibility workload, and with financial targets set, target cost reductions fall out of that equation.

Rolls-Royce has initiated a comprehensive company-wide programme, 'Better Performance Faster', a series of initiatives to improve productivity in systems, plant and equipment throughout the group, making it the most efficient supplier in its target market sectors. In one such venture Rolls-Royce has outsourced all of its IT to consultants EDS, who are also participating on a risk/reward basis, in 'Better Performance Faster'.

Keeping customers satisfied is arguably the number one challenge, and Rolls-Royce is doing a good job. A broader product range and better access to customers represents opportunity, but also provides more scope to get it wrong. Rolls-Royce, with that superlative brand name, could be judged by its weakest product. It must therefore make sure that the quality associated with the name is integrated across the entire product range. Excellent Rolls-Royce performance – of engines and financial results – looks set to continue for a long time.

J. Rothschild Assurance

J. Rothschild Assurance began life in 1991 as a joint venture between St James's Place Capital, Scottish Amicable and its management team. In 1997, St James's acquired the full share capital of the J. Rothschild Assurance Group, which then became its principal operating company. The main business is the provision of advice on personal financial services through approximately 900 'partners', who retain self-employed status. The company has grown steadily, increasing both premium income, assets under management and profitability.

Scorecard:

Flexibility	★★★
Innovation	★★★
Human resources	★★★★
Growth markets	★★★★
Quality of management	★★★★★
International orientation	★★★

Biggest Plus:
The company has secured a superbly profitable niche

Biggest Minus:
Regulation continues to weigh heavily on the life industry

Key Figures:
(to 31 December 1998)

Annual turnover	£494 million
Operating profit	n/a
Pre-tax profit	£42.9 million
Employees worldwide	289
Employees UK	281

J. Rothschild Assurance
Dollar Street
Cirencester
Gloucestershire GL7 2AQ
Tel: 01285 640302
Fax: 01285 642772

J. ROTHSCHILD
ASSURANCE GROUP

J. Rothschild Assurance

Company Background

J. Rothschild Assurance operates in the fiercely competitive UK life assurance and personal investment industry. Its senior managers have impressive pedigrees within the market, having built up their previous companies into dominant players. In the years since J. Rothschild Assurance was created in 1991, they have repeated the trick, and now run a profitable, highly respected company with a market capitalisation of over £1 billion.

The holding company of the business is St James's Place Capital, which was established in 1980 by Jacob, now Lord Rothschild of the eponymous banking dynasty. The company is conscious of the cachet which attaches to the Rothschild name and all its actions are designed 'to protect and enhance it at every opportunity'. The main target audience for J. Rothschild Assurance's products is individuals with incomes of around £40,000 or more or who have capital, excluding the value of their main residence, of around £150,000 and upwards.

Operations and Markets

The J. Rothschild Assurance Group, which is the principal business of St James's Place Capital plc, consists of three companies:

J. Rothschild Assurance plc, which provides insurance, investment and pension products. These products are distributed through a network of approximately 900 self-employed 'partners' who are recruited from the cream of UK life assurance salesmen and women. Areas of particular speciality include retirement planning, business assurances, corporate and personal tax planning and mitigation, school fees planning and protection against sickness and disability.

J. Rothschild International Assurance plc, which is based in Dublin and which offers tax-efficient 'offshore' investment and insurance products for UK residents and expatriates.

St James's Place Unit Trust Group Limited, which offers a range of unit trust funds. Management of these funds is outsourced to external organisations whose performance is monitored to ensure acceptable standards are maintained. The investment specialists include Taube Hodson Stonex Partners, M&G Investment Management, Schroder Investment Management and Cazenove Fund Management.

The company defines its clients as, typically, professionals running their own businesses or in management roles in large organisations. They tend to fall into the category 'higher net worth', which means they have considerable income or wealth, a fair understanding of the types of product and service they require, and exacting standards in terms of what they expect from their product provider. The company's mission statement is: 'To be regarded by all our target audiences as the most service-oriented and professional provider of personal financial services in the UK today.'

Strategy and Management

The success of J. Rothschild Assurance can be attributed in large part to the experience and expertise of its senior managers, all of whom enjoy glittering track records in the UK financial services industry. Particular mention should be made of Sir Mark Weinberg, chairman, and Michael Wilson, chief executive, both of whom were instrumental in the remarkable success of Hambro Life (later renamed Allied Dunbar) in the 1970s and 1980s.

When these key individuals conceived J. Rothschild Assurance, the idea was not simply to create yet another direct sales-oriented life office, but to establish new benchmarks for quality of service and product performance. This led to the partnership concept, whereby self-employed individuals identify potential clients, introduce the company and, where appropriate, distribute its products. Personal recommendation and investment seminars generate the bulk of the company's 'leads', as opposed to the much-maligned direct sales technique of 'cold-calling', where introductions are sought through telephone calls to previously unknown individuals.

As Michael Wilson explains, the calibre of the partners is of paramount importance and individuals must demonstrate their capabilities before being granted partner status: 'They must have a minimum three years' experience at the top of their trade, have minimum previous earnings of £32,000 per annum and must have a proven track record in terms of productivity and persistency.'

'Persistency' is one of the life assurance industry's buzzwords. Of the many products sold by the industry as a whole, a high proportion lapse after a short time; those which are maintained by satisfied policyholders are said to 'persist'. Thus J. Rothschild Assurance is interested not in high volumes of sales that fail to stick to the books, but in quality business which signifies an enduring relationship with the client.

The emphasis on high quality sales staff is also evident in the fact that there is relatively little staff turnover. In other life offices, as many as 50 % of the people who join a sales force will leave and be replaced each year. At J. Rothschild Assurance, the figure is much lower, confirming the stature and ability of the individuals involved.

A key element of the company's strategy is to outsource its back office administration and investment functions so that it is free to concentrate on sales and marketing. Mike Wilson explains the thinking behind this revolutionary approach to structuring a life office: 'We acknowledge that no one organisation can excel at everything, so we buy in expertise to supplement our strengths.

'In terms of investment, again no one company has a monopoly of expertise. Different investment sectors require different skills. This is why we subcontract our fund management to a select number of highly respected groups with distinctive investment styles. This is the best way to offer our clients the best opportunity of obtaining consistent, superior investment performance over the long term.'

J. Rothschild Assurance has an Investment Performance Monitoring Committee which receives a presentation from each of the four investment management groups each quarter. The aim is not to influence investment policy but to hold the managers accountable for their performance. The fact that the strategy has teeth was evidenced in 1997 when Scottish Amicable was replaced by Cazenove.

Another vital part of the J. Rothschild Assurance philosophy is the desire to be responsive to changing customer needs and aspirations. Michael Wilson says the company's partners are a superb channel for client feedback: 'Their livelihoods depend on us delivering the right products, services and performance so if there are any problems or opportunities, they are very quick to tell us. The partners are sensitive to the needs of the client and their input has been instrumental in shaping both the products we provide and the company as a whole.'

To facilitate this approach, J. Rothschild Assurance operates a flat management structure which provides its senior members with 'No Hiding Place'. Under this initiative, the various telephone numbers and contact details of all senior executives are made available to the partners so that communication can take place at the partners' behest. 'We have an open approach,' says Wilson. 'We share ideas and are always receptive to suggestions for change and improvement. We give credit where credit is due and we work hard to recognise individual performance.'

Change has swept through the life insurance and investment markets in recent years, not least because of the welter of regulation that has been imposed by central authorities. But for J. Rothschild Assurance the fundamentals remain the same: the provision of a highly professional, high-performance service by experienced individuals who endeavour to build long-term relationships with their clients.

The Future

It is generally agreed that the UK population is under-insured, under-invested and under-pensioned, so there is considerable scope for companies such as J. Rothschild Assurance to continue to grow their business. The increasing inability of the state to provide for the welfare of individuals will also boost the role of the private sector, further strengthening sales of 'protection' policies. The company's target market of reasonably affluent prospects should assist the marketing of investment products.

There are many other influences affecting the shape and direction of the insurance and investment industries. The number of life insurers in the UK has shrunk from over 100 in 1992 to around 60 today and further consolidation is expected. The number of sales jobs has fallen by 50,000 during the 1990s and the number of companies running direct sales forces has decreased from 30 to 18. This is due at least in part to the close regulation of the industry, which imposes substantial costs on companies and requires them to act within rigidly defined operating parameters.

Mike Wilson says that 'the only way to win is by playing within the rules'. In other words, a well-managed, well-resourced business which constantly strives to deliver improvements to the customers should be able to achieve compliance with the regulations and go on to enjoy commercial success.

J. Rothschild Assurance's prospects and potential have recently been given a positive appraisal by the independent ratings organisation Standard & Poor's. In its 1999 UK Life Financial Strength Digest, which covers 47 life companies, J. Rothschild Assurance was the only one whose rating improved. At the same time, the ratings of four were lowered. This objective endorsement of J. Rothschild's strategy confirms its standing in the premier league of UK life assurers.

S & J (Chatteris) Limited

S & J (Chatteris) Limited offers clients a complete building service: architecture, project management, the design and installation of all-metal roofing and wall-cladding systems, the design and installation of structural steelwork, comprehensive construction skills, glazing, maintenance and refurbishment. As well as operating throughout the UK, the company has a base in Belfast and is opening another in Poland.

Scorecard:

Flexibility	★★★★
Innovation	★★★★
Human resources	★★★★
Growth markets	★★★★
Quality of management	★★★★
International orientation	★★

Biggest Plus:
Unique in the UK for its range of in-house services

Biggest Minus:
Building work is always dependent upon macroeconomic factors

Key Figures:
(to 31 March 1998)

Turnover	£35 million
Pre-tax profits:	£1.5 million
Employees:	300

S & J (Chatteris) Limited
Number One
Fenton Way Business Park
Fenton Way
Chatteris
Cambridgeshire PE16 6US
Tel: 01354 694000
Fax: 01354 695000

S & J (Chatteris) Limited

Company Background

The company was formed in 1974 by the current chairman, Swales Hammond. The business then was simply a small, local business contractor, operating in groundwork mainly within the agricultural market. Then, four years ago, the company acquired an interest in a national roofing and cladding company. The current managing director, Mark Langley, joined the organisation at the same time.

Since then, growth has been nothing short of phenomenal. From an annual turnover of just £800,000 four years ago, S & J (Chatteris) now turns over more than 40 times this amount – and forecasts that the current figure of £35 million will double within the next five years. No surprise then that the company was placed 70th in the Virgin Fast Track 100 in 1997 and 20th in 1998.

One of the reasons for this success is the high quality of the company's work. Its excellent reputation is its only means of gaining new clients, since it has never employed a new business sales person. The company's complete skill set is undoubtedly another factor. It offers a full range of business services through an array of separate trading companies. Each has its own trading discipline, but each shares the culture of the group.

Operations and Markets

The organisation currently comprises ten companies, headed by a holding company that carries out all common accounting and administration services for the group.

S & J (Chatteris) Cladding Limited specialises in the design, supply and installation of all-metal roofing and wall-cladding systems, and is one of the group's main businesses as well as being one of the largest privately owned roofing and cladding companies in the UK. Projects include the construction of a new conference centre for Nigeria in 1991 and work on the Thetford Power Station. Job values range from £70,000 to £3 million.

Currently based at St Ives in Cambridgeshire but planning to move to a purpose-built facility next to the head office, S & J (Chatteris) Steelwork Limited handles the design, manufacture and installation of structural steelwork. The business, assisted by state-of-the-art equipment, works directly for most national contractors but also works closely with the cladding company and other group members.

S & J (Chatteris) Construction Limited operates as specialist groundwork contractors through to main contractors. Its highly skilled workforce includes ground workers, plasterers, concrete finishers, bricklayers, carpenters and joiners. Recent work includes the construction of a £3.6 million cold storage facility for Turners (Soham) Limited and an extension to the Frank Lee Sports and Leisure Complex at Addenbrookes Hospital in Cambridge.

Formed to handle small works cladding as well as maintenance and refurbishment projects, S & J (Chatteris) Special Projects Limited has expertise in all aspects of cladding and building maintenance, from full site inspections to detailed recommendations. Clients include Securicor and Glaxo Wellcome.

Specialist Glazing Systems Limited is an approved dealer for a wide range of curtain wall and roof glazing systems. It is currently refurbishing all the roof glazing at London's Charing Cross main railway station.

A recent addition to the group, Specialist Finishing Systems Limited works in the refurbishment market. Its activities include vacuum blasting of steelwork and repainting with specialist coatings; vacuum blasting of other surfaces including stone, brick, aluminium and stainless steel; and repair work to glass facades.

Christopher Davis Architecture Limited is the group's own architectural design company. It uses its skills within the group and also provides external design services for an array of residential, commercial and industrial projects. Additionally it acts as a project supervisor for in-house design-and-build projects.

The two remaining companies are S & J (Ireland) Limited and S & J (Polska) spzo.o. The former was recently set up to operate as a roofing and cladding contractor in both the Republic of Ireland and Northern Ireland and is based outside Belfast. This formation was a logical move since the group has worked in the Irish market for some time but has always serviced its operations from mainland Britain. The local base will bring the company much closer to its clients.

S & J (Polska) spzo.o is currently being formed. Based in Kalisz, a town positioned between Warsaw, Poznan and Wroclaw, this company is well placed to benefit from Poland's strong economic growth rate (forecast to hit 7% in 1999). Again, the new formation builds on previous group work, such as constructing roofing and cladding for Cadbury's new chocolate factory in Wroclaw.

Strategy and Management

Mark Langley: 'We have worked very hard to ensure that we offer a service second to none. The key element in our strategy is to offer clients a true single-source contract for the building frame, the envelope and the glazing. In short, everything from concept and design to the finished building. Others claim to offer a similar service, but generally subcontract a number of their services. But all of ours are in-house, which lets us control the quality of our workforce – and, of course, continue to train them to an ever-higher standard.'

Growth strategy has been about both growing with existing clients and finding new ones – the latter, as stated, through reputation and word of mouth. The structure of the company allows cross-feeding of clients. For instance, roofing and cladding often opens up new markets that the other group members can enter. There are also projects which draw on the resources of most or even all of the group, such as a recent contract for the BBC which is a complete turnkey project.

As the group grows, its capacity to handle larger projects inevitably increases. This has already been seen with the steelworks company which is now able to handle far larger jobs than in the past. An important part of group strategy will be to bring the other companies up to the level whereby they can handle considerably more substantial projects.

Company strategy does not rule out further additions to the group. Mark Langley: 'We would consider adding a company where we currently have large amounts of expenditure going outside the group. The obvious examples would be a scaffolding company and a plant-hire and access equipment company. Again, such companies could work within the group and also offer services to outside clients.' Another source of growth could come by acquiring other companies which have good quality staff, thereby adding to market share.

The company acknowledges that its meteoric rate of growth in the past four years has led to some things being, if not left aside, certainly given less importance. One is staff training. The organisation has an existing training programme for all its site and office people, but wants to add to this by adding appropriate training packages. It is also looking at Investors In People accreditation. Its employees are vitally important to the company's future, and it recognises that their commitment has been a big factor in its impressive growth to date.

The Future

Mark Langley remains sanguine about the company's prospects. 'There has been lots of talk of recession, but from what we've seen, our business will not suffer in 1999 – nor in subsequent years, unless recession becomes a complete nationwide depression. We started 1999 with nearly 50% of our turnover target secured in one month – particularly impressive given our short lead-ins.'

Such confidence looks well-founded. Given the wide spread of the group's operations and its uncompromisingly high standards across that range, success looks assured. Its own forecasts back this up, predicting that it will be a £70 million turnover company in five years, employing from 600 to 700 people.

Its operations outside the UK are also positive factors for the future. Poland, for instance, has seen huge external and internal investment in recent years, including the building of 20 new Tesco stores; and its desire to join the European Community will lead to further spending. It has also remained largely unaffected by the crisis in Russia.

The only real challenge for the company would appear to be a potential lack of sufficiently skilled people. It can be difficult to fill posts, especially in computer-aided design. Even here, however, the company operates through a spread of UK offices. This means that it can draw on different talent pools. This factor, coupled with its other advantages, suggests that the future for S & J (Chatteris) Limited will continue to be bright.

Sage Group

The Sage Group provides business solutions, predominantly accounting and payroll software, for small to medium-sized businesses in over 100 countries. Its main operating centres are the UK, France, Germany and the US, with international expansion facilitated through organic growth and acquisition. The company has 2,500 employees worldwide, including 700 in the UK, and services 1.2 million customers through an extensive, 15,000-strong re-seller network, retailers and a direct sales operation.

Scorecard:

Flexibility	★★★★
Innovation	★★★★★
Human resources	★★★
Growth markets	★★★★
Quality of management	★★★★
International orientation	★★★★★

Biggest Plus:
Demand for Sage products can only increase

Biggest Minus:
Sage is having to manage sustained international growth

Key Figures:
(year to 30 September 1998)

Annual turnover:	£191 million
Operating profit:	n/a
Pre-tax profit:	£47 million
Annual investment:	n/a
Employees worldwide:	2,500
Employees UK:	700

Sage Group plc
Sage House
Benton Park Road
Newcastle-upon-Tyne NE7 7LZ
Tel: 0191 255 3000
Fax: 0191 255 0308
website: www.sage.com

Sage Group

Company Background

The Sage Group, which was founded in 1981, manufactures and sells business solutions, predominantly accounting and payroll software, for use on personal computers. Its market comprises small to medium-sized enterprises (up to 100 employees) and has over 1.2 million customers worldwide. It has grown steadily, both organically and through a programme of acquisition, which has seen expansion into mainland Europe and America. Recent acquisitions include State Of The Art and Prosoft in the US, KHK in Germany, Sybel in France and PASE and PACS in the UK.

Sage has also forged a number of strategic alliances with blue-chip organisations such as Microsoft, IBM, Compaq and Novell in order to increase its market penetration. Turnover in 1997/98 moved from £152 million to £191 million, while pre-tax profit, at £47 million, was 25% higher than the previous year's £38 million. The company achieved a stock market flotation in 1989, since when its share price has risen steadily, indicating the buoyancy of the information technology market in general and the particular strengths of the group.

Operations and Markets

The Sage Group targets a precise sector of the business community with its business solutions: smaller to medium-sized enterprises with between one and 100 employees. That said, it should be remembered that this market segment accounts for around 99% of all companies and so represents a massive marketplace. What is more, the market is far from saturated, with many businesses still using manual or outmoded computer systems. Sage naturally identifies every start-up business as a potential customer.

In addition to strategic partnerships with the likes of Microsoft and IBM, Sage works with over 500 'Developers', who devise vertical market applications using Sage development tools. This helps increase the relevance of Sage products to a wider audience and generates additional income through licensing agreements. These Sage products are distributed through 'Value Added Resellers', with the balance of sales coming through conventional retailers. The company maintains an extensive support facility to advise and assist existing users.

While the overall policy is to purchase proven companies and to allow them to continue largely unmolested, Sage is conscious of the strength of its international brand and is working to develop this further. Sage products are now in use in over 100 countries and the company continues to be on the look-out for further acquisition opportunities.

Strategy and Management

Given the rapid and continuing growth of Sage both in the UK and internationally, there is a clear need for strong central management to maintain consistency of approach and to provide leadership. While newly acquired businesses are expected to continue operating successfully, there is no doubt that they are an integral part of the overall Sage business and serve as ambassadors for the global brand. The senior management, headquartered at Newcastle in the UK, therefore provides structural focus and direction while encouraging staff throughout the organisation to be self-determined, self-motivated and creative.

The powerful Sage brand is a key asset of the company and in 1997 the various international subsidiaries were brought together under the common identity. This was done primarily to satisfy customer demand for a brand which had international credibility. Paul Walker, chief executive, says customers obtain peace of mind from working with a familiar name which has demonstrably sound finances: 'They feel reassured to be dealing with a vendor which is stable, which is at the leading edge of technological development and which can be relied upon to support the customer for years to come.'

Sage is nothing if not flexible, however. It happily exploits the strength of existing brands when it acquires companies overseas, integrating the suggestion of local knowledge and expertise with the security and commercial muscle associated with a well-established international organisation.

Sage has developed close working relationships with other software providers and developers in order to develop its market penetration. These 'co-operative marketing initiatives' extend the reach of the company both horizontally, in terms of increasing the total number of users, and vertically, by increasing the number of applications used by each customer. Such arrangements will be nurtured and fresh opportunities explored as and when they arise.

Sage is determined that it should be viewed not merely as a provider of software products but as a provider of business solutions. It sees itself as helping those with little or no technical knowledge to squeeze maximum benefit from the extraordinary capabilities of modern computers. It therefore runs training programmes for users and operates the Sage Helpline, which provides its SageCover clients with access to almost 200 specialists in its accounting and payroll software products. It can also provide business stationery which is specifically designed for use with the company software.

The broader business issues being addressed by Sage include new legislation on late payment, the national minimum wage, the Year 2000 and the euro, to name just a few. The company sees itself as the friend of the smaller enterprise and wants to provide advice as well as product. This sort of brand reinforcement is an important element of the overall strategy of making Sage the automatic first choice of its target client group across the world.

The Future

Sage has invested heavily in market research to help determine future strategy. According to Paul Walker, chief executive, it is an effective way to keep in touch with consumer attitudes: 'The information technology marketplace changes at a bewildering pace and, as a supplier, it is sometimes easy to get carried away with developing technology for technology's sake. Talking to customers and researching new product concepts with them helps to keep our feet on the ground and ensures products are relevant and appropriate.'

With numerous small to medium-sized businesses in each of its geographical markets yet to computerise, Sage has no shortage of prospective customers. Its efforts to consolidate its various operating companies under the Sage brand should enhance its standing as a global player and facilitate further international expansion, both within Europe and North America as well as in the Far East. Strategic alliances with household name computer companies should also confirm perceptions of Sage as a major presence on the world stage.

While undoubtedly a dynamic company with its finger on the pulse of technological development, Sage never forgets that its customers are generally conservative when it comes to using today's business solutions. It is therefore careful not to alienate those who are getting to grips with technology for the first time. 'It is a question of delivering the right product to the right audience at the right time,' says Paul Walker.

However, businesses in the future will be run by people who grew up using computers and whose needs and aspirations will be dramatically different. This means the company's fortunes will depend to a degree on its ability to remain at the cutting edge of product development.

To ensure it achieves this, it invests heavily in its own research and development staff as well as working with other companies to expand the range and capabilities of its products.

Particular attention is currently being paid to commercial applications of the Internet and to electronic commerce in general. As yet, the full potential of these innovations has yet to be realised, but Sage is determined to be at the forefront of development work so that it will be well placed to take full advantage of every emerging market.

The Sheridan Group

The Sheridan Group was formed in 1989 'to pursue the development and operation of unique, integrated urban entertainment centres in Ireland and the UK'. It is now the biggest leisure-oriented development company in Ireland and a leading player in Great Britain and further afield, bringing imaginative new concepts to the entertainment world through harnessing world-leading technology and offering local investors exciting joint venture opportunities.

Scorecard:

Flexibility	★★★★★
Innovation	★★★★
Human resources	★★★
Growth markets	★★★
Quality of management	★★★★
International orientation	★★★

Biggest Plus:
Entrepreneurial vision and agility harnessed to financial acumen

Biggest Minus:
Financial and executive restructuring required to cope with future growth

Key Figures:
(year ended 30 September 1998)

Annual turnover	£17.1 million
Operating profit	£5.2 million
Pre-tax profit	£2.3 million
Annual investment	£12.5 million
Employees worldwide	260

The Sheridan Group
35 Bedford Street
Belfast BT2 7EJ
Tel: 01232 244211
Fax: 01232 233946

Sheridan Group

The Sheridan Group

Company Background

The true entrepreneur is born, not made, but the factors that kick-start their drive to success are as varied as the individual. In Peter Curistan's case it was a depressing wet night in Belfast – and an ability to detect a small, feeble spark of life in something considered to be as dead as a dodo.

The seeds of the Sheridan Group were sown in 1986 when Curistan, a successful Price Waterhouse accountant, had to stand in the rain in a queue of 600 to see *Crocodile Dundee*, which he describes as 'the first good quality film after two decades of "King Fu Charlie" garbage films', and after the novelty of TV had virtually killed off the film industry.

As he queued, Curistan realised two things: that people *would* leave their homes to see films worth seeing and cinema need not die; but he also saw that entertainment had to be *more* than that, that cinema could be revived if it was part of a package that attracted people out of their homes, with comfortable multi-screen choice, and included bars, restaurants and secure, convenient parking.

His answer was a £12 million project (with £20,000 of his own money – all he had) but it took him more than six years of 'perseverance, tenacity and doggedness' to overcome bureaucratic inertia, business scepticism and banking disinterest before Ireland's first integrated urban entertainment centre opened in Belfast comprising a Virgin multiplex cinema, themed bars, restaurants, a nightclub, and a multistorey car park.

This was the start. From a cold, wet stand outside a run-down Belfast cinema, an empire was born.

Operations and Markets

The Sheridan Group officially came into being in 1989 when everything was finally in place for the building of the Virgin (at that time the MGM) Centre in Belfast 'to pursue the development and operation of unique, integrated urban entertainment centres in Ireland and the United Kingdom'.

With two centres now up and running in Belfast and Dublin, two major new millennium projects under its belt in England and Scotland, and another six under negotiation, Sheridan Group's remit and reputation has now spread beyond its home market. Companies in countries as diverse as South Africa, Poland and Hong Kong are now talking to Peter Curistan about development and equity partnerships.

Its operations have now, almost by default, widened into areas that Curistan never envisaged at the start, particularly into hotel and residential development. Lucrative and prestigious as these can be, however, Curistan says that he does not envisage them forming more than about 20% of the group's total activity. Entertainment will remain the core.

He also operates a range of theme bars and restaurants (some as franchises), multistorey car parks, nightclubs and family entertainment centres in Belfast and Dublin.

But the activity probably dearest to his heart is the IMAX, giant-screen 3D film theatre. Curistan opened the first of these in Europe in June 1998 in his huge Parnell Centre in Dublin, which has a Virgin multiplex as the anchor tenant as well as 40,000 sq. ft of shopping, restaurants, 10,000 sq. ft of theme bars, a Virtual Voyages simulation theatre, a Century City family entertainment centre, multistorey car parking and more than 100 apartments. IMAX uses an 18×20 metre screen 'wrapped around' the tiered audience, providing people with the most mind-blowing cinema experience ever.

Sheridan's first foothold in Great Britain came with the development contract for the 70,000 sq. ft seafront entertainment centre due to open in Bournemouth in the summer of 1999. It will be anchored by an IMAX theatre and house a range of theme restaurants. He has plans for at least five other similar complexes in England, all centred round an IMAX theatre.

Of considerable pride to Curistan, and which won an international accolade, was the award of a contract in 1998 to operate the visitor attraction centre in the £60 million tourism development planned for the southern shore of Loch Lomond, forecast to attract 1.2 million visitors a year.

But the jewel in the Sheridan crown, and its biggest project to date and probably for some time, is the £100 million Odyssey Centre, an educational sports and entertainment complex rising from the side of the River Lagan in Belfast and Northern Ireland's 'landmark' millennium project. It is the biggest-ever building project in Ireland. His partners are the government and the Ulster Museum and the project will give Northern Ireland, for the first time, facilities to host world-class sports events and live performances attracting audiences of up to 10,000.

A strategically located plot of land within walking distance of Belfast city centre opened the way for another phase of Sheridan's development. In spring 1998, it announced plans to build a 170-bedroom hotel, conference centre and fitness/leisure suite for Granada's Posthouse Forte chain. The £16 million complex will also contain commercial units and apartments.

Part of this deal involved the purchase by Sheridan of an existing Forte Hotel at Dunmurry in South Belfast, which was past its use-by date and no longer viable. The building and car parks are surrounded by an estate of beautiful woodland, however, and Curistan plans to replace it with a residential 'retreat' of apartments and town houses offering an up-market, secure 'tennis-club' lifestyle. Granada is already talking to him about further hotel developments in England and Scotland.

Strategy and Management

In building the Sheridan empire, Peter Curistan has been an entrepreneur, but not a buccaneer. His grounding in accountancy, where he worked with a number of blue-chip companies, has taught him to watch his financial back.

The projects in which Sheridan is involved and their logical development from each other demonstrates the evolutionary rather than revolutionary management strategy which drives the group.

So careful is Curistan to avoid doing anything smacking of the gamble, he maintains that his present activities, dramatic though they may be, are not in fact entrepreneurial at all but copper-bottomed investments.

'We tie-in an anchor tenant right at the start, which takes most of the risk out of it,' he says. 'In Bournemouth, the first thing we did was to secure five anchor tenants and then we sold the development to a pension fund for £2.5 million profit before a sod was turned.'

His drive to see Sheridan become a leading leisure development company in Britain and further afield will be underpinned by a level of credibility that will ensure he does not have to worry about getting financial backing for the next step.

'When you reach the right level of credibility, the big leisure players come to you saying, "We'd like to be involved in your schemes." If you have delivered successfully a few times it speeds everything up. You get through to the top people right away; it becomes easier.'

Curistan operates through a small team of key executives in driving the group forward, although he admits that as projects get bigger and more complex, this team is going to have to grow – the problem, he says, is getting the right people.

The Future

Peter Curistan admits that the Sheridan Group is at a crossroads. The question is not which direction to go – that will continue to be upwards – but in which type of vehicle to make the journey.

Growth will come from appreciating values of developments at home and by developing opportunities worldwide for the application of its unrivalled experience and technical expertise in creating integrated urban entertainment centres through partnerships with companies that bring local knowledge, and equity, to the project.

This exponential growth and the changing financial conditions it implies for the management of the group underlie difficult decisions that Curistan knows he will have to make in the next few years to ensure that its financial and organisational structure is appropriate. The bigger you get, the more critical it becomes to get capital financing right.

Currently he sees the joint venture approach to project development as a failsafe way forward but as the company grows he knows that, reluctant as he may be to give up the fast response flexibility that his 100% control gives him, he may have to learn to share. He has a number of options at the back of his mind, but he is not in any hurry to make change.

'I'd never rule out floating but it's unlikely in the near future. We don't need to,' he says.

Standard Life

Founded in Edinburgh in 1825, Standard Life is one of the world's leading mutual financial services companies, with its activities ranging from the provision of traditional life assurance and savings, pensions and mortgage repayment plans to the management of pension funds, unit trusts, mortgages, banking products and health insurance.

Scorecard:

Flexibility	★★★★
Innovation	★★★★
Human resources	★★★★
Growth markets	★★★★
Quality of management	★★★★
International orientation	★★★

Biggest Plus:
Despite its age and size bold enough to try new ventures

Biggest Minus:
Its perceived virtue of being risk-averse could stifle even more adventurous moves

Key Figures:
(to year end 15 November 1998)

New business:	£3.5 billion
Funds under management:	
	In excess of £65 billion
Employees worldwide:	10,000
Employees UK:	8,000

Standard Life
Standard Life House
30 Lothian Road
Edinburgh
EH1 2DH
Tel: 0131 245 4020
Fax: 0131 220 1534
website: www.standardlife.com/UK

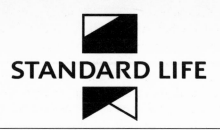

Standard Life

Company Background

Standard Life is one of the largest investors in the UK equity market. It invests over £50 million each week and manages the equivalent of more than 2% of the All Share Index. It is one of only a handful of life assurance companies in the world to hold Triple A ratings for financial strength by the US credit rating agencies, Standard & Poor's and Moody's.

It is a company with no shareholders – it is owned by its 'with profit' policyholders. That means that all profits can be distributed to its with profit policyholders (shareholders usually require 10% of all profits). This mutual status is frequently questioned by those who see a listing as the way to advance and expand in the financial services world.

Standard Life says it is not married to the mutuality concept and will continue to keep an open mind while conceding that if somebody came along with an 'out-of-this-world' offer it would have to put it to its policyholder owners.

Operations and Markets

A company of this size and experience is expected to set standards. And it does. But that was not always the case. Chief Executive of UK operations Jim Stretton recalls that when he and group managing director Scott Bell took over the helm about ten years ago they did a bit of research to find out what people thought about Standard Life. The answer: 'They thought we were arrogant and distant and they did business with us because they had to because we were big and strong.'

Jim Stretton states: 'We said that this could not go on. You can't run a company with people doing business with you because they feel they must.'

So they set about putting things right. Senior management, in tranches, visited the United States to see how they did things and they came back impressed and determined to pursue a policy of total customer focus – a strategy which has transformed Standard Life.

Total Customer Satisfaction (TCS) has changed beyond measure the reputation the company has in the market. It has won a raft of awards at a time when the pensions industry has suffered damage and much adverse publicity as a result of the mis-selling of personal pensions, although Standard Life remains virtually unscathed by this debacle. Most of its business is done through independent financial advisers, with the company not responsible for the advice given on its products. But as one of the leaders of the industry it is an issue it takes seriously. It has worked hard to ensure that life, pension and associated products offer genuine value for money.

Standard Life has what it calls an extremely regulatory compliant culture and the astute leadership of its management team has seen the company change direction and carefully extend its grasp.

After the Second World War it cut back on its international activities to concentrate on the home market while maintaining a strong presence in Ireland and Canada. It is back on the international trail again as might be expected of a company of this size and ambition. It now operates in Spain, where it made a small acquisition, and Germany, has two representative offices in China, sells its products in Austria from its German base and has established a joint venture in India.

It has launched the hugely successful Standard Life Bank which, after a year of raking in deposits, has moved into the mortgage market with matching success. It has set up Standard Life Investments as an independent company, selling the company's investment expertise, and early on it bought Prime Health, a medical insurance company.

All this is in line with what in many ways is a simple business philosophy: being there for major financial events in people's lives, such as taking out a mortgage, investing money, arranging a pension, personal banking.

Strategy and Management

In the last five years Standard Life has moved into new areas of product provision and investment while staying faithful to the need to be trusty custodians of policyholders' money. This has led some to claim that the company is risk-averse, sometimes to its detriment, but the company's answer is simple: 'We are shrewd not foolish investors. We don't do silly things.'

It has 10,000 people on its books and holds to the firm belief that for a company which prides itself on its investment expertise the prudent investment in staff is one of its priorities.

Jim Stretton puts it this way: 'We are a big, successful and innovative organisation with developing international presence and exciting ideas for the future. We are doing things today unthought of five years ago. Visionary companies like ours need the injection of new, young talent and we can provide the opportunities that ambitious people in a hurry expect.'

The company accepts that despite its award-winning approach to giving quality service to the customer it still has a long way to go. The better the service the higher the customer expectation, and the company believes that quality of service will remain the real differential in its marketplace.

It has followed up its North American learning visit at the start of the decade with another visit by its top people to study the North American approach, with 12 senior executives visiting 22 American companies to look and learn. They say they returned with a briefcase full of ideas.

Implementing them will not necessarily be easy in such a vast company but their track record shows it is possible as the company seeks to strengthen its position in the UK market while developing its overseas presence.

The company also believes that part of its new look has to be a better understanding of press and public relations. For years this financial giant was aloof and unapproachable. Now it courts press coverage in the belief that this helps spread the brand name, creating the correct environment in which to sell. It also believes this fosters the 'feel-good' factor in staff, taking pride in seeing their company enter into debate and receive third-party endorsement.

This is only part of the brand-building challenge that faces the company. Despite its size and reputation the company name itself is under-used. It is hardly recognised south of the border where the company does the bulk of its business. Overseas it means even less.

The company strategy is to develop that brand name, which is steeped in the Scottish tradition of the successful husbandry of people's money and financial aspirations. The Scottish card is played carefully – Standard Life is a company which just happens to have its head-quarters in Scotland and, while proud of its heritage, does not see itself as a Scottish company. The brand has powerful potential, like the company itself.

The Future

A company of this size and stature has nothing but growth and success ahead, but it is taking nothing for granted.

It will be in the spotlight as the biggest private sector employer in Edinburgh at the time of the establishment of a Scottish parliament. It says that this event will have a negligible effect on Standard Life or on its customers, but many will nonetheless look to the company to provide a lead on a number of issues.

The company is moving towards its goal of becoming a global operation once again but one wonders whether this is being done as part of a carefully worked out global strategy or if it is simply seeking to take advantage of opportunities as and when they appear.

The brand name itself is a mighty weapon still to be wielded effectively nationally and internationally.

The company has shown its tremendous ability to move into new but compatible areas of business, making cutting-edge decisions and competing with the best while remaining true to its policyholders and to its mutual status. It operates in a market bristling with opportunities and has already set itself some hard acts to follow.

Sun Microsystems

Sun Microsystems is a worldwide leader in network computing technologies, systems, software and services. It is recognised as one of the premier providers of open network computing solutions.

Scorecard:

Flexibility	★★★★★
Innovation	★★★★★
Human resources	★★★★
Growth markets	★★★★★
Quality of management	★★★★
International orientation	★★★★★

Biggest Plus:
A highly successful future-shaping company with
a strong vision

Biggest Minus:
Operates in a highly competitive marketplace

Key Figures:
(to 31 March 1998)

Net revenues:	$9.7 billion
Operating income:	$1.1 billion
Net income:	$762 million
Total assets:	$5.7 billion
Employees worldwide:	26,000

Sun Microsystems Limited
Bagshot Manor
Green Lane
Bagshot
Surrey GU19 5NL
Tel: 01276 451440
Fax: 01276 416707
website: www.sun.co.uk

microsystems

Sun Microsystems

Company Background

Sun Microsystems was founded in 1982. Its name derives from 'Stanford University Network', and the company still maintains a link with the academic establishment. From its relatively recent formation, the company has grown into a ten billion dollar business which trades in more than 150 countries worldwide.

The company is a world leader in UNIX servers: first in workgroup servers, first in midrange servers and third at the high end (from not even featuring in the previous year). In data storage, it is first in UNIX storage and fifth overall. It now sells devices which work in mixed-platform environments, thanks to its acquisition of Encore in 1998. Sun remains the leading UNIX workstation vendor by a wide margin, and is first in 10 of the top 17 technical markets where these systems are used.

Above all, Sun leads the way with its widely adopted Java technologies. This platform is already the standard for the smart-card industry and for leading Web phone manufacturers, and is being widely deployed in home banking, retail point-of-sale applications and major segments of the telecommunications industry. As chairman and CEO Scott McNealy puts it: 'Others make the devices. We make them possible by selling them network enabling components.'

Operations and Markets

The UK operation is the second largest part of Sun Microsystems worldwide. In its first quarter of fiscal 1998 it grew by around 49% compared to Q1 fiscal 1997 – phenomenal growth by any standards. This is fuelled by two key factors. First, the company has a clear vision: it knows where it is going, how it sees the industry and what it delivers to its customers.

Jon Tutcher, PR and corporate affairs manager: 'We don't think our customers should be bothered by the complexities of all this technology. Our vision is in effect to take computing to the masses. We adopt a model from the utilities industry. As a customer, you want water on tap and electricity at the flick of a switch, but you don't want or need a sewage works in your garden or a power plant in your garage! It's the same with us. We keep all the complexity at the centre of the network. As a result customers will increasingly see simpler devices, fuelled by our technology such as Java. Our goal – not too far off – is to have a world where you can access the computer network from anywhere and use it to do whatever you want. For instance, you could use your mobile phone to turn your central heating on, pre-heat your oven or whatever. Computing as we see it will be in lots of different forms, not just boxes on desks.'

The second factor is that Sun is an exceedingly open company. This runs right through its culture. Its main route to the market is through partners; it doesn't produce word processors or ledgers for software. Instead, it partners with companies such as Oracle. It publishes all the programming interfaces that others need to work with – a refreshing change for buyers. Rather than insisting on being one vendor, Sun Microsystems' philosophy is all about helping its customers solve problems.

Sun is undeniably effective in finding opportunities and creating marketplaces. It created the workstation marketplace single-handedly 15 years ago and is still the largest player. It is also first or second in all the countries it operates in for enterprise-class servers. Having only just entered the mainframe market, it is already second or third here. And so the story continues. It intends to be first in all the markets in which it competes, and its strong growth, powerful vision and committed people suggest that this ambition is certainly achievable.

In terms of structure, Sun has a number of teams which focus on separate markets: for example, telecoms, finance and so on. This allows its sales people to talk the same language as their customers and to understand those industries inside out. As a result, the company is able to add more value to those customers. In the UK, these include such major names as British Airways, NatWest Bank, Rover, News International, British Gas, CCTA, Glaxo Wellcome, Virgin Records and many more.

Around 1,500 people in the UK work on sales, service and support, with 800 more in the company's factory in Linlithgow, Scotland. This provides the majority of the products for Europe and Japan, building everything from workstations to mainframes. A truly world-class facility, this is responsible for around 45% of the company's total output. Rather than operating in traditional style, the factory is structured around cells which allow much more intelligent working and help reduce the timeframe within the supply chain. There are 14 offices around the UK, including six in the Thames Valley which will be consolidated in mid 2000 into a $100 million campus in Farnborough.

Until the last six months, the company operated on a country basis. There is now a regional structure, with the UK part of the Europe, Middle East and Africa region. Virtual teams now work across Europe, replicating the best practice across countries. Structurally, the company is divided into computer systems, enterprise services, professional services and a software business. In the UK, Sun ships 20% of its products to end-users, with the other 80% going through its partners. The company's flexibility ensures that its customers can buy from other suppliers; Sun will make sure all systems talk to each other. The result is the best of all worlds for the customer.

Strategy and Management

The strategic questions for the UK business's executive committee are: how does it take US technology and apply it to its own markets, and what resources are needed to make this happen effectively?

In the UK, as elsewhere in the world, the company is aided by a very flat structure and rapid decision-taking processes. Jon Tutcher: 'This is essential for us, because our customers continually challenge us. Product cycles are moving ever faster. Innovation is also speeding up. Yet customers want stability as well. At Sun, part of our strategy is to find that balance between innovation and stability, and I believe our rapid growth suggests that our customers feel we've got that balance right.'

For Sun as a whole, the strategy is the same: finding the best ways to deliver solutions to customers. To do so, it is committed to seeing things from the customer viewpoint. Jon Tutcher: 'People buy IT as a strategic purchase. We therefore have to have a close working partnership with our clients. The message from us is simple: we will be your enterprise supplier, and you can rely on us.'

Of course, strategy has to evolve rapidly when marketplaces are subject to such change. Sun takes advantage of this rapid pace by considering all implications of Internet growth and advising its clients. For instance, wider Internet use may make the current vast networks of clearing bank branches unnecessary, or at least reduce branch numbers and change their function into higher-value transaction bases.

The last but by no means least aspect of company management is to look after its staff. Sun Microsystems is the only major IT company with Investors in People accreditation. Its people enjoy great working conditions, excellent remuneration and career development, and the chance to work in a cutting-edge industry for an industry leader at a particularly interesting time.

The Future

The single major threat to the company is Microsoft. This works both ways, however! Bill Gates, Microsoft's chairman, recently paid tribute to Sun in a speech by calling the company its second most feared competitor after IBM. Indeed, Sun can be seen as a much more viable threat to Microsoft now than just 18 months ago. Increasingly, Sun Microsystems is moving into the software market, led there by the success of Java, Jini and other technological advances. There is an evolution in where Sun Microsystems puts its resources.

Overall, the future looks rosy for Sun. Jon Tutcher: 'The pieces of the technological jigsaw are now falling into place. Everything has changed in a very short space of time – but we are helping to shape those changes. We have the technology, the understanding of our markets and above all the right people to make the most of this fast-moving world.'

Taylor Nelson Sofres

Taylor Nelson Sofres is one of the world's largest market information services groups with particular specialisation in consumer products, media, healthcare, business and finance, automotive, IT and telecommunications sectors. The 1997 merger of Britain's Taylor Nelson AGB and Sofres of France created a group with combined sales of £300 million and businesses in 33 countries.

Scorecard:

Flexibility	★★★
Innovation	★★★★★
Human resources	★★★
Growth markets	★★★
Quality of management	★★★
International orientation	★★★

Biggest Plus:
A commanding position in an expanding and high yielding field

Biggest Minus:
Needs to build greater scale in important US market

Key Figures:

Turnover (1997)*	£111.6 million
Pre-tax profit (1997)	£12.2 million
Capital expenditure (1997)	£4.3 million
Employees (1998)	4,600
Offices worldwide (1998)	more than 100

*includes only one month's contribution from Sofres. Pro-forma sales were £296 million

Taylor Nelson Sofres
Westgate
London W5 1UA
Tel: 0181 967 0007
Fax: 0181 967 4060
e-mail: Enquiries@tnsofres.com

Taylor Nelson Sofres

Company Background

Taylor Nelson Sofres is a market information company which aims to provide businesses ranging from drugs giants to high street fashion chains with up-to-the-minute commercial information. The group, which evolved into its present form following the 1992 acquisition of AGB from Maxwell Communication Corporation and the 1997 merger with Sofres, now ranks as the fourth largest group in what is estimated to be an $11 billion a year industry.

The company's revenues are derived partly from long-term syndicated business, whereby the same information is sold to 30 or 40 separate subscribers, and from more customised contracts, probably one half of which are long term in nature.

Underlying revenues have doubled in the past five years while profits have trebled to £12.2 million. Nearly 30% of turnover is generated in France, 29% in the UK, 22% in the rest of Europe, 12% in the US and 8% in the Far East.

Operations and Markets

Like many other providers of services to business, Taylor Nelson Sofres has been expanding rapidly around the world to keep pace with the demands of multinational customers such as Coca-Cola, Ford, Unilever and International Business Machines, which want information on a global basis.

In response to these demands, Taylor Nelson Sofres has made a spate of acquisitions and now has operations in 33 different countries. Such a global spread acts as a high barrier to entry for would-be competitors, providing a degree of protection.

The group specialises in a number of sectors where it is confident of maintaining a commanding market position including:

Media – the particular strength here lies in TV audience measurement and related research and technology. In the UK, for example, the company holds the BARB audience measurement contract while its innovative Picture Matching technique, for measuring digital, cable and satellite TV audiences, is now being introduced into a number of countries around the world.

Consumer – the group is a world leader in setting-up and running consumer product panels, for example FashionTrak, the bespoke information system for high street outlets which has now become the industry standard with almost all retailers buying the service. It also provides a range of custom research products.

Healthcare – the group has a dominant position in the custom market but mergers between the big drug companies could make the going tougher.

Business services and finance – the group provides customised research through branded products. Again, the pace of global rationalisation among banks and building societies is tremendous, although the company's BrandVision technique for tracking advertising is picking up clients.

Information technology and automotive are examples of other growing sectors in which the group specialises.

Strategy and Management

The company is convinced it must be a world provider of information and must be in the top three or four players in all the territories in which it operates. The merger of Taylor Nelson and Sofres was an almost ideal geographical fit, although the group probably still feels it lacks sufficient scale in the important US market.

The decision to specialise in particular sectors makes global supremacy in these fields more attainable. The company's staff know their business sectors intimately and are able to offer consultancy and analysis as well as more impartial information provision.

Although the business information market, valued at $11 billion, is reckoned to be growing at something like $1 billion a year, the prospect of recession has prompted some commentators to fear that Taylor Nelson Sofres's business growth will slow. However, experience of the UK and French recessions of the early 1990s and even the economic meltdown in Asia during 1998 suggests these worries are overdone and that while growth may go out of some parts of the business, they will not experience decline. Tony Cowling, the group's executive chairman, expects the 10–11% growth rate of recent years to continue for some time.

A key to the group's continued steady growth is its ability to win syndicated contracts whereby it extracts information which is then sold to 30 or 40 different subscribers. But this means Taylor Nelson

Sofres has to be exceptionally inventive and pro-active in suggesting information services which customers will pay for (and the margins on syndicated business can be up to 15% compared with about 9% for ad hoc work).

Tony Cowling points out that nearly all the group's research and development spending (about 4% of total expenditure) is devoted to projects such as these. The company does, however, have a strong track record for innovation. FashionTrak is one such product devised for an industry which suffered from weak information systems.

Taylor Nelson has established a panel of 6,000 shoppers from which it collects purchasing information which is then analysed and passed on to clients. In just three years since its software designers signed off the project, FashionTrak has gained 50 clients including powerful fashion names such as Next and Gap. It has also become a valuable tool for Marks & Spencer.

Products such as FashionTrak not only ensure that the company's earnings stream continues, but as they become akin to an 'industry bible', they effectively block competition. Neilsen Media has achieved something similar in the US while IMS has an almost impregnable position in the measurement of doctors' prescription information. In this position, the information providers can hike the price to the top of what they regard as a sustainable range.

Tony Cowling admits, however, there are disadvantages in such market dominance. Firstly major corporates have a natural anxiety about restricted choice and tend to try to encourage competition. Secondly, even though the barriers to entry are high, a competitor will try to enter a field if the incumbent becomes too greedy.

Specialisation has an added advantage in terms of group human resources – a factor which Taylor Nelson Sofres is seeking to exploit. The company encourages its executives to become expert and to take charge of financial units whose performance can then be monitored. Staff are given a good degree of autonomy, the ability to recruit and devise strategic plans, the success of which can form the basis for bonuses. Impressed by the ambition of the people now being recruited in the company's offices around the world, Tony Cowling is creating a network of high flyers, giving them the opportunity to work around the world. The business is managed within specialist sectors and the group is bringing together people from different countries who work in the same sector to share resource, development, marketing and training.

The Future

The information market is one of the fastest moving of global business sectors and there could be considerable discomfort for the major players if the recent strategy of specialisation and thereby avoiding head-to-head confrontation breaks down.

Tony Cowling, who has no doubts that big business will always want to be told what competitors and customers are up to as quickly as possible, does foresee some rationalisation among the industry's leaders. He stresses that Taylor Nelson Sofres must 'run fast enough to ensure we are in one of the top three places'.

A stronger share price would help to give the company greater financial room to manoeuvre in takeovers but Taylor Nelson Sofres has suffered recently in the eyes of the City, which does not have a clear enough grasp of the group and the dynamics of its business. The group is seeking to address this weakness with the appointment of its first specialist investor relations executive.

The group will continue to increase the volume of its business from syndicated contracts in step with the increased pace of mergers and acquisitions between the group's major global customers. If a syndicated survey loses one customer because it is taken over that is not too punishing, but if one of only a handful of ad hoc contract buyers disappears that can dent the business.

Although Taylor Nelson Sofres is still in the early stages of digesting its merger, it is clear that the company's determination to build its presence in important territories such as the US and Asia will drive further acquisitions as well as greenfield office openings.

TNT UK Limited

TNT UK Limited is a market leader in time-certain express delivery and logistics services in the United Kingdom. The company employs 12,000 people and is part of the TNT Post Group which employs 100,000 people worldwide.

Scorecard:

Flexibility	★★★★★
Innovation	★★★★★
Human resources	★★★★★
Growth markets	★★★★
Quality of management	★★★★★
International orientation	★★★★★

Biggest Plus:
An environment where everyone can succeed and everyone is valued

Biggest Minus:
Operates in a hugely competitive marketplace

Key Figures:
(to year ending 31 March 1998)

Turnover:	£850 million
Pre-tax profit:	£54 million
Number of employees:	12,000

TNT United Kingdom
TNT Express House
Holly Lane
Atherstone
Warwickshire
CV9 2RY
Tel: 01827 303030
Fax: 01827 713746
website: www.tnt.co.uk

TNT UK Limited

Company Background

TNT UK Limited started trading in 1978 when TNT acquired Inter County Express Limited, a successful carrier providing a profitable three-day parcels delivery service.

Almost from the first day, TNT UK was noted as an innovator. When it began, no parcel carrier in the country provided nationwide on-demand, next-day-delivery services, and real-time communication with drivers on the road was almost unknown. Its TNT Overnite service, launched in 1980, offered both through a fleet of radio-equipped vehicles. This service was supplemented two years later with the introduction of TNT Sameday (the first nationwide door-to-door immediate delivery service), and by a range of other new services throughout the 1980s and 1990s.

TNT UK is the only organisation to have won four European Quality Prizes (in 1995, 1996, 1997 and 1998) for business excellence. These awards, given by the European Foundation for Quality Management, are widely regarded as the pinnacle of achievement in Total Quality Management. The best company among the prizewinners is also honoured with the European Quality Award, which TNT UK won in 1998.

The company has also won 15 Motor Transport Industry Awards in the last 13 years; the 1997 Management Today/Unisys Business to Business Overall Service Excellence Award: and was voted by 2000 members of the Institute of Transport Management as the 1998 Express Parcels Carrier of the Year. TNT UK has Investors in People status, one of the few multi-site businesses to win company-wide recognition. It was also one of only two companies highly commended for best practice in people management in 1997 by that organisation and is the winner of the Investors in People 1998 Key Champions Award.

Operations and Markets

The company is made up of a range of businesses. The principle behind this approach is to build the businesses up from nothing into units capable of becoming major players or market leaders in their sectors. As Alan Jones, MD of TNT UK, puts it: 'The idea is to innovate with a unique service and then offer outstanding customer satisfaction. For example, we pioneered national newspaper distribution by road instead of rail. Soon after, we had cut transit times by approximately one hour across the country and also reduced costs by eliminating intermediate handling processes.'

TNT UK now consists of 19 separate businesses. These include TNT Express, the fastest provider of nationwide door-to-door on-demand overnight delivery services for parcels and other items of small freight; TNT Sameday for nationwide immediate collection and instant direct delivery; TNT Newsfast, which handles newspaper and magazine distribution; and TNT Mail Services, offering tailored solutions for the movement of inter-office mail and post-room management. TNT Supamail offers next-morning express delivery services for business mail, documents and small parcels.

TNT Logistics works closely with clients to manage and improve all or part of large-scale, complex supply chains, and this includes providing reliable transport, warehousing and other customer-liveried services. TNT Storapart is a fully integrated rapid response local storage and distribution network providing round-the-clock delivery services. TNT Parcel Office is a unique national network of over 80 parcel reception points, offering customers the full range of TNT Express, TNT Supamail and TNT Sameday services. TNT UK Limited also offers print handling for time-critical printed matter, a next-working-day delivery service for the medical and healthcare industries, an autoparts delivery service, distribution solutions for high-tech companies, security services, European and international delivery facilities, and a myriad of other logistics services.

The company's achievements speak for themselves. TNT UK now has nearly 80% of the national newspaper market, around 80% of the UK magazine market, 50% of garment distribution, and is the largest carrier and storer of tyres and also of packaged lubricants. All of the share certificates traded on the London Stock Exchange are handled by TNT on behalf of Crestco. TNT vehicles carry over one million loaves of bread every day, and the company is the biggest carrier of automotive parts as well as being the largest carrier of computers in the UK. It is the official handling agent for the Farnborough Air Show; it runs the logistics for the London Marathon ... The list could be added to almost endlessly. Suffice it to say that TNT UK is either market leader or close to that position in a large number of its operational sectors.

TNT provides services for almost every company listed in the FT-100. Alan Jones: 'We have more vehicles in other companies' livery than in our own. Each of these operations is a unique contract. We are able to offer tailormade solutions by understanding our clients' needs and giving them a better service than they could provide themselves. These activities – running warehousing, transportation and other key services – are crucial to a company's success. Our impressive organic growth, as instanced by the fact that we have doubled our revenue and profits over the last five years, results from exactly meeting those client needs.'

Strategy and Management

The company's strategy is straightforward: to be the best player and the market leader in every field in which it operates. It aims to achieve that objective through a four-part approach. First is an absolute focus on its customers and provision of outstanding levels of client satisfaction. TNT goes out of its way to offer higher quality service than any of the other carriers, and the organisation thereby wins and retains the loyalty of its clients.

The second strategic strand is to involve everyone in the company. Alan Jones: 'We want all our staff to take part in setting the policy for the business – which means empowering people to do their jobs. I firmly believe that the role of managers should be to give our people the tools and the training to do their jobs – and to create a climate of enthusiasm and success in which everyone can flourish.' As part of this belief, TNT UK virtually never appoints senior people from outside the company. This means that anyone with ability, commitment and drive can go all the way to the top. Indeed, many of the company's top managers started out as drivers.

Continuous improvement is the third element. The aim is to inspire everyone within the company to beat their previous best performance, and this produces considerable personal satisfaction as well as overall company improvement. The company approach to improvement is also bound up with continuously identifying the changing needs of TNT's customers, and finding ever more effective ways to meet those needs.

Perhaps the most important element of strategy is the company's ability to make things happen against seemingly impossible odds. The company definitely engenders a belief that there is nothing that cannot be achieved; and that, with the right mindset, you can do anything. Alan Jones: 'A key part of our strategy is to provide absolute reliability. Customers pay us for reliable service, and they need to feel certain that we will deliver. Faced with unusually demanding problems, our people make extraordinary efforts. The "must get through" attitude for which TNT UK is famous has helped us win a competitive advantage, and I am sure it will stand us in equally good stead in the years to come.'

As well as putting these strategic goals in place, the company is almost fanatical about measuring key outcomes for improvement. TNT UK monitors its on-time delivery performance relentlessly. Underlying this activity is the belief that 'What happen are the things we inspect rather than the things we expect to happen. And so our main area of focus is the quality of service provided by the company for customers.'

The Future

The future for TNT UK will undoubtedly be a case of more of the same: sticking to its basics, providing an outstanding service for customers, growing organically, and continuing to innovate and stay at the leading edge of the market. TNT UK is already the market leader in many of its sectors: it will need to maintain and build on that position. Doing so requires constant dialogue with customers, which is something TNT is clearly very good at.

There are two main challenges for the company. The first is the intensely competitive nature of the market. Alan Jones: 'We never rest on our laurels. At the moment, we don't have any real competitors – only weak opposition. But weak opposition can turn into strong competition tomorrow if you let it. That's why complacency is taboo.'

Creating sufficient expansion to satisfy the aspirations of its people is TNT's other major challenge. TNT UK can only promote high-performing people and give them long-term careers if the organisation grows. However, the company's deep-rooted desires to be the best in everything it does and to continually improve its already impressive practices make its future look assured.

UNISYS

Unisys

Company Background

Unisys can trace its corporate roots back over 100 years to Burroughs Corporation, which invented the world's first commercial adding machine. In 1986 Burroughs merged with Sperry Corporation (which invented Eniac, the USA's first computer) to create the second largest mainframe company in the world. The debt created by this merger, increased by some other acquisitions, was a major problem in the early 1990s as world interest rates rose sharply. As a result the company made significant losses in the early 1990s, an additional cause being the fact that 80% of its revenues were sourced from mainframe sales at a time when customers were moving towards lower margin products and seeking service solutions from technology companies.

The company was also relatively unfocused. For instance, until 1995, each of its 16 European country operations was run on a semi-autonomous basis, with its own CEO, sales director, finance director, and so on. Each country had a very broad spread of programmes to sell, from hardware to systems to maintenance.

To improve this situation, Unisys embarked on a major reorganisation at the end of 1995. It removed much of the individual country management in Europe, thus cutting back heavily on the bureaucracy and becoming more responsive to the market. It also began the move from being a seller of hardware to being a solutions provider.

This strategy was implemented but the initial execution was flawed, and after 18 months of slow progress Unisys appointed a new chairman and chief executive, Lawrence Weinbach, in September 1997. Formerly the managing partner/chief executive of Andersen Worldwide, he had turned it into the world's largest professional services firm and quintupled its revenues. He was therefore well placed not only to transform Unisys, but to take an unemotional look at all its operations. Weinbach: 'The products were very good and the service capability was very good. The way the company went about expanding its product base and getting into the service business was not so good, and because of that, the company got into trouble.'

Unisys

Unisys is a major international information technology and computer services company. Unisys operates globally and is represented in 16 European countries.

Scorecard:

Flexibility	★★★★★
Innovation	★★★★★
Human resources	★★★★
Growth markets	★★★★★
Quality of management	★★★★★
International orientation	★★★★★

Biggest Plus:
A focused, well-managed company with a clear direction

Biggest Minus:
Still has large corporate debt but now at a much more manageable level

Key Figures:
(year to 31 March 1998)

Global revenue:	$6.6 billion
Global gross profit:	$2.2 billion
Net income:	$199 million
Employees worldwide:	32,600
Employees UK:	4,000

Unisys
Bakers Court
Bakers Road
Uxbridge UB8 1RG
Tel: 01895 237237
Fax: 01895 862093
website: www.unisys.com

When Weinbach joined, the company was saddled with $2.3 billion in debt. It was also losing money in its personal computers and small servers area, had a tarnished reputation and a demoralised workforce. Weinbach promised to shave $1 billion off the Unisys debt and by December 1998 had reduced it by $1.1 billion (saving over $60 million a year in interest). He also took the company out of personal computers, outsourcing production to Hewlett Packard. Above all, he refocused the company. The stock price soared and the 1998 third quarter results (net income $250 million compared to $112 million in 1997 Q3) were the best for a decade. Not surprisingly, the company's reputation is revitalised and demoralisation is no longer an issue.

Operations and Markets

Unisys has three divisions: Unisys Computer Systems (which sells hardware and related software), Unisys Information Systems and Unisys Global Customer Services. Increasingly, services make up a rising proportion of revenue compared to products. In 1992, 43% of revenue came from services. This figure was 63% in 1997 and is forecast to be 70–75% by 2000.

The Information Systems division sells tailor-made solutions to well-defined market sectors. These are predominantly repeatable solutions, where the core remains the same but the front-end is tailored to the particular client's needs. The four main markets are: financial services (retail banking, wholesale banking and life assurance); transportation (largely airlines: systems for seat reservations, passenger check-in, plane loading, airport management and air traffic control); telecommunications (most telecommunications companies in Europe use Unisys products, especially the new mobile, digital operators – and it is also a big player in installing call centres); and the commercial and public sector (criminal justice systems, publishing systems – most major titles in Europe either use Unisys or are moving to it – hospitality and leisure, for example bar management, and project management for construction).

The Global Customer Services division has grown into a healthy networking business on a worldwide basis, buying in components from other suppliers and integrating them into systems. This includes distributed computer support services, where the company manages desktop environments for clients who prefer not to employ in-house staff, and providing warranty and maintenance services to companies which sell computers but have no engineering coverage.

Strategy and Management

The repositioning of the company points the way ahead. The strategy has been focused on three strands: technical excellence (in terms of products built and the technical understanding of the employees); creativity; and tenacity – in other words, sticking with a problem until it is solved to the complete satisfaction of the client. Above all, Unisys is a people company. With a rising source of revenue from solutions, the company's people are vital.

The focus will continue to be on the company's key market areas. Weinbach's philosophy here is for Unisys to be 'an inch wide and a mile deep' in its selected markets. The company now recognises it cannot be good at everything (personal computers, for instance) but it is increasingly overcoming this by selecting partners and working closely with them: Intel, Microsoft, Oracle, and others. It is also very good in its chosen markets. Those markets are largely infrastructure systems: banking, transportation, publishing and the like. As such, they are fundamental to the way countries operate.

Unisys only enters markets where it holds or can obtain a dominant position. This allows continual improvement in its activities, with more and more satisfied clients as a result. It also allows it to help shape the future of its markets. For instance, call centres were unknown in the UK a few years back. Unisys has helped drive this trend forward.

In terms of hardware products, the company will remain firmly at the high end of the business: enterprise server and mainframe equipment. Most of its research and development investment goes into developing its high-end servers. The company's ClearPath product had already sold $2 billion by March 1998.

The services business will continue to predominate over products, and in recent years has been fuelled by two issues in particular: the year 2000 problem, and the introduction of the euro.

The UK company, far from having a different strategy, exemplifies it. It was already ahead of the game when the reorganisation began worldwide. Since then, growth has accelerated, with the UK company growing by 20% in both 1997 and 1998. Its 4,000 staff make up over one third of the entire Unisys European workforce and the company contributes over 33% of the region's revenue. This growth has been assisted by the setting up of a subsidiary in 1995, Unisys Payment Services Limited (UPSL). This company processes documents on behalf of financial institutions and is already the largest third-party processing company in the UK.

Other areas where the UK leads the way in Europe for Unisys is the move away from traditional offices to business centres. Many Unisys staff are away from their desks for long periods – and in the past, this meant that they had no access to office facilities while out of the building. Business centres in major cities allow staff to book desk space, computers, telephones, etc., whenever they need them, together with full secretarial support. They can also work more easily from home using the Unisys global in-house telephone network. This has made the company far more effective, as well as bringing major savings in rental costs. A telling statistic here is that, in the last two years in the UK, office space has fallen by 30% while staff have increased by 20%. This system, pioneered in the UK, is now being rolled out across Europe.

Unisys also offers to its employees an attractive share scheme (15% discount on the market rate, with employees able to spend up to 10% of their salary each month this way), which was introduced in September 1998.

The Future

Unisys is now a radically improved company. 'Increasingly, clients see us as a solutions provider rather than a box maker,' says Martin Sexton, VP of corporate communications for Unisys EMEA. 'We're also much more dynamic, far more focused, and very much a people company. I feel very bullish about the future – probably more so than at any time in my 36 years here! We already had great products, loyal clients and excellent people, coupled with a strategy that was right for the changing marketplace. What we've added to that is outstanding leadership and an even sharper sense of direction. I feel confident that we're well placed for an exciting, stimulating and successful period of sustained growth.'

United Utilities

United Utilities is a business providing services in water, wastewater, electricity distribution, electricity and gas supply, telecommunications and business operations outsourcing. The company is a £2 billion turnover business based in the North-west of England but with additional national and international activities. The company was the UK's first multi-utility, starting life as North West Water before privatisation at the start of the 1990s.

Scorecard:

Flexibility	★★★★
Innovation	★★★
Human resources	★★★★
Growth markets	★★★★
Quality of management	★★★★
International orientation	★★★★

Biggest Plus:
Focused strategy. A company that knows where it wants to be.

Biggest Minus:
Likelihood of diminishing profits due to water price review.

Key Figures:
(1997/98)

Turnover	£2,150.2 million
Operating profit	£601.7 million
Pre-tax profit	£460.5 million
Annual investment	£750 million
Employees worldwide	9,902
Employees UK	9,811

United Utilities
Birchwood Point Business Park
Birchwood Boulevard
Birchwood
Warrington
WA3 7WB
Tel: 01925 285000
Fax: 01925 285199
website: www.united-utilities.co.uk

United Utilities

United Utilities

Company Background

United Utilities is a new breed of company, the first UK multi-utility to evolve and one that is rapidly establishing itself as a progressive business. It provides services in water, wastewater, electricity and gas supply, electricity distribution, telecommunications and business management.

Based firmly in the North-west of England, the company has grown from the roots of the former publicly owned business North West Water, which was privatised nine years ago. It acquired regional electricity company Norweb for £1.826 billion after a sharply contested takeover battle that ended in November 1995.

The first UK 'superutility' was born into a world of unrelenting controversy under feisty former chairman Sir Desmond Pitcher. Boardroom wrangles, sackings, intense media publicity over rewards to directors and shareholders were all features of the fledgling years at United Utilities. When Sir Desmond left in 1998 he was replaced by Sir Christopher Harding, who provided stability as executives focused the corporate strategy for the next phase of the company's development.

In the 1997/98 financial year, the business reported operating profits of £585.5 million, up 29.1%, on a turnover of £2.150 billion. A windfall tax of £415 million has been taken by the government, while further uncertainty has been fuelled by regulator Ofwat's price review and competition in the fuel markets.

Operations and Markets

United Utilities' six key businesses are managed under their own brand names each with their own specific goals and markets. North West Water serves 2.8 million domestic and business customers, providing both water supply and wastewater disposal. The industry price review will determine the level of future profits and investment in services. Over the period 1995–2000 North West Water is expecting to spend a total of £1.4 billion on wastewater assets to improve inland, estuarial and coastal waters and to maintain existing facilities, while extensive attempts to reduce leakage have been commended by Ofwat.

Norweb, the electricity distribution company, delivers power to 2.2 million customers in the North-west and is particularly proud of its impressive reliability levels. ENERGi was formed to fight for new customers in the deregulated gas and electricity sectors and is strongly positioned to win substantial business, say the company's executives. It already offers attractive savings on dual fuel deals and incorporates Tesco Clubcard points and, in addition, Freedom Pounds, which provides big discounts on holidays.

Meanwhile, Norweb Communications is a new growing business venture that has moved into profitability within three years. The aim is to develop a customer base in the area around its North-west fibre optic cable network. Senior management is keen, however, to create partnerships with other companies to pool expertise and resources. One example is the link-up with Northern Telecom of Canada to offer telephony and transmission data services over conventional electric wires. This prevents the need to dig up roads or lay cables, thus giving an obvious cost-saving advantage. Data can be transmitted at high speeds using Digital Powerline technology that is ten times faster than ISDN, for instance.

Vertex began life in April 1996 as a major business operations outsourcing company. Its initial responsibility was to manage a wide range of non-core activities for United Utilities as part of a large-scale outsourcing contract. This included customer contact management, billing and payment services, field services, procurement, accounting, training and information technology. In addition to managing these activities for United Utilities, the company is also well positioned to take advantage of the rapidly growing UK business operations outsourcing market. It has recently recorded a number of notable external contract wins from organisations such as Littlewoods, Independent Energy and the London Borough of Ealing.

United Utilities International is a significant but focused player in emerging markets where UK expertise in both power and water is much coveted. US Water supplies services in the United States while other operations are found in Australia, Mexico, Argentina and the Philippines. A project in Bangkok was less successful as the business took an £83 million hit but company chiefs say that a partnership with Bechtel the construction company will ensure that such errors are not repeated. The board is aware that it has a steady income in its core services but growth in other areas is essential if the ambition to become the pre-eminent superutility is to be achieved.

In January 1998, an American Depository Receipt Programme was launched with a listing on the New York Stock Exchange. In March,

$500m was raised in 10-year US bonds with proceeds and obligations swapped into sterling.

United Utilities' financial performance in 1997/98 saw profits before tax and exceptionals rise 3.7% to £460.5 million, adjusted earnings per share increase 6.1% to 81.9p, and the underlying full year dividend of 40.8p was up 7%. Equity shareholders' funds stood at £2,045.5 million with gearing at 104.6%. Payment of the final dividend was held until April 1999 to manage group corporation tax, although a shares alternative to the cash dividend was offered.

Strategy and Management

United Utilities undertook a comprehensive review of operations in 1998. Under chief executive Derek Green it was decided that the fundamental direction of the business was right but that there needed to be a more dynamic and focused plan. Reducing corporate costs and producing efficiency savings amounting to £40 million by the end of 1999 are high on the agenda. Maximising current skills and expertise to win customers and realising the synergies between the businesses is an important commitment.

Research is being carried out in the area of telecommunications and a major technological breakthrough has already been achieved. More use must be made of the computerised facilities at Vertex which is geared to large-scale contracts.

The company can only be made more flexible by encouraging a motivated workforce and managers are sure this is firmly on track. After all, there has been a dramatic culture transformation since the days before privatisation and many employees from that period still remain. This may be why there are still sporadic difficulties with unions in the area of industrial relations, but in the main, job satisfaction levels of over 80% indicate that the foundations are strong.

Around £3 million will have been spent on staff training in 1998/99 and a performance appraisal scheme involves both managers and employees agreeing on objectives. All play a role in community schemes that act as a basis for a united approach to social responsibility. Sir Christopher Harding's assertion that people come first shows a realisation that business targets can only be reached with the close involvement of staff and customers. Clive Elphick recognises that they must reverse the impression that the company's goal is solely to enhance shareholder value: 'There has been this impression admittedly, but we have been equally concerned with customers and if you look at our track record closely we believe we have done that.'

And indeed, customer satisfaction is on the rise – no mean feat in the utilities sector. Since the departure of Sir Desmond Pitcher, the board appears more willing to listen to constructive criticism and less prone to inviting damaging publicity.

Financial controls have been strongly targeted by CEO Derek Green and there is no doubt that the savings to be achieved in 1999 will provide a bedrock for further improvements.

The Future

United Utilities is well placed to push its brands into ever more competitive markets at home and abroad. A diligent and progressive management is well equipped to give the business a real foothold in lucrative areas.

In the UK it can focus on creating more businesses away from its North-west heartland in business and management services as well as in the utilities marketplace. Overseas there is no reason why international operations cannot be a substantial generator of profits. The foundation has been laid and with steady progress success should follow.

Other multi-utilities have similar aims but United Utilities would do well to concentrate on the quality of its products and services rather than attempting to opt for quantity. The management is convinced the correct strategy is in place – the future is in their hands.

Vanco Euronet

Vanco Euronet designs and manages wide area networks for companies throughout Europe. It has offices in the UK, France, Germany, Italy, the Netherlands and Spain, and an array of support locations from Athens to Zurich.

Scorecard:

Flexibility	★★★★★
Innovation	★★★★★
Human resources	★★★★
Growth markets	★★★★
Quality of management	★★★★★
International orientation	★★★★

Biggest Plus:
Operates in a huge and growing marketplace

Biggest Minus:
Finding enough high-calibre people to sustain growth could be a challenge

Key Figures:
(to year end 31 January 1999)

Pre-tax profit:	£1.6 million
Turnover:	£20 million
Contracted revenue:	£28.4 million
Employees:	150

Vanco Euronet
John Busch House
277 London Road
Isleworth
Middlesex TW7 5AX
Tel: 0181 380 1000
Fax: 0181 380 1001
website: www.vancoeuronet.com

Vanco Euronet

Company Background

Chairman and managing director Allen Timpany formed Vanco Euronet to take advantage of a massive new industry created by four market developments. These are: the liberalisation of telecommunications monopolies throughout Europe; the expansion of businesses to become pan-European players in the European Union; the need for greater business efficiency through the use of telecommunications; and the dramatic advances in the functionality and cost-efficiency of equipment and circuits.

Indeed, it would be hard to overestimate the opportunity. In the 1970s, the back-office automation spending was around $50 billion a year. The PC and front-office revolution increased this to $500 billion a year; and the networking of IT is increasing this at the beginning of the new millennium to $800 billion a year. Vanco Euronet is a key enabler in this massively growing market.

European deregulation of telecommunications companies is certainly one of the key drivers. In the UK, where there was previously one licensed operator – BT – there are now 168. Less dramatic but still significant growth is evident in continental Europe where numbers have burgeoned from 20 to 260. Vanco Euronet was formed to take advantage of this and other market opportunities. The essentials of the company are to offer businesses solutions and provide business benefits through a team of high-calibre, highly intelligent network people who understand fully the needs of their corporate customers.

Operations and Markets

The market for Vanco Euronet is in rationalising: delivering real benefit which companies are looking for from network solutions. Increasingly, companies are choosing to outsource their wide area networks in order to obtain the maximum benefit from telecommunications, but which operator do they select? The market choice can be bewildering. But more and more of those companies are going with Vanco Euronet, thanks to its ability to simplify that decision-making process.

Allen Timpany: 'We offer genuinely impartial advice: we can repackage elements from different PTTs and other suppliers to add value for our clients. We also have enormous experience, diverse knowledge, and flexibility: we often know very quickly which is the most appropriate configuration of hardware, software and circuits for a client's needs. We guarantee high service quality. Even more importantly, we give our customers the opportunity to enjoy continual and dynamic network improvements over the lifetime of their contracts.'

The effectiveness of the company in getting under the surface of its clients' needs, coupled with its dedication to meeting those needs, is becoming widely appreciated. Robert Edmondson-Jones, group information systems manager for international leisurewear manufacturer Lee Cooper, one of its customers, commented: 'The implementation of our new network went smoothly because the same technical consultant was responsible throughout. The migration from our existing European network to the new one was planned and executed very well. Their commitment to meeting our business needs was such that they even obtained a link to an important manufacturing plant in Tunisia where others had failed.'

Optimising networks will certainly be a key factor in the most successful companies of the future. Vanco Euronet facilitates that process by taking an end-to-end risk position. It provides the usual consultancy services, but also has contracts with both its customers and the PTTs. Vanco Euronet provides the opportunity for a client to change the circuit supplier element of a network agreement, which means that the company is always at the top end of service and of cost-effectiveness.

The importance of the company's people cannot be over-stressed. Everything else is simply a commodity – the hardware, the software, the circuitry – but the people put those commodities together into tailored solutions for their clients. Vanco Euronet attracts the best people in the industry and it invests considerable resources in ongoing training. They remain close to their customers, giving guidance, support, and management of electronic commerce across Europe. The 150 current employees will soon become 1,000, working in teams across the continent.

The company already trades in 19 European countries, with £30 million of contracted business to its name. Its customers include *Financial Times* Information, where Vanco Euronet manages the stock exchange network for information services; First Group; OTIS; Airtours; Tibbett & Britten; Chrysler; Phillips; and a range of other blue-chip clients.

Strategy and Management

In Allen Timpany's words, the approach of the company is 'To go to the heart of a business and enable it to operate more efficiently.' It does this by designing, providing and managing high-quality and high-availability Wide Area Networks to medium-sized corporate customers across Europe. This means designing the network – and then providing the circuits and equipment, installing, testing and maintaining the network over the lifetime of the contract. That lifetime is typically from three to five years, during which period Vanco Euronet will refresh and upgrade the system whenever appropriate.

Outsourcing of networks is growing, one reason being the current shortage of network-skilled people, which in turn is raising significantly the strategic costs of in-house operation. Vanco Euronet can offer clients some savings in their online costs, and will also help to optimise their capital equipment spending. But where the company really comes into its own is helping to slash strategic costs by offering substantial economies of scale. Because it is not restricted to selling a specific networking product, its network consultants are free to meet client needs with the most effective product or combination of products on the market. Allen Timpany comments: 'It is obviously not prudent to sign up with BT for a five-year contract when there are hundreds of competitors becoming more credible every day. Through Vanco Euronet we can supply a BT service at the same price but give the customer flexibility to change if a competing carrier becomes a better option.'

Having designed, delivered, installed and maintained the network, Vanco Euronet can underwrite its performance with meaningful financial guarantees. The result is a least-risk guaranteed business solution for the client. Its customers who select the highest service level enjoy aggregate network availability of over 99.9%, and 60% of faults are resolved within five minutes. This impressive rate results from building resiliency into network designs, using the best equipment, and hiring and retaining the most skilled teams of managers and engineers.

This strategy is clearly working well. Over 70% of its customers tried other suppliers before switching to Vanco. The company's success has also been recognised by its winning the Wide Area Networking Outsourcing Supplier of the Year Award two years in succession.

An important part of the company's current strategy is its desire to grow as fast as possible, in order to maximise the pan-European opportunities and to consolidate its lead over potential future rivals. Vanco Euronet is taking a long-term approach with substantial investment in the business to maximise long-term growth. As a result, Allen Timpany says, 'As we are a services business based on people we do not require massive capital, and we have a realistic opportunity of building a substantial global business.'

Vanco Euronet has an interesting structure, with its people divided into small working units in which they have a shareholding. Each workgroup contains its own account managers, salespeople, finance, technical and administrative staff: and is effectively a company in its own right. This puts a premium on effective teamworking, but then that is very much a Vanco strength. It also allows quick distillation of information, rapid response and close co-operation with the customer at every level.

The Future

Not surprisingly, Allen Timpany is enthusiastic about the future of his company. It is operating in what is today the world's biggest market-place, and doing so with great success. Business opportunities in Europe can only continue to expand, and Vanco Euronet is very well placed to take advantage of those.

The company will remain focused on the European opportunity for the time being. It already has offices in Amsterdam, Paris, Frankfurt, London, Madrid, Milan, Copenhagen, Manchester and Prague. Over the next year it plans to add Athens and Warsaw, together with another 20 locations with mobile sites in places such as Stockholm. It also aims to expand its UK offices.

The challenge for the company will be finding sufficient numbers of the right people in order to maintain its impressive growth rate sustained to date. Allen Timpany: 'The problem for the company creates an opportunity for the individual. The right people have almost boundless opportunities here, and their future success is clearly linked to the success of the company. It will be difficult, but not impossible, to find enough top-rate people to go forward at the rate we would wish.'

Certainly, the success of the company so far, its distinctive strategy, its effective cost-savings and financial guarantees to its clients, and its fast-moving, entrepreneurial spirit, stand it in good stead in the years to come. It has identified a highly profitable market and has come a long way in a short time to create an enviable reputation for itself. The future looks bright for Vanco Euronet and everyone who works for it.

Virgin

Virgin is one of the UK's largest private groups of companies, bound together by one of the most powerful brand names around. Virgin Group has grown 30 times in size over the last 14 years through a series of alliances, joint ventures and outsourcing, catapulting it from a modest music and entertainment company with revenues of £50 million to a diversified global conglomerate with revenues in excess of £2.5 billion. The group of Virgin companies and their joint ventures currently operate in at least 24 countries with a mix of media, entertainment, retailing, publishing, financial services, merchandising and travel activities.

Scorecard:

Flexibility	★★★★★
Innovation	★★★★★
Human resources	★★★★
Growth markets	★★★
Quality of management	★★★★★
International orientation	★★★★

Biggest Plus:
One of the strongest brand names around, with each business financed independently

Biggest Minus:
The brand is strongly associated with one individual and stands or falls on that reputation

Key Figures:
(1999, estimated)

Revenue	£2.8 billion
Operating profit	£730 million
Pre-tax profit	£290 million
Annual investment currently	£600 million
Employees worldwide	24,000
Employees UK	18,000

Virgin Management
120 Campden Hill Road
London W8 7AR
Tel: 0171 229 4738
Fax: 0171 229 5834
website: www.virgin.com

Virgin

Company Background

According to a recent survey, 96% of British consumers have heard of Virgin and 95% can correctly name Richard Branson – 'Richard' to everyone – as its founder. People know about Virgin and expect extraordinary things from it, which puts Virgin in a unique position of trust and strength, but also gives it the responsibility not to disappoint.

Virgin started from a public phone booth while Branson was at university. From a student magazine and a small mail-order record business, Virgin has grown into a worldwide group which leads the way in such diverse areas as air travel, cola, radio and entertainment, cosmetics, music, financial services, retailing, trains and bridal wear.

Virgin is not really a 'group' as such – financial results are not aggregated centrally – and each business runs its own affairs. But there is a collection of shared ownership, shared leadership, and shared values. In many respects, Virgin resembles a *keiretsu* – a society of business. The Japanese think so anyway.

Richard Branson's business style has sometimes been viewed as slightly eccentric, but few can deny his success. Virgin has a sizeable global presence, and incredible name recognition. It is profitable and growing fast, entering new markets and quickly claiming a significant share. But all this has come about without most of the trappings of the multinational. There is no head office, board meetings are often held in a pub or someone's living room, there is little sense of management hierarchy and the minimum of corporate bureaucracy. This is the ultimate lean enterprise.

Operations and Markets

Virgin companies are almost too numerous to list – it's easier to visit the website! The companies are organised into at least eight main divisions: Virgin Communications, Virgin Retail, Virgin Travel, Voyager Investments and Virgin Hotels Group, Virgin Radio, Virgin Cinemas and Virgin Direct. Each business group operates autonomously, and there are many other stand-alone companies.

But all Virgin businesses grow around a name which must stand for something. Anything which employees do must fit the corporate brand values, which is how the Virgin 'group' works. Virgin is not a brand extension, however – as a 'house' brand, it adapts to diverse types of businesses and services.

In terms of size, Virgin Atlantic Airways is the largest, with turnover of around £680 million; Virgin Holidays adds another £180 million turnover to the wholly owned Virgin Travel Group, which in total has over 5,000 employees. In 1998 the company turned in a profit of £89 million.

Virgin Direct, a 50:50 joint venture with AMP, had gross sales of £608 million in 1998 and this figure is increasing all the time. Virgin Entertainment, with its portfolio of cinemas and Megastores in Europe, the US and Japan, has turnover in excess of £400 million and some 1,600 employees. The UK Megastores are found separately in Virgin Retail, which also includes the Our Price chain of music stores.

Virgin Rail is a more recent venture, and this recently privatised train operating company, which runs the West Coast line, has annual turnover of around £430 million and 3,450 employees.

Other companies including Virgin Radio, the V Entertainment Group, Virgin Cola, Virgin Hotels, the London Broncos, Storm Model Agency, and Virgin Net just highlight the diversity.

Virgin focuses on businesses that can generate their own growth potential. So it is easy to see why some of Virgin's target markets are those occupied by near-monopolies or where cartel-like behaviour is evident. Not only are there fat margins to cut into, but you can be the people's champion while you are doing it.

According to Rowan Gormley, managing director, Virgin Direct: 'When we said we were going into the personal financial services market, a lot of people said, "Whatever for? It's a dreary, discredited business." And we said, "Yeah, that's why."'

Virgin Atlantic Airways has really flown the flag of the underdog in its struggles with the major airlines. Virgin Direct confounded the conventional industry wisdom that you cannot sell non-obligatory financial services over the telephone, by introducing its own PEP. Virgin Cola, in a joint venture with Canadian partner Cott Corporation, took on Coke and Pepsi (one of the world's most entrenched duopolies) and shifted £50 million of product after three months with only four employees.

Working through joint ventures, alliances and outsourced operations is integral to Virgin's culture, and imbues the style in which people work. Each business inevitably has its own manifestation of the Virgin culture, but most employees of joint ventures think that they work for Virgin. Identifying with the Virgin group – or the Virgin name – instils confidence, a belief that they cannot fail to succeed, as well as helping to open doors.

Strategy and Management

Richard Branson identifies the key Virgin values which must be instilled in any new business venture: 'Virgin is about doing things which really work, not just looking the part. We are passionate about running our businesses as well as we can, which means treating our customers with respect, giving them good value and high quality, and making the whole process as much fun as it can be.'

But it is the Virgin brand, so carefully nurtured by Branson, that holds the key. As Branson explains: 'If we launch a new product, people know that we will come up with something a bit different. They also assume that we will give them better quality and value than the establishment, as well as more fun and entertainment. The value of the name is enormous, but so is the responsibility it confers. We get asked to put the Virgin name to many things, but we say "no" to most of them.'

Virgin has managed to achieve success in so many different markets because it remains true to its brand values, and to its promises. As Will Whitehorn, Virgin's director of corporate affairs, Virgin Management, puts it: 'At Virgin we know what the brand means and when we put our brand name on something, we're making a promise. It's a promise we've always kept and always will. It's harder work keeping promises than making them, but there is no secret formula. Virgin sticks to its principles and keeps its promises.'

Virgin businesses are constantly on the look-out for ways to re-energise themselves, to be more interesting. It's a process of continuous improvement. Amusing, innovative thinking can turn problems into benefits. Supervisors on Virgin Atlantic flights noticed that the salt and pepper shakers were always disappearing. The airline had the bottom of each shaker engraved with the words: 'Pinched from Virgin Atlantic'. The problem was transformed into a joke which pleased passengers and ensured their loyalty.

One of Branson's philosophies in building the record business was instead of trying to make a good business even larger, he preferred to start a new one and take the management team with it. A regular diet of fresh challenges is one reason why he has kept his management team together for so long. In a way, the *keiretsu* developed naturally, without anyone ever realising it was becoming one.

The speed of Virgin's growth has impressed the business world, particularly because it has been achieved by having good business ideas and managing them according to strong Virgin principles, rather than by acquisition. Professor George Foster of Stanford Business School said: 'Virgin's management style empowers and encourages fresh ideas. It demands excellence of itself in everything it does.'

It's possible to conclude that the Virgin formula would make every new business venture an automatic winner. Virgin Direct for example, took £40 million of funds management in its first month, while Virgin Cola sold seven million cans in its first week.

But nothing is inevitable. Behind Virgin's glamorous, laid-back image there is a great deal of hard work and pure number crunching that go into each new venture. New joiners often remark on the energy of its research and the depth of analysis.

The Future

Virgin managers believe passionately in the Virgin values and in what they are doing, and are convinced that together they can build a British, truly global brand name. Realising this ambition is a highly motivating challenge.

Things just keep happening at Virgin, and the pace shows no signs of abating. Virgin Atlantic is taking on another 1,500 staff before spring 2000. 'We're backing young British people to help us take on rival airlines from the UK and around the world,' says Richard Branson. Other radical new ventures are started all the time.

Virgin probably has its work cut out most in the much-scrutinised UK rail industry, particularly on its high-profile West Coast line. But ever on the side of the customer, many will be backing Virgin to get it right. Virgin has already launched Millennium Drivers, an initiative to provide some 2,200 new train drivers by 2006 for all the train companies from three new training centres in the UK.

But one thing is virtually certain – the Virgin *keiretsu* will make a high-profile impact whatever it does and wherever it goes.

Vodafone Group

Vodafone is the world's largest mobile telecommunications company. Vodafone's annual turnover in 1997/98 was in excess of £2.4 billion, representing growth of 41%, with profits growing at similar levels. Vodafone is the leading service provider in the UK with unbeaten coverage and some 40% of the market, and the company has expanded into twelve other countries, from France to Fiji, implementing and developing comprehensive networks. Vodafone had over 9.1 million customers worldwide at the beginning of 1999, some 59% higher than the previous year and a figure that is rising all the time.

Scorecard:

Flexibility	★★★★★
Innovation	★★★★★
Human resources	★★★★
Growth markets	★★★★★
Quality of management	★★★★
International orientation	★★★★

Biggest Plus:
The leading company in a very fast-growing market

Biggest Minus:
Inevitable, increasing competition, and regulatory uncertainties

Key Figures:
(year to 31 March 1998)

Revenue	£2,471 million
Operating profit	£686 million
Pre-tax profit	£650 million
Employees worldwide	12,000
Employees UK	7,000

Vodafone Group plc
The Courtyard
2–4 London Road
Newbury
Berkshire RG14 1JX
Tel: 01635 33251
Fax: 01635 45713
website: www.vodafone.co.uk

Vodafone Group

Company Background

Vodafone is a very young company – not something obviously apparent from its current position in the top 10 companies by market capitalisation in the FTSE-100 index. But this is a tremendous success story – a story that is a long way from over.

Vodafone was formed in 1983 as a subsidiary of Racal Electronics. Sir Ernest Harrison, then chairman and chief executive of the parent company, ensured that the development of the Vodafone network was given the highest priority in terms of financial and human resources and he moved with Vodafone Group when it floated on the London Stock Exchange in October 1988 with a value of £1.7 billion. Vodafone was de-merged from the Racal Group in September 1991 'in order to create increased shareholder value'. By early 1999, Vodafone's market capitalisation had reached £30 billion.

The company has grown phenomenally on the back of the explosion in mobile telecommunications. It is the undisputed market leader in the UK, and growing its networks overseas all the time.

Operations and Markets

In the UK Vodafone accounts for at least 28% of all new connections. It now has more than 5 million UK customers, representing a market share of 40%. Vodafone's operations in the UK continue to be the mainstay of the group's turnover and profitability, despite increasing competition and Vodafone's spiralling investment in overseas markets.

Around 4.2 million of this 5 million figure subscribe to digital services. Digital customers now account for 82% of the UK market and have increased to 80% of the Vodafone customer base as migration from the analogue network continues to be encouraged.

Analogue 'churn' continues to be high, but these customers are tending to churn to digital rather than migrate to Vodafone's competitors. Digital churn remains at 20% annually, but Vodafone is promoting a number of loyalty schemes, increasingly competitive tariffs and enhanced customer service to reduce future levels of churn.

Vodafone's average revenue per customer (excluding 'Pay As You Talk') remained constant at £427 over 1997/98 despite tariff reduction – 'highly significant' says Vodafone – and ahead of its key competitors on a like for-like basis.

In addition to its core UK network and service provider activities, Vodafone's activities comprise cellular, paging and packet radio data services and value added network services. These are provided by the group companies Vodafone Value Added and Data Services Limited and Vodafone Paging Limited.

Vodafone continues to develop its highly successful 'Recall' voice messaging service, which now has approximately two million users, making it one of the UK's leading providers of voicemail and a significant contributor to network traffic.

Many might be surprised to learn that the UK, at 19%, is only the twentieth most highly penetrated mobile market; Finland, the number one market, has at least twice this level of mobile ownership, and other markets are not far behind. The UK is expected to achieve levels of penetration not dissimilar to Finland's by 2002, according to stock-broking analysts at SG Securities in July 1998.

Growth in the international market is beginning to accelerate. At the end of 1997 there were around 208 million customers worldwide. By 2002, it is anticipated that this could be 800 million. Europe has overtaken America as the largest market, with nearly 70 million mobile customers.

By 1999, Vodafone had over 4 million customers outside the UK, representing 41% of the group's total, although UK activities account for around 70% of group turnover. Vodafone presently operates in France, Germany, the Netherlands, Sweden, Greece, Malta, Australia, New Zealand, Fiji, South Africa, Gibraltar and Egypt. These investments in networks became profitable very quickly.

Many of Vodafone's overseas markets are expected to grow strongly, and overall profits are expected to grow 'massively' over the next five years. This will produce a correspondingly huge increase in free cash flows and how Vodafone spend this money will determine the next stages of the company's tremendous growth.

Strategy and Management

Vodafone's strategy is, quite simply, to concentrate on providing mobile telecommunications services worldwide.

There's a huge demand to satisfy. In the words of Chris Gent, chief executive, 'We now expect total market penetration in all the major markets in which we operate to reach 50% by the end of 2003, a year earlier than we projected in 1997. Mobile telephony is becoming the preferred means of personal communications and Vodafone is at the leading edge of the industry's development.'

Obviously, extending and advancing international operations is crucial. Vodafone's strategy for international investments is to develop further its existing businesses, build shareholdings in associates and, where appropriate, bid for new licences and make acquisitions.

This is happening already. In its 1997/98 year, Vodafone signed up more than 1.25 million international customers, and international operations contributed 17.8% of total group operating profit, against 3.3% in the previous year.

In the UK, Vodafone is committed to maintaining the strength of its core business, in terms of technical efficiency, customer needs and market opportunity.

Voice telephony is 'going mobile' in the widest sense. The challenge for companies like Vodafone is to not only grow their own market, but also to erode the PTA's traditional core business.

Over 1996–98, Vodafone acquired all the various service providers with disparate brand names that connected people to the Vodafone network. In 1998, Vodafone completed the conversion of these operations and retail shops to a single new format under the Vodafone brand, and also reduced the number of billing and administration systems from five to one.

The business was also rationalised to provide three discrete channels of distribution. These are Vodafone's own retail operations, a channel to meet the needs of corporate customers and a channel to sell through independent distributors and the retail multiples.

Marketing strategy shifted to focus not only on the increasingly mature business market but also on the fast-growing mass consumer sector. Cue the communication of simplified and reduced tariffs and the introduction of the 'Pay As You Talk' service, designed cleverly to expand the use of mobile phones into a new segment of the market.

The Vodafone digital network continues to grow. Over 1997/98, Vodafone added over 1,030 base stations in the UK, bringing the total in operation for the GSM network to over 3,800. This includes base stations installed in 'key' areas such as the terminal buildings at Heathrow Airport and at the NEC and Olympia exhibition centres.

Vodafone even had time to come up with a new corporate identity, following extensive research into the way it was perceived in the marketplace and how its core identity could be more powerfully expressed. Few can remember the old one.

Vodafone says that it is 'firmly focused on customer service, total quality and value for money'. Customers may not always agree, but shareholders are not complaining.

The Future

Vodafone's outstanding financial performance continues to surpass the expectations of even the most optimistic analysts and forecasters. There is a growing belief that all estimates for the international mobile telecommunications market might be too conservative.

Vodafone's launch of 'Pay As You Talk' at the end of 1997, the upgraded version of its original 'prepay' service launched a year before, is set to revolutionise the mobile telecommunications sector, making mobile telephony accessible to a whole new sector of the market. It's already enjoying significant success.

While subscriber numbers climb relentlessly, many people feel that a mobile phone is something they 'must have' but that they are still being stung quite hard, especially in the UK, by the high level of mobile phone charges. Competition will force these prices down. Vodafone will be asked to 'walk the talk' when it says it aims to be recognised as 'the best value for money', especially when many Vodafone subscribers say they choose Vodafone only because of its network's better quality coverage of the UK. But Vodafone has said that it is committed to matching tariff reductions by competitors in order to remain the clear market leader.

Deregulation and increasing competition are creating uncertainty in many major European markets, for both fixed and mobile telecommunications. Vodafone has got a wealth of experience already under its belt in competing in a diverse range of markets. This differentiates it from most of its peer group and leaves it better positioned to cope with a market which is likely to become more competitive and less predictable. In the UK, its main competitor Cellnet surely cannot deliver as lacklustre a performance as it did in 1997/98.

But at the start of the 1990s, it was not immediately obvious that mobile phones would become an everyday item. They did, and how. Voice communication is going mobile and 100% penetration – not 50% or even more conservative forecasts made previously – may be feasible for some markets. Vodafone has achieved its market position entirely on its own merits and seems poised to profit substantially from the explosive growth of mobile telecommunications worldwide.

Waymade Healthcare plc

Waymade Healthcare plc is a significant niche player in the pharmaceutical industry. Waymade's core business is supplying prescription medicines to retail pharmacies throughout the UK. It also acquires, develops and licenses generic medicines. Two other areas of business are Woundcare and Medical Devices.

Scorecard:

Flexibility	★★★★★
Innovation	★★★★★
Human resources	★★★★
Growth markets	★★★★
Quality of management	★★★★
International orientation	★★★

Biggest Plus:
A flexible, fast-moving and rapidly growing company

Biggest Minus:
Not yet a truly international operation

Key Figures:
(year to 31 March 1998)

Turnover:	£85.5 million
Gross profit:	£9.9 million
Net profit:	£3.6 million
Net assets:	£5.9 million
Employees UK:	300

Waymade Healthcare plc
Sovereign House
Miles Gray Road
Basildon
Essex SS14 3FR
Tel: 01268 535200
Fax: 01268 535299
website: www.waymadehealthcare.plc.uk

Waymade Healthcare plc

Company Background

Waymade Healthcare's roots go back to 1975. In that year, Vijay Patel qualified as a pharmacist and set up his first retail pharmacy outlet. This quickly grew into a small chain which prompted a move into distribution. Vijay's insight was that he could source and supply cost-effective medicines – not only to his own chain, but to a growing number of independent pharmacies. In 1982 Vijay was joined by his brother Bhikhu, and the company became a plc in 1984.

In 1989, the retail chain expanded to 15; in 1991, Sovereign Surgical was formed; and in 1992, the company established its own salesforce. As well as Waymade Healthcare plc, the Patel brothers also own Chemys, a chain of dispensing chemists; a property portfolio; and Sovereign Alliance, a joint venture.

Since 1982, performance of Waymade Healthcare has been impressive, to say the least: consistent year-on-year growth in sales and profits have averaged over 30% a year. Recently, even this excellent result has been eclipsed: 1997 saw a growth rate of 65%, and 1998's figure looks set to be around 60%, with projected sales of £135 million.

Operations and Markets

As marketing director Brian McEwan says, 'In one sense our customer is the patient; in another, it's the retail pharmacist.' Waymade's core business is supplying prescription medicines to retail pharmacies throughout the UK. The company has developed considerable expertise in sourcing branded pharmaceutical products from throughout the EEC, importing them and distributing them to retail pharmacists. The wide range of products offered at cost-effective prices can help to enhance the profits of the high street pharmacy and help to control the NHS drug bill.

Furthermore, Waymade has made a significant investment in acquiring, developing and licensing generic (i.e. off-patent) medicines. This is a fiercely competitive area but also a high growth sector. Waymade has developed a number of new products for launch, to add to its range over the coming years.

Two other areas of business are Woundcare and Medical Devices. Under the Sovereign Surgical banner, the company produces and distributes a range of basic woundcare products. A recent addition is a high-tech glycerine gel-based wound dressing with several innovative features, for which the company has acquired UK rights. Medical Devices include a number of patent-protected, innovative pieces of equipment researched and developed by the company. These include an electronic Peak Flow Meter for the management of asthma and other respiratory diseases, and a safety syringe designed to be non-reusable and prevent needle-stick injury, for use in high-risk areas of medicine such as HIV and hepatitis.

Strategy and Management

The company's goal is ambitious: to evolve into a fully integrated pharmaceutical company. 'Long-term, pharmaceuticals has been and will be an attractive growth market to be in,' says chief executive Vijay Patel. 'Despite lots of consolidation worldwide, the industry is still fragmented; the biggest company has no more than a 5–6% market share. This trend of consolidation will continue, with the biggest companies chasing a share of 10%. Indeed, the pundits predict that, by the year 2010, the upper end of the market will consist of just twenty mega-houses. But there will always be room for smaller players – and in this market, "smaller" companies can be very large indeed!'

The company's challenge is to take advantage of the current opportunities. These include opportunities in pharmaceuticals and also in delivery as a number of governments look at disease management systems involving the holistic management of patients. In the UK, the government has made changes to the structure of the healthcare market by introducing primary care groups. These and other trends create a climate where the dynamics of the market are constantly changing. A flexible company such as Waymade Healthcare is ideally placed to maximise such opportunities.

Dr Brian McEwan: 'One strategy is to use differentiation in order to grow. We don't just compete on price. Instead, we see ourselves as a service company. We have high levels of customer contact and service, and our telesales and field sales people work together to ensure optimum customer satisfaction.'

Another strategy is to increase the product range in the generics sector. 'Our aim is to grow the customer with us,' says Vijay Patel. 'We aim to continue expanding our customer base by offering a very wide product range. If we can sell one product to a given client, we can potentially sell twenty. This reduces our marginal costs while still offering attractive deals to our customers.'

A third strand of Waymade's strategy is to enter into partnerships, both with customers and other companies. Brian McEwan: 'We don't just sell products, we look at the individual needs of our customers and segment them by need. Larger customers have very different requirements. With clients such as Boots, for instance, we talk to them commercially but also in terms of regulatory and quality levels. It's all about reassuring such customers that our total package meets exactly their needs.'

Waymade also explores partnerships with other companies. Its distribution strength is well known in its marketplace, so it makes sense for other companies to use this to gain outlets for their products. It also shares development of products with other companies to provide a balanced risk portfolio, particularly where complementary skills exist. This helps obtain services at competitive prices and also dilute overheads – a process aided by the current oversupply of manufacturing capacity in the UK.

The company is undoubtedly a flexible, innovative and entrepreneurial company, as recognised by being elected to Europe's 500 Dynamic Entrepreneurs (a European Union initiative which whittled the field down from 12 million companies!) in 1995, 1997 and in 1999. It is also, in the *Independent on Sunday*/Price Waterhouse Middle Market 50, and in *Enterprise* magazine's Top 100 Entrepreneurs. This widely-acknowledged flexibility will stand the company in good stead. As Brian McEwan says, 'We look at products that aren't just big potential but are also difficult to make. This creates entry barriers for us – typical niche operating, in fact – ensuring our margins are more attractive.'

Overall, the company is following what might be called backward vertical integration. The pharmaceutical value chain runs from research and development to registration, manufacturing, marketing, wholesale and retail. Waymade has followed the reverse route – and has done so very successfully. The ultimate aim is to produce new chemical entities, but this may still be some way off since the average cost of doing so is estimated to be around $500 million. The rewards can often far exceed the outlay, of course, hence the company's desire to ultimately pursue this route.

This trend is likely to be accompanied by a growing international presence. Waymade currently has partnerships with a number of European and Far Eastern companies. The latter makes excellent commercial sense, since perhaps fifty Indian PhDs can be hired for the cost of five in the UK. Further international presence is a definite strategic goal.

The Future

Waymade Healthcare has a refreshing approach to success and failure. As Vijay Patel says, 'Nothing is a bigger burden than a proven record of success!' Having said this, the company aims to retain its entrepreneurial, flexible approach as it expands, growing its core of talented people with strong complementary skills – 'Sharing the vision,' as Vijay aptly puts it.

In the past few years, a key drive has been strengthening the company's senior management team. The aim here is undoubtedly to control, but not stifle, the creative process – in essence, to give people the tools and the freedom to give of their best.

Brian McEwan concurs. 'We recognise that we can't get it right every time. But, unlike some monolithic multinationals, we reserve the right to make wrong decisions. In other words, if something goes wrong, we can change track. Similarly, if we start down one route and discover something potentially more marketable en route, we can divert resources into that. It's all about balanced, measured risk. We remain confident that we will have the right people, the right processes and the right products in place to take us where we want to go in the next millennium.'

WHSmith Group

WHSmith is the UK's leading seller of books, newspapers, magazines and stationery and supplies more magazines and newspapers to retailers than any other organisation. WHSmith is one of the most recognisable and reliable retailers on the high street and has successfully exported its retailing skills into travel niches in the USA, Europe and beyond and developed these as separate operations. It also owns an online book-selling company.

Scorecard:

Flexibility	★★★★★
Innovation	★★★
Human resources	★★★★
Growth markets	★★★
Quality of management	★★★★
International orientation	★★★

Biggest Plus:
A clear focus on its core brand

Biggest Minus:
A long way to go

Key Figures:
(15 months to 31 August 1998)

Revenue (Sales)	£2,649 million
Operating profit	£104 million
Pre-tax profit*	£145 million
Employees worldwide	n/a
Employees UK	n/a

*(continuing activities, before exceptional items)

WH Smith Group plc
Nations House
13 Wigmore Street
London W1H 0WH
Tel: 0171 409 3222
Fax: 0171 629 3600
website: www.whsmithgroup.com

WHSmith Group

Company Background

WHSmith is without doubt one of the most familiar names on the British High Street, where it has been represented for 203 years. Yet recent times have been turbulent, and have seen WHSmith divest some non-core businesses to concentrate instead on its core brand.

A good starting point for the refocused WHSmith is 1995, when a profit warning and City uncertainty effectively forced a management shake-up. Bill Cockburn was made chief executive, and promptly sold the Do It All and Business Supplies operations, and looked to expand the remaining businesses. But Cockburn resigned in 1997 and a successor was found in Richard Handover, previously managing director of the WHSmith News business.

WHSmith then took the decision to focus on a core of businesses comprising the WHSmith high street chain, WHSmith News, WHSmith USA Travel Retail and WHSmith Europe Travel Retail. Specialist retail operations Waterstones (book chain), Virgin Megastores and Our Price (music stores) and The Wall (music stores in the USA) were all sold. In the other direction, WHSmith bought the John Menzies retail chain and the Internet Bookshop.

Operations and Markets

The four core businesses of the WHSmith Group today are very autonomous, each with its own executive management and business strategy.

WHSmith High Street remains one of the best-known retail names in the UK. It has over 550 stores with the inclusion of the John Menzies chain of 158 stores, and better geographical coverage (Menzies has a strong presence in Scotland).

Books, newspapers, magazines and stationery are the main products sold. WHSmith is essentially a 'popular specialist', focusing on books in the education, travel, popular fiction, cookery and garden ranges. WHSmith sells more books than any other retailer in the UK does.

WHSmith is also the leading UK high street multi-media products retailer.

WHSmith Europe Travel Retail consists of 184 stores and concessions located in UK and European stations, airports and hospitals. Recognising that customers in these locations have very different needs and mindsets to customers in high street stores, this operation was spun off from the WHSmith High Street business in 1998.

In 1948 WHSmith was the first retailer to open at London's Heathrow Airport and nearly fifty years later, was among the first retailers to open a store at the Eurostar terminal at London Waterloo International. WHSmith Europe Travel Retail includes former John Menzies stores and the first of these to be refitted as a WHSmith outlet opened at London Paddington station in 1998. By 1999, WHSmith stores could be found in all London mainline stations.

WHSmith News delivers newspapers to its 24,000 customers who consist of independent newsagents and multiple retailers. WHSmith News is the biggest wholesaler of newspapers and magazines in the UK, delivering 34% and 36% respectively in what remains a complex and time-sensitive business.

WHSmith USA Travel Retail currently has 409 stores in airports and hotels across the United States, Canada, the Caribbean and Southeast Asia. The stores located in hotels are centred around holiday and gaming resorts and convention centres in prominent locations such as Chicago, Atlanta, New Orleans, British Columbia, Hawaii, Singapore and Puerto Rico. WHSmith recently won the contract to operate five news and gifts stores in the new Hong Kong airport.

WHSmith USA Travel Retail specialises in bespoke retailing and many of its USA outlets are not branded as WHSmith shops. For example, in the New York, New York casino in Las Vegas, the shops trade under the 'SoHo Village' and 'I love New York' names.

The Internet Bookshop – www.bookshop.co.uk – is the leading European Internet bookseller currently offering 1.4 million titles from the UK and USA. Established in 1994 and based in Oxford, the Internet Bookshop reported tremendous sales growth of 269% to £2.1 million in the twelve months to December 1997.

Strategy and Management

WHSmith's strategy is now focused clearly on exploiting the strengths, power and potential of its brand to the best advantage of shareholders, customers and the wider community. Current management concluded that the WHSmith brand was the jewel in the crown and had perhaps been neglected.

The John Menzies retail outlets in England and Wales are being re-badged as 'WHSmith', although this decision has not been taken for stores in Scotland and will be driven by consumer sentiment.

A new generation of stores is being rolled out across the WHSmith Europe Travel Retail chain. The first of these 'new look' stores opened at London Gatwick Airport and London King's Cross station. In-store initiatives include the country's leading book promotion 'Read of the Week' and the weekly news promotion 'Hot off the Press' featuring the best edition of any magazine in any particular week.

Recently WHSmith News has started to target independent retail customers to provide them with extra support and advice on selecting the range of magazines that they offer to their customers to help them compete more effectively and improve sales and profit.

WHSmith's purchase of the Internet Bookshop was a natural extension of its commitment to bring its customers the most advantageous and convenient methods of buying products. Effectively, WHSmith bought the people, systems and expertise – not the brand – and can easily graft on the WHSmith brand. The Internet Bookshop has built strategic partnerships with AOL.UK, Lycos, MSN, Yell and Condé Nast to develop a market-leading 'retail engine' which enables the site to offer additional products in various languages. Although the current Internet market is relatively small, it is expected to develop significantly over the next few years.

WHSmith is dedicated to helping improve education standards in the UK. Its Ready Steady Read! initiative is providing £1.5 million worth of books to 75,000 children across the UK over the next five years, helping deliver a better standard of literacy among the nation's children.

Management style under Richard Handover has become much more informal, and the old 'Eton and Guards' tag has gone for ever. WHSmith now has much more of a team-based culture, and in the process, has also become more customer focused and results oriented.

'Customer service excellence across the range of our operations is vital to our future. We want to be one of the best companies in the world,' says Richard Handover. 'We aim to please our customers by providing a standard of service that is consistently better than our competitors'.

'Our people are very much a part of the mission of the company and our human resources policy is bound into our overall business philosophy. The reason is simple. There's a clear link between satisfied staff and satisfied customers,' adds Richard Handover.

The company is developing a flatter management structure. 'We say that everyone can make a contribution, so we need an organisational structure that puts this into action,' says Richard Handover. The businesses have been brought much closer together, and management spend more time together mixing, sharing experiences and ideas, and cultivating Richard Handover's message of 'one brand, one company'.

Recognising that step, rather than incremental, change was needed to achieve real results, WHSmith has initiated a comprehensive business transformation programme. An antidote to the adage that 'the fish rots from the head', the programme will broaden from top management to the next level of 500 managers as part of a three-year plan which will embrace everyone in the organisation. Staff throughout the group are aware, even if not yet themselves an integral part of the change process, that change is happening. Management is spending much more time in the stores and communication is rife.

The Future

WHSmith expects revenue growth to come from two streams. The first is 'more of the same', but better. If that sounds a little obvious, it is. Simply doing retailing better is a constant challenge, and supply chain management can be improved.

The second is to extend the brand. And if there is one brand value that WHSmith wants to nurture, it is 'trust'. Already focused on the education segment of the market, its market research reveals that consumers trust WHSmith on education and the company believes it can exploit this potential further over time. The success of other promotional initiatives such as 'Read of the Week' suggest that there is also wider customer trust in the WHSmith brand.

Short term, WHSmith faces uncertain consumer demand. But the company is in a robust state, with cash in the bank and no debt, and remains committed to high street retailing.

There is a huge opportunity to develop the travel retailing market. In airports, WHSmith Europe Travel Retail is expanding at double the rate of the UK High Street business and is growing by around 10% each year in Europe. Its other international operations offer good scope for further expansion, but with the Asian economic crisis, plans to roll out the WHSmith brand around the world will be longer term in nature.

In theory, everything that WHSmith retails could be sold over the Internet. No-one knows how quickly online commerce will develop, but WHSmith is in there, and with the right brand. Its future looks brighter than for a long time.

Willis Corroon

Willis Corroon is a worldwide knowledge-based company providing risk management solutions, risk transfer expertise and specialist consultancy services.

Scorecard:

Flexibility	★★★★★
Innovation	★★★★
Human resources	★★★★
Growth markets	★★★★
Quality of management	★★★★
International orientation	★★★★★

Biggest Plus:
Among the very best in all its chosen markets

Biggest Minus:
Still undergoing cultural transition

Key Figures:
Global gross premiums handled annually:	£8 billion
Global pre-tax profit:	£95.5 million
Continuing operations (brokerage and fees):	£692 million
Employees worldwide:	11,500

Willis Corroon
Ten Trinity Square
London EC3P 3AX
Tel: 0171–488 8111
Fax: 0171–488 8223
website: www.williscorroon.com

Willis Corroon

Company Background

London insurance brokerage Henry Willis & Co. was founded in 1828. This was the starting point for the British company Willis Faber. It merged with US brokerage RA Corroon & Co. in 1990, a company whose roots went back to 1905. The merger created Willis Corroon Group, now one of only three insurance brokers with a truly global basis of operations. Today, it operates in 250 locations in 69 countries, and has additional representation in 53 locations in 24 countries. It transacts business in over 150 currencies.

Throughout the 1990s, Willis Corroon has been making the transition from a more traditional insurance and reinsurance broker to a professional service firm focused more on risk management advice. The reason for this transition is clear. Peter Stevens, director, Corporate Communications: 'Insurance markets operate on the basis of a price for their product, and the risk transfer price has been falling for many years. This is likely to remain the case for the foreseeable future. As a result, there is pressure on the revenues of insurance brokers. Our response was to increase the proportion of our work which is advisory or consultatory in nature, while continuing to offer more traditional services to clients who wanted them.'

The most recent, and most important, change for the company was the leveraged buy-out of 1998. This removed the company from the public arena and gave it more freedom and flexibility to pursue its chosen goals. It also allowed it to incentivise its leading managers and directors far more effectively through the use of equity buy-ins.

Operations and Markets

The company has six main areas of operation. The first is global reinsurance. Willis Faber Re is the group's specialist reinsurance intermediary business, providing risk analysis, consultancy and transactional capabilities to insurers worldwide. This division also includes Willis Corroon Catastrophe Management Limited. The second area is global specialities, which provides specialist broking and consulting services to clients with large or unusual risks. The third is UK retail, dominated by Willis Corroon Limited, the largest risk management consultant and insurance broker in the UK. The fourth is North American retail, served by Willis Corroon Americas, the third largest retail broker in the USA. The fifth is US wholesale, wherein an array of companies provide specialist services to US clients. Sixth and last is international, accounting for 20% of the group's brokerage and fee revenue.

One part of the operation is a pure research and development business for its reinsurance clients. This is about providing research and development which can be sold to clients: matrix modelling, flood modelling, catastrophe planning, etc. Peter Stevens: 'One can then help to influence the business which insurance companies are writing in the first place, giving them help in risk management in effect. As an intermediary, we are ideally placed to do that because we see such events many times and from many different angles.'

The group always aims to be within the top three companies in any market segment in which it chooses to compete. This may be a business specialisation or a geographic area. In terms of international expansion, the group has now reached an ideal position within the European marketplace. The next target area is Latin America, where the scope for insurance broking is increasing. Brazil and Mexico lead this trend; other countries in the region are still moving from a situation where such services were nationally owned and controlled. A further target area is Asia/Pacific. Willis Corroon has a number of offices in the region already, but growth here is frequently hampered by national restrictions on open insurance markets. In few countries does the insurance broker operate fully, in the traditional UK or US sense – Singapore being a notable exception. However, the company has a strong position in Japan, one which no other broker can emulate. Expanding the company's presence into full broking offices in such countries as Korea, Thailand, Malaysia, China and Taiwan will largely depend on those economies opening up.

Strategy and Management

Dominating the company's strategy at present is its desire to become a professional service firm, shifting emphasis away from traditional insurance broking to develop its risk management advisory and consultancy services. Peter Stevens: 'Within the UK and the US, insurance brokers have operated in their fullest and least trammelled way. There is a steady move in those countries towards providing a fee-based advisory service. Our strategy is to drive that trend forward at a pace fast enough to meet the needs of those clients who wish to use such services, without losing clients who prefer to move more slowly.'

Underpinning this trend is the company's extensive market research programme. As Peter Stevens comments, 'Willis Corroon has undertaken a very detailed market research effort aimed at understanding the needs of our clients. We then use this information to segment clients in terms of buying behaviour. What type of service do they want from their insurance broker? Do they want a full service consultative relationship, and are they prepared to pay for it? This is the type of question we have been addressing, allowing us to offer a different service to different market segments.'

While the transition to a professional service firm continues, the company is also focusing on doing what it does from day to day as well as it can be done. It is going to great lengths to import best practices into all elements of transactional work, which still accounts for the majority of the company's business. This is all about embracing change and instilling a desire in the company's people for continual improvement. Peter Stevens: 'Part of our strategy is about changing the way our people operate. We want them to look at everything they do and change anything that needs changing to enhance our efficiency. Change is part of their jobs, and they need to recognise and indeed welcome that fact.'

Changes can be made externally as well as internally. Willis Corroon is working with insurance carriers to improve the processes whereby the industry operates overall to its clients. This is about speeding up response times, cutting down errors and avoiding duplication. Central to this role is the use of IT as a vehicle. The practical outcome of this move is to create a secure environment for electronic commerce for the insurance industry. This network, sponsored by three shareholding brokers, is already extremely secure and dedicated to the insurance industry as a whole.

Another challenge is to remain adaptable in such a fast-developing market. The role of the insurance intermediary is changing rapidly. One source of pressure is the growing use of the capital markets for the transfer of risk. Peter Stevens: 'We want to be up with that trend and be able to use those markets for clients if they are suitable for their needs. We have that expertise already in place and we will continue to build it as necessary.'

The conventional insurance industry has tended to focus on pure risks: risks to the company's property, those affecting employers, customers, products, and so on. This has left uncovered whole areas of risk. A growing trend is the need for so-called holistic risk management, devoted to covering the whole gamut of risk facing financial directors and looking at those risks as one. Willis Corroon is becoming increasingly involved in this area for its larger clients.

The Future

The leveraged buy-out is key to the company's future. The buy-out gives the company a tremendous advantage: it takes it out of the public arena and therefore allows it to effect change faster and without media analysis. It is therefore able to build and recruit when its competitors are consciously trying to reduce their operations. It gives it stability of ownership, and also access to more financial resources if required. Peter Stevens: 'Although the future is always hard to predict, I am confident that Willis Corroon will be a larger and an even more successful organisation in three to five years' time, due to both the buy-out and our ongoing strategic shift to a professional services company.'

WPP Group plc

WPP is one of the world's largest advertising and marketing services groups. The 60 companies in the group offer clients – local, multinational and global – a comprehensive and, when appropriate, an integrated range of marketing services, including advertising, market research, media consultancy, public relations, sales promotion, direct marketing, identity and design, and other specialist communications.

Scorecard:

Flexibility	★★★★
Innovation	★★★★
Human resources	★★★★
Growth markets	★★★
Quality of management	★★★★
International orientation	★★★★★

Biggest Plus:
Strong balance sheet, sharp focus on efficiency

Biggest Minus:
Marketing services often vulnerable during recessions

Key Figures:
(to 31 December 1997)

Revenue	£1,747 million
Operating profit	£206 million
Pre-tax profit	£177 million
Employees worldwide	30,000
Employees UK	3,600

WPP Group plc
27 Farm Street
London W1X 6RD
Tel: 0171 408 2204
Fax: 0171 493 6819
e-mail: esalama@wpp.com
website: www.wpp.com

WPP Group plc

WPP Group plc

Company Background

WPP Group provides communications services to clients throughout the world, including more than 300 of the *Fortune 500* companies and more than 60 of the FTSE-100 in 1997. The group's 30,000 people work out of 835 offices in 91 countries. Disciplines range from advertising and market research to public relations and specialist communications, including many of the 'new media'.

Each WPP company is a distinctive brand in its own right, with its own identity and own area of expertise. They all share intelligence, creative talent and experience with the aim of bringing competitive advantage to their clients. Within the fold are prominent names like J. Walter Thompson, Ogilvy & Mather, Hill & Knowlton, Enterprise IG, Millward Brown, Research International, CommonHealth, and the Henley Centre, as well as many niche specialists.

WPP has grown revenue, operating profit and operating margins and earnings per share year-on-year, for the last five years. WPP Group also maintains a strong balance sheet. Average net debt has reduced over the same period, reaching £135 million (in constant currency) in 1998 with interest cover of over seven times. This is after share purchases and acquisition payments which totalled £167 million in the twelve months to October 1998.

Operations and Markets

Advertising remains WPP's dominant sector, accounting for 54% of revenue and 64% of operating profit. The proportions for its other business sectors are information and consultancy (16% and 13%), public relations and public affairs (7% and 4%) and specialist communications (23% and 19%).

The group also has genuine global reach to match the breadth of its services. North America is the most important market, representing around 40% of revenue, with roughly 20% coming from each of the

UK, Continental Europe and the rest of the world (Asia Pacific, Latin America, Africa and the Middle East).

Placing greater emphasis on revenue growth, WPP is focusing its portfolio on those geographical and functional areas that are growing fastest. Asia Pacific, Latin America, Africa and the Middle East, Central and Eastern Europe account for more than 20% of group revenues compared to 11% a few years ago. It expects this figure to rise to nearer 33% in five years. WPP views the present difficulties in Asia as offering 'buying opportunities'.

Information and consultancy, public relations and public affairs, and specialist communications presently account for 45% of group revenues, and it expects this percentage to rise to 55% over a similar period.

Strategy and Management

WPP's operating businesses are autonomous, but increasingly the parent company is doing more at the centre. 'We continue to seek ways of unlocking added value for our clients and our people and proving the real value in WPP and its strategy,' says chief executive Martin Sorrell. 'Our goal remains to become the world's most successful and preferred provider of communications services to both multinational and national companies.'

This dictates monitoring consumer and business trends very carefully. One important trend is the increasing number of clients which are thinking about or actively seeking integrated solutions to marketing issues. WPP has therefore put in place mechanisms where different disciplines can work together. Already major clients are utilising multi-disciplines of WPP companies for advertising, direct marketing, promotions and interactive media, for example.

This is just one area where WPP as the parent company intervenes as a facilitator between the different parts of the group. Chief executive Martin Sorrell has worked hard to improve the degree of co-operation among the many disparate parts of the WPP empire. Much effort has gone into helping individual operating companies improve the quality of their service offer, and into facilitating cross-company partnerships and initiatives including training, recruitment, career development, incentive and stock-ownership schemes, information technology, property, procurement and practice development.

Many WPP clients – including those with major marketing spends – are already headed along the globalisation path. WPP's geographical reach is already extensive. 'We are already everywhere we want to be,' says Eric Salama, strategy director at WPP Group, 'although we could be better in some markets and sectors.' Infill acquisitions will continue to be made in functional areas where WPP is under-represented, and in new areas, such as employee behaviour, interactive marketing and internal communications.

While the current problems in Asia, and to a lesser extent North America, are of concern, these will remain very important markets with a high proportion of the world's communications services spend. WPP has recently announced a deal in Japan – the last major market where it wasn't substantially represented – forming a strategic alliance with Asatsu, the third largest advertising and communications agency in Japan. And WPP is the leading marketing services company in China and India, two very big markets that have hardly been hit by the Asia crisis.

For some time now companies have looked at cutting costs, and for many, the scope for further efficiency improvements is limited. More are realising that to make 'a breakthrough', they will now have to inspire consumers and grow markets rather than market share. Creativity remains absolutely inherent to everything that WPP does, and time, money and considerable effort goes into recruiting and retaining the brightest, smartest people who want to pursue a career in a creative services company as an alternative to investment banking or management consultancy.

WPP recently launched at group level a major project called 'BRANDZ', a detailed research study on 3,500 brands worldwide. This has served not only as a database attraction to clients, but WPP knows that when you can quantify these areas, you have a firmer basis for making recommendations to clients.

WPP regards itself as already being in the consultancy business, and sees no reason to formalise its offer in the so-called 'third-generation consultancy' proposition being touted by other management and marketing service consultancies.

Much of WPP's strategy will necessarily be evolutionary, as this is a marketing services company already with considerable strengths. It owns high-quality individual companies, and the parent company has applied an infrastructure which allows and encourages them to work together.

WPP Group is committed to deploying technology to its advantage. It spends some $65 annually on computer hardware, software and information technology salaries. Its aims are to provide a coherent strategy and framework and prevent wasteful duplication and unnecessary reinventing of wheels in various parts of the organisation.

But it is people which represent the critical factor. They form 60% of WPP's total costs, and although systems are important, if WPP is to help its clients grow revenue rather than cut costs, the key determinant will be the quality of its people.

WPP strives to deliver value to clients with fewer people who are more productive and better paid. Staff cost-to-revenue ratios have fallen by over 7% during the 1990s, while profit margins have improved by even more than this. Yet the top 400 people earn considerably more, largely due to rapidly increasing incentive remuneration. WPP spent £52 million on incentives in 1997, rewarding key people for superior performance. WPP judges people only on what they contribute to the business, indicating a strong belief in the potential of the individual to make a difference and its wish for everyone to think and act like an owner.

WPP is publicly committed to wider internal share ownership, and various programmes have been developed to enable a large number of WPP professionals to participate actively in the growing value of the company. In 1997 WPP introduced its Worldwide Ownership Program and granted stock options to 12,000 people, including special executive option programmes for the top 400 people.

The Future

WPP has some fairly specific financial objectives. It aims to improve operating margins by 1% each year, pursuing the higher margins of some of the other media giants in its peer group. WPP also uses its free cashflow to enhance shareowner value, and expects to spend £50 million on this activity in 1998.

Arguably, marketing services always has a future, with companies needing constantly to innovate, create or grow markets, and grab market share. Although these budgets are sometimes regarded as discretionary, or even vulnerable, the global trend has been upwards for years. Non-media advertising businesses are expected to grow faster than advertising, and communications services will grow faster outside the US than inside. WPP is well positioned in this context.

WPP will continue to develop its portfolio of businesses in high-revenue geographical and functional areas, and improve the creative quality of all of its businesses. Some sectors, such as healthcare and technology, will become increasingly important and increasingly specialised.

Meanwhile, the marketing services sector is consolidating, and WPP knows that it is likely to face a fewer number of tougher competitors in the future. 'We will have to work hard just to stand still, and even harder to progress,' according to Eric Salama.

WPP has a series of qualitative measures to see how it is progressing against its intended strategy. But revenue is regarded as the real test of success in its qualitative work and turning revenue into profits will be the ultimate test of how well the business is being run.